Forced Migration and Global Politics

Alexander Betts

WILEY-BLACKWELL

A John Wiley & Sons, Ltd., Publication

This edition first published 2009
© 2009 Alexander Betts

Blackwell Publishing was acquired by John Wiley & Sons in February 2007. Blackwell's publishing program has been merged with Wiley's global Scientific, Technical, and Medical business to form Wiley-Blackwell.

Registered Office
John Wiley & Sons Ltd, The Atrium, Southern Gate, Chichester, West Sussex, PO19 8SQ, United Kingdom

Editorial Offices
350 Main Street, Malden, MA 02148-5020, USA
9600 Garsington Road, Oxford, OX4 2DQ, UK
The Atrium, Southern Gate, Chichester, West Sussex, PO19 8SQ, UK

For details of our global editorial offices, for customer services, and for information about how to apply for permission to reuse the copyright material in this book please see our website at www.wiley.com/wiley-blackwell.

The right of Alexander Betts to be identified as the author of this work has been asserted in accordance with the Copyright, Designs and Patents Act 1988.

Library of Congress Cataloging-in-Publication Data

Betts, Alexander, 1980–
    Forced migration and global politics / Alexander Betts.
        p. cm.
    Includes bibliographical references and index.
    ISBN 978-1-4051-8031-3 (hardcover : alk. paper) – ISBN 978-1-4051-8032-0 (pbk. : alk. paper)
    1. Refugees–Government policy. 2.   Refugees–International cooperation. I. Title.
    HV640.B48 2009
    325–dc22

                                                    2009000847

A catalogue record for this book is available from the British Library.

Set in 10/12.5pt Sabon by SPi Publisher Services, Pondicherry, India
Printed in Singapore by Ho Printing Singapore Pte Ltd

1   2009

Forced Migration and Global Politics

This book is dedicated to the memory of my father,
John Hamilton Betts (31 March 1940–25 January 2008),
who committed much of his life to teaching and publishing books that
made academic work accessible to students.

Contents

Acknowledgments   vi

Introduction   1

1. International Relations Theories   18

2. Sovereignty and the State System   43

3. Security   60

4. International Cooperation   80

5. Global Governance   99

6. North–South Relations and the International Political Economy   127

7. Globalization   145

8. Regionalism   164

Bibliography   185

Index   200

Acknowledgments

The content of this book is based on the graduate course on "International Relations and Forced Migration" that I teach at the Refugee Studies Centre, at the University of Oxford. It was in preparing the syllabus for the course that it occurred to me that there was a significant gap in the literature. Despite the important relationship between forced migration and global politics, there was no single textbook that applied the concepts of International Relations to the empirical context of forced migration. Given the growing number of graduate courses that touch upon aspects of this relationship between forced migration and global politics, it seemed like a worthwhile project to write up my lectures into a resource that other people might be able to use. I am particularly indebted to three colleagues in Oxford who have played a significant role in enabling this book to come into existence. Matthew Gibney, as the director of the MSc in Forced Migration, gave me the opportunity to design and teach the course on which this book is based, and offered invaluable advice on the content and structure of both the course and the book. Gil Loescher, as my long-time mentor in International Relations and Forced Migration, has been an endless source of inspiration and guidance. Andrew Hurrell, first as my doctoral supervisor and then as a colleague, has shaped my understanding of International Relations more than anyone else. The fact that this book covers such a broad conceptual terrain is testimony to his teaching and longstanding critical engagement with my work.

A number of other colleagues in Oxford have been a great source of inspiration and have contributed to the development of some of the ideas in the book. Oxford truly is the most appropriate place in the world to write a book such as this, which attempts to bridge the divide between two areas in which Oxford excels. Not only am I blessed with having excellent colleagues in the Department of Politics and International Relations but Oxford also represents a world-class hub for the study of migration in general and forced migration in particular. Without listing everyone, Stephen Castles, Jean-François Durieux, Jason Hart, Eva-Lotta Hedman, Esra Kaytaz, Neil MacFarlane, Kalypso Nicolaïdes, Jochen Prantl, Anne Roemer-Mahler, Martin Ruhs, Sibylle Scheipers, Devi Sridhar, Nick Van Hear, Ngaire Woods, and Roger Zetter have been an invaluable source of ideas, wisdom, and constructive comments. Outside of Oxford, a host of colleagues who work on issues relating to forced migration and global politics have contributed in different ways to the development of this book. I am particularly grateful for discussions with B. S. Chimni, Jeff Crisp, Sarah Cross, James Hollifield, Robert Keohane, Rey Koslowski, Susan Martin, James Milner, Phil Orchard, Anna Schmidt, and Eiko Thielemann.

The chapters in the book benefited greatly from the feedback of an excellent group of graduate students who took the course on "International Relations and Forced Migration" in its first year. I am particularly grateful for the input of Thais Bessa, Miriam Bradley, Neil Howard, Eveliina Lyytinen, Ann McKittrick, Stephanie Silverman, and Bea Trichachawanwong. Miriam Bradley also provided excellent research assistance in tidying up references and preparing the bibliography for the book. On a practical level, I wish to acknowledge the Rose Research Fellowship at Lady Margaret Hall, the Hedley Bull Research Fellowship in the Department of Politics and International Relations, and the MacArthur Foundation for providing financial support during various stages of the planning and writing of the book. I also wish to thank the Guggenheim Museum in New York for allowing me to use Picasso's "The End of the Road" in the cover design. At Wiley-Blackwell, I am grateful to Nick Bellorini for showing great belief in this project from its inception, and Liz Cremona, Ginny Graham and Louise Spencely for helping to transform the manuscript into a book. Lastly, but definitely not least, I am grateful to my mum, Hilary, for love, support, and aesthetic advice on the cover design.

Introduction

Forced migration has been a major feature of the twentieth and early twenty-first centuries. Around the world, people have been forced to flee their homes as a result of political persecution, conflict, and natural and man-made disasters. The two world wars, the colonial liberation wars, the proxy conflicts of the Cold War, a range of internal conflicts in the Balkans, Africa, and the Caucasus in the aftermath of the Cold War, occupation in Afghanistan and Iraq in the context of the "War on Terror," state partitions and nationalist claims to territory in South Asia and the Middle East, authoritarian regimes, human rights violations, large-scale development projects, and environmental disasters resulting from hurricanes, tsunamis, and climate change have all contributed to people leaving their own communities in search of protection elsewhere. Most notably, refugees have been displaced across international borders, fleeing political persecution by traveling into neighboring states or moving long distances to states in other continents in search of international protection. Other people have been displaced across borders as stateless or environmentally displaced people. In addition to refugees and other people who have crossed an international border, an even greater number of people have been displaced from their homes but have remained within their country of origin as internally displaced persons.

What these categories of people have had in common is that, as a result of an existential threat, they have faced significant constraints in their ability to remain within their home communities. They have consequently been compelled to seek access to rights and entitlements, or "protection," outside their home community. Whether it involves the crossing of international borders or not, forced migration lies at the heart of global politics. Refugee movements are inherently political – involving the competing interests and rights of citizens and non-citizens – and inherently international – involving the cross-border movement of people. However, even internal displacement has dynamics that place it squarely within global politics. There has been increasing recognition that where an individual's country of origin is unable or unwilling to ensure his or her access to a certain set of basic rights, then there is a wider international responsibility to ensure that such individuals or groups receive protection. Debates on issues such as humanitarian intervention, humanitarian assistance, and the so-called "responsibility to protect" have been closely intertwined with internal displacement. Whether forced migration involves displacement across borders or within a state, its causes, consequences, and states' responses to it have been inextricable from global politics.

Despite the political and international nature of forced migration, issues relating to refugees and internal displacement have rarely been addressed by scholars of International Relations. The discipline of International Relations has expanded its empirical focus beyond analyzing war and peace and issues relating to military security to address a range of areas such as the global economy, environment, human rights, and international trade. However, it has paid relatively little attention to the international politics of forced migration. Where it has done so, the work has emerged in relatively isolated pockets. These have mainly concentrated on analyzing the relationship between forced migration and security and providing historical accounts of the emergence of the global refugee and IDP (Internally Displaced Persons) regimes. Yet the study of forced migration has enormous relevance for IR. It touches upon issues relating to international cooperation, globalization, global public goods, ethnicity and nationalism, sovereignty, international organizations, regime complexity, security, the role of non-state actors, interdependence, regionalism, and North–South relations, for example. Making the study of forced migration part of the mainstream study of International Relations has a potentially wide-ranging theoretical contribution to make to the discipline.

Meanwhile, the discipline of Forced Migration Studies has rarely drawn upon the tools offered by International Relations to inform its analysis. Forced Migration Studies has predominantly drawn upon disciplines such as anthropology, sociology, geography, and law to analyze the causes and consequences of human displacement. It has generally offered a "bottom-up" perspective which places displaced people at the center of its analysis. Although exploring the perspective of forced migrants is crucial, and should not be neglected, there is also a need for a "top-down" level of analysis in order to understand the macro-level structures that influence states' responses to forced migration. This is crucial because it is often the choices of states and other political actors that determine outcomes for the displaced. Bringing the tools of International Relations into the field of Forced Migration Studies therefore has an important contribution to make to the study and practice of forced migration.

This volume therefore attempts to close the gap between Forced Migration Studies and International Relations. For the first time, it brings together the literature on International Relations and the literature on Forced Migration and integrates them within a single volume. It explores what International Relations theory might offer the study of Forced Migration, and vice versa. The main aim of the book is to offer an analytical tool kit for studying the politics of forced migration, and to explore what potential IR has for understanding states' responses to forced migration.

The book has been written primarily as a textbook for undergraduate and graduate courses in International Relations and Forced Migration. However, it is also intended to make a broader academic contribution to International Relations. It attempts to set out a research agenda for how International Relations can approach the study of forced migration and integrate an awareness of forced migration into broader work relating to a range of other areas such as international political economy, security, and international cooperation. Applying IR's core debates to a relatively uncharted empirical terrain also offers an opportunity to push those debates in new directions and to explore them in an applied context. The book represents an opportunity to engage in applied International Relations and explore how a number of the discipline's core concepts can be operationalized in a specific empirical context.

The approach of the book is to take a series of the main topics within International Relations and to apply their core concepts to the study of forced migration. The topics are not intended to be exhaustive. Rather, they are used to highlight and question the relevance of some of the core aspects of the subject for understanding the international politics of human displacement. The concepts that are included in the book are particularly chosen for their ability to shed light on how states respond to forced migration. While it is also important to understand the behavior of other actors and also the underlying causes of displacement, the concepts that are chosen are primarily those that address how states respond to human displacement. The topics covered represent a range of the most relevant aspects of contemporary International Relations for forced migration.

Each chapter sets out a number of key concepts and debates in International Relations and explains their relevance to the international politics of forced migration. It goes through a number of areas: IR Theories, Statehood and Sovereignty, Security, International Cooperation, Global Governance, North–South Relations and the International Political Economy, Globalization, and Regionalism. The chapters then attempt to integrate the concepts drawn from International Relations with the wider Forced Migration literature through a number of case studies involving the politics of contemporary human displacement. Since refugees have the most obvious relevance for international politics due to crossing international borders, most of the case studies relate to the politics of asylum and refugee protection. However, examples are also used that relate to conflict-induced internal displacement, development-induced displacement, and environmental displacement.

This introduction contextualizes the book. Firstly, it offers an overview of forced migration. Secondly, it explains the relationship between forced migration and global politics. Thirdly, it examines how International Relations and Forced Migration Studies have so far addressed questions relating to the international politics of forced migration. Finally, the introduction concludes by explaining the content and approach of the book.

Categories of Forced Migration

The study of forced migration is premised upon the distinction between forced migration and voluntary migration. The separation of these categories emerges largely from policy categories designed to distinguish between and prioritize the rights of different groups of people. Forced migration is often assumed to have a political basis, being based on flight from persecution or conflict; voluntary migration is generally assumed to be underpinned by economic motives. However, in practice, this distinction is problematic; it is not possible to distinguish sharply between volition and coercion, and they exist on a spectrum. In practice, most migration has elements of both coercion and volition, and is likely to be motivated by a mixture of economic and political factors. All migrating individuals face structural constraints and all retain a degree of agency to choose between different options. For example, while refugees face severe political constraints, they often retain choice over a range of options about where and when to move. Similarly, even "economic migrants" often face serious structural constraints as a result of, for example, a lack of livelihood opportunities in their home country.

Nevertheless, even though the forced/voluntary distinction represents a spectrum rather than a clear dichotomy, which is inadequately captured by existing policy categories, it remains an important and useful distinction for analytical purposes. This is the case for two reasons. Firstly, despite the problematic nature of the dichotomy, and the challenge of knowing "where to draw the line," there are certain categories of people whose basic rights their own states are unwilling or unable to provide, and who are therefore compelled to leave their homes. Secondly, because existing policy categories are based on the distinction, the international politics of forced migration is generally distinct from the politics of other aspects of human mobility. This book is therefore premised upon the idea that it makes some sense to distinguish analytically between forced and voluntary migration but acknowledges the problematic nature of the distinction. It takes forced migration to be defined by movement that takes place under significant structural constraints that result from an existential threat.

Academic concern with forced migration has been notably concentrated within what has been termed Forced Migration Studies. The traditional concern of Forced Migration Studies has been refugees as people who, owing to a well-founded fear of political persecution, leave their country of origin. However, with time, there has been a growing recognition that, aside from people who cross international borders for reasons of political persecution, there are other groups of people who can legitimately be considered to be forced migrants, even if they have not crossed an international border or may be fleeing for reasons other than those that define refugee status. This section briefly outlines the main categories of forced migration that are addressed by this book.

Refugees

The most high profile and highly researched category of forced migration is refugees. Refugees are defined as people who "owing to a well-founded fear of persecution, on the grounds of race, religion, nationality or membership of a social group, find themselves outside their country of origin, and are unable or unwilling to avail themselves of the protection of that country" (Article 1a of the 1951 Convention on the Status of Refugees). Because they flee persecution and conflict, and cross international borders, they are often colloquially referred to as "human rights abuses made visible," and the number of refugees fleeing a country is often taken to be a proxy measure for the degree to which that country respects human rights. In 2007 there were 11.4 million refugees of concern to the United Nations High Commissioner for Refugees (UNHCR 2008). They are most frequently hosted in camps or settlements in countries that neighbor their country of origin. For example, the most prominent refugee situations include Somalis in Kenya, Burundians in Tanzania, Afghans in Iran and Pakistan, Burmese in Thailand, Iraqis in Syria and Jordan, and Sudanese in Chad and Uganda. In addition, there were estimated to be around 5 million Palestinian refugees in the Occupied Territories and the Middle East (Dumper 2008).

In contrast to other areas of forced migration, there is a clearly defined international regime governing states' responses to refugees. The 1951 Convention on the Status of Refugees sets out a definition of a refugee and the rights to which refugees are entitled. The original 1951 Convention was confined to geographical Europe but its scope was made universal through the 1967 Protocol to the Convention. The core principle underpinning the regime is *non-refoulement*, which prohibits states from forcibly returning an individual to a country in which he or she faces a well-founded fear of persecution. Responsibility for monitoring and overseeing the implementation of the 1951 Convention lies with the Office of the United Nations High Commissioner for Refugees (UNHCR). Under the Office's 1950 Statute UNHCR has explicit supervisory responsibility for ensuring that states party to the Convention comply with its obligations. Refugee protection is the only area of forced migration which has historically had a specialized UN agency. The refugee regime has been supplemented by a series of regional agreements on refugee protection, such as the 1969 Organization of African Unity (OAU) Convention, the 1984 Cartagena Declaration in Latin America, and the 2004 European Council Directive. As well as international refugee law, sources of refugees' rights (and hence states' obligations towards refugees) can also be found embedded in other areas of law such as international human rights law, which offers a complementary source of legal protection for refugees.

The international politics of the refugee regime represents the main focus of this book, and the majority of case studies used to illustrate the international relations concepts introduced by the book relate to refugee protection. This is because refugees have been a central part of world politics. Because they cross international borders and so have implications for state sovereignty, because they symbolically serve to discredit or legitimate certain Governments by allowing people to "vote with their feet," and because refugee protection has been subject to regulation by international institutions, refugees have a clear and obvious relationship to international politics. The combination of cross-border movement and the political motives for that movement have made refugees a central part of global politics during the twentieth and early twenty-first centuries. The way in which states have selectively engaged with refugees has been a barometer of wider political trends during the inter-war years, the Cold War, the aftermath of the Cold War, and the so-called "post 9/11 era."

However, although refugees are the central empirical focus of this book, they are by no means the only group of forced migrants who are central to world politics. Indeed, the academic and policy-level focus on refugees has been claimed to highlight an exilic bias. In other words, the refugee regime and the focus on refugees serves to hone attention on those forced migrants who have crossed an international border, to the detriment of focusing on other categories of forced migration such as internally displaced persons (IDPs). While IDPs and other categories of forced migrant may not have been such a prominent part of modern international political history, they nevertheless also have significant political implications that can be explored using the tools of International Relations.

Conflict-induced internal displacement

During the latter part of the twentieth century, there was increasing recognition that people could be "in a refugee-like situation" and be in need of international protection without having crossed an international border. People facing political persecution or fleeing conflict might move to a different part of their own state rather than travel across an international border. IDPs can be defined as "persons or groups of persons who have been forced or obliged to flee or to leave their homes or places of habitual residence, in particular as a result of or in order to avoid the effects of armed conflict, situations of generalised violence, violations of human rights or natural or man-made disasters, and who have not crossed an internationally recognised State border" (*Guiding Principles on Internal Displacement*, Introduction, para. 2). There are currently around 25 million conflict-induced IDPs in the world, in countries such as Colombia, Sudan, Iraq, Uganda, and Chechnya (Weiss and Korn 2006).

Yet until the end of the twentieth century, there was very little awareness of, or international response to, the situation of IDPs. From the early 1970s, UNHCR began, on an *ad hoc* basis, to provide some protection and assistance to IDPs when doing so was inextricably linked to refugee protection, the work fell within the Office's expertise, and the Office had the permission of the host state. Over time, however, a growing body of academic work and advocacy campaigns began to focus on IDPs and to argue for a more predictable and comprehensive international response to internal displacement. In 1992, the UN Secretary-General appointed the Representative of the Secretary-General on Internally Displaced Persons in order to contribute to awareness of the plight of conflict-induced IDPs and to work towards the development of a legal and normative framework for the protection of IDPs. This culminated in 1997 in the creation of the so-called "Guiding Principles on Internal Displacement" which, drawing upon states' existing obligations under international human rights law and international humanitarian law, created a soft law framework, defining states' obligations towards IDPs (Bagshaw 2005; Phuong 2004).

Following the creation of these principles, an international institutional framework has begun to emerge. Initially, UN agencies attempted to coordinate their responses to IDPs through a so-called "collaborative" approach in which they would jointly engage in IDP protection under the aegis of the UN's humanitarian assistance coordinators. In 2006, this division of responsibility was made less vague and the so-called "cluster" approach was created. Under this, different UN agencies share responsibility for responding to different aspects of the needs of IDPs. Since 2006, UNHCR has taken responsibility for IDP protection in conflict situations, while the WFP (World Food Programme) takes responsibility for IDPs' food and nutrition and UNICEF for child protection, for example.

Since the creation of the Guiding Principles, states are showing an increasingly significant commitment to IDP protection. The "soft law" principles have been incorporated into the municipal law of some states and the African Union (AU) has pioneered an attempt to develop the world's first "hard law" international legal framework on internal displacement. However, IDP protection continues to be politically controversial. Foreign states engage selectively in IDP protection, in practice only being able to assist IDPs with the permission of the host country. In the context of Chechnya, for example, there has been little means to address internal displacement in the absence of support from the Russian Government. Although internal displacement does not involve those fleeing conflict or persecution crossing a border, it nevertheless has significant implications for state sovereignty. An international response necessarily requires international actors – whether states, international organizations, or NGOs – crossing an international border. In other words, because the displaced do not cross the border, international actors often have to cross the border in the other direction instead. IDP protection therefore lies at the heart of debates relating to state sovereignty and the circumstances under which outsiders have a responsibility to protect individuals whose own governments cannot ensure their safety.

Development-induced displacement

Development-induced displacement and resettlement (DIDR) occurs when, as a result of a change in land use, people are forced to leave their homes either because of direct physical displacement or because of indirect livelihood displacement. DIDR results from a large range of different development projects. The most common source of DIDR is the construction of large dams which submerge villages in rural areas in order to provide irrigation and hydro-electric power needs. However, other development projects such as extraction, conservation programs, urban development projects, and transportation projects have also led to the forced displacement of people. The reason large-scale development projects often lead to displacement is that governments use the principle of "eminent domain" to assert a legal claim over land which is needed for "the collective interest" (de Wet 2006; Khagram 2004).

The majority of DIDR takes place in the developing world. The World Bank conducted a large-scale survey in 1993 and estimated that 80–90 million people were displaced by development projects between 1986 and 1993. It also estimated that, on average, 300 new large dams displace around 4 million people each year. India has historically had the most numerically significant DIDR, displacing between 1951 and 1990 an estimated 20 million people, 16.4 million of whom were displaced by large dams (World Bank 1994). China's development projects such as the Three Gorges Dam on the Yangtze River have also been implicated in causing massive displacement. Such projects, and the displacement they cause, are frequently justified as being in the "national interest" and necessary for "national development." However, while a simple cost-benefit analysis may indeed suggest that displacement is justified by the economic benefits of the project, this ignores the political economy of DIDR. In practice, DIDR has redistributive consequences, generally redistributing resources from the marginalized to the powerful. DIDR places costs disproportionately on politically and economically marginalized groups such as indigenous populations, and its benefits, while often justified as being in the "national interest," frequently accrue to elites and the private sector (Roy 1999).

DIDR takes on a range of international political dimensions. Because many large-scale development projects are funded by international development organizations or regional development banks, these bodies play an important role in regulating how states address DIDR. Development agencies' lending guidelines have become the main means of mitigating the most serious consequences of DIDR and of ensuring that, where people are displaced, they receive rehabilitation and compensation. The World Bank in particular has been heavily criticised for funding projects that led to significant displacement, and, in response, has developed a series of operational guidelines and directives based on its in-house "Impoverishment Risks and Reconstruction Model" (Cernea 2000). The World Bank's lending criteria on DIDR have also shaped the lending conditionality of other development agencies and regional development banks, compelling borrower governments to adopt appropriate reconstruction and resettlement plans. In the absence of an alternative way to enforce human rights guidelines relevant to DIDR – compiled by the UN Commission on Human Rights in its "Comprehensive Human Rights Guidelines on Development-Based Displacement" – these lending criteria represent the dominant "soft law" framework that regulates how states respond to DIDR (Barutciski 2006).

Furthermore, DIDR involves a range of trans-national non-state actors in displacement. Private sector actors have frequently been involved in the development projects that have led to displacement. For example, a number of US and Europe-based MNCs (Multinational Corporations) have held contracts in relation to large-scale dam projects that have led to displacement in the developing world. Furthermore, DIDR has implicated trans-national civil society. Many of the development projects that have led to displacement have inspired significant resistance. In response to the high profile Sardar Sarovar Dam in India, for example, the so-called Narmada Bachao Andolan (NBA) resistance movement has organized strategic non-violent resistance. The NBA has mobilized support, publicity, and funding for its campaigns through trans-national civil society, leading to the creation of, for example, The Friends of River Narmada and Narmada Solidarity Society movements.

Environmental displacement

A new and emerging category of forced migration is that of environmental displacement. With climate change and the possibility of sinking islands in the Pacific Ocean such as Kiribati, and increased risks of flooding in countries such as Bangladesh, there has been growing speculation about the implications of climate change for human displacement. At the extreme end of the spectrum, where islands disappear and resettlement is required, it may be possible to attribute displacement to climate change. However, beyond the stark examples of sinking islands, attribution may be less clear cut. Indeed, environmental change is more likely to represent a multiplier for other sources of human mobility than a source of forced migration in its own right. As environmental change takes place, it may exacerbate other factors that underlie the movement of people. For example, it may combine with other causes of movement by affecting access to livelihoods, competition for resources, and conflict. Estimates of the impact of climate change on human displacement are contested and vary radically but it is clear that it will be both a source of forced migration in its own right and, more significantly, a multiplier for other underlying causes of forced migration (Myers 1997; Piguet 2008).

On a related theme, natural disasters such as the tsunami in Southeast Asia in December 2004 and Hurricane Katrina in the US in 2006, also frequently compel people to move. Sometimes countries are able to address the human consequences of these disasters in isolation. At other times, an outside response is required. Sometimes assistance is gladly accepted – as in Sri Lanka and Indonesia post-tsunami – and at other times it is resisted – as in Burma in 2008. Increasingly, UNHCR and other humanitarian actors are being drawn into addressing humanitarian crisis and displacement created by serious natural disasters. There is consequently a growing recognition that the environment and human displacement are closely related and that there is a need to address this relationship on an international political level.

The Relationship Between Forced Migration and Global Politics

Forced migration lies at the heart of global politics. The relationship between forced migration and global politics can be identified on three different levels: the *causes* of forced migration, the *consequences* of forced migration, and *responses* to forced migration. On each of these three levels, the concepts of International Relations have a contribution to make to understanding forced migration and forced migration has a contribution to understanding world politics. This section explains each of these levels at which the relationship exists.

Causes

The underlying causes of forced migration are highly political. Analytically, if displacement is seen as a dependent variable, political factors represent important independent variables in explaining displacement. The causes of human displacement are closely connected with trends in the international system, geopolitics, and the global political economy. These broader macro-level trends may in turn shape the country conditions that lead to human displacement. For example, wider inter-state relationships between countries of origin and great powers or former colonizers may sustain oppressive, authoritarian governments that persecute their populations; environmental trends at the global level may mean people are compelled to leave their homes; an international demand for raw materials or commodities such as diamonds may fuel or mitigate conflicts that lead to displacement; the role of multinational corporations may contribute to the type of development project that leads to displacement. In other words, in order to understand why forced migration occurs, it is likely to be insufficient to look at trends within the country in which displacement takes place. Instead, there is a need to also look at global political trends. A number of these relationships can be explored.

Oppressive regimes may be supported or installed by major powers or former colonizers. Internal conflicts, which lead refugees to cross international borders or IDPs to move to other parts of the country may be connected to wider international political issues. They may be triggered or exacerbated by military intervention, occupation, colonialism, or the global political economy. During the Cold War, the proxy conflicts of the 1970s, in which the superpower rivalry between the US and the USSR was played out in the developing world, led to massive displacement in, for example, the Horn of Africa, Southern Africa, Indo-china, and Central America. Today, the involvement of large powers such as China in Sudan and the US in Iraq and Afghanistan indirectly contributes to human displacement. Colonialism has a relationship to displacement. The postcolonial regimes installed in countries like Rwanda, the Cote d'Ivoire, and Zimbabwe have contributed to social conflicts that underlie forced migration. Meanwhile, economic links between developing countries and developed countries have often contributed to creating the conditions for displacement. The diamond trade from Sierra Leone or oil in Angola have been factors underlying conflicts that have led to both internal displacement and refugee movements.

The consumption and production choices of consumers and corporations may also have a significant relationship to displacement. Environmental change within one state may result from the emissions of other states. For example, greenhouse gas emissions in the developed world may ultimately underlie displacement in the developing world by submerging islands in the Pacific or by radically changing livelihood opportunities on Sub-Saharan Africa. Meanwhile dams and major development projects may result from the foreign direct investment of multinational corporations. Many of the large-scale development projects that have led to human displacement in states in Asia and Africa have been funded by MNCs or through international development organizations. The World Bank and North American and European MNCs have been implicated in large dam-building projects in India and China.

Consequences

It is not just the case that scholars and policy-makers with an interest in forced migration should be concerned with understanding its relationship to global politics. Forced migration may also have an impact on other areas of international politics. In other words, human displacement may be an important independent variable in explaining other issues within global politics. It may, for example, be one factor amongst other variables, that has a significant effect on conflict, peace-building, state-building, terrorist recruitment, sources of foreign direct investment, trans-national crime, or even interest group formation and voting patterns in domestic politics. Some of these relationships are explained below.

Forced migration has an important and inextricable relationship with conflict. During the Cold War, refugees were often supported by the superpowers to fight or offer support to combatants in the proxy conflicts in the developing world. Similarly, the colonial liberation wars were often waged by nationalist groups in exile. The Rwandan Patriotic Front (RPF) in Uganda from the 1970s until the early 1990s, the African National Congress (ANC) in other parts of Southern Africa in the 1970s and 1980s, the Nicaraguan

Contras in Honduras in the 1980s, for example, highlight the role that exiles and refugees play in developing opposition movements that engage in fighting the government in the country of origin. In the Cold War context the phrase "refugee warriors" was frequently used to describe the relationship between guerrilla movements and refugees in the Cold War proxy conflicts. Refugee camps often serve as sanctuaries and bases for combatants. For example, following the Rwandan genocide, many of the Hutu *interahamwe* implicated in the genocide sought refuge in the camps of Eastern Democratic Republic of Congo (DRC). Furthermore, refugees have often been identified as potential "spoilers" in peace deals. The repatriation of groups in exile, the existence of refugee camps that serve as rebel bases, and cross-border smuggling facilitated by refugee camps, can all undermine the prospects for peace. Refugees and returnees have, for example, been regarded as "spoilers" in attempted peace-building in West Africa and the Great Lakes region.

Furthermore, refugees and displaced people are frequently part of trans-national networks in ways that have significant cross-border effects. Refugee camps and protracted refugee situations are potential sources of radicalization and terrorism. With few prospects for education, livelihood opportunities, or freedom of movement, young people in protracted refugee situations may represent a pool of potential recruits for terrorists. The refugee camps that host Palestinian refugees in the Middle East or Somali refugees in East Africa or Afghan refugees in Pakistan, for example, have been identified by Western governments as sources of Islamic radicalization and sources of recruitment for terrorist cells.

In other areas, the trans-national networks created by refugee movements, and their links with diaspora groups, may have significant political effects. For example, in many cases refugees represent a significant source of foreign direct investment. Refugees frequently engage in remittance sending which, for countries under stress such as Somalia, represents one of the biggest sources of overseas income. Refugee flows are also associated with other trans-boundary movements such as organized crime and the demand for trafficking and smuggling networks. These types of trans-national networks, whether positive or negative in their effects, can feed into domestic politics by defining voting behavior, influencing the perception held by electorates of foreigners in general, and introducing a focus on asylum, immigration and trans-nationalism to the domestic political process.

Responses

Beyond seeing forced migration itself as either a dependent or independent variable in global politics, there is also a need to understand how states respond to forced migration. The way in which states respond to forced migrants – whether they have crossed borders as refugees or remain within their country of origin – is highly political. It involves a decision on how to weigh the rights of citizens versus non-citizens. Indeed, the decision of states to provide protection, contribute to durable solutions for refugees or IDPs, or to address the root causes of displacement through military intervention, diplomacy, development, post-conflict reconstruction, or peace-building, are all highly political. Understanding the conditions under which there is variation in states' (and other actors') responses to forced migration is a crucial part of understanding how to reduce the negative human consequences of displacement.

When states decide to provide protection to refugees or IDPs from or within another state, they choose to allocate scarce resources to non-citizens. They may contribute to protection either through offering asylum or resettlement, or by making financial contributions through humanitarian organizations, for example. Empirically, states' contributions to protection have generally been highly selective and have rarely been motivated exclusively by humanitarian or altruistic concerns. There is therefore a need to understand the range of political motives that underlie states' selective contributions to supporting displaced people who are in need of international protection.

States respond to forced migration not only by offering protection; they may also contribute to durable solutions for refugees or IDPs in terms of supporting resettlement, local integration, or repatriation. However, states have been increasingly reluctant to provide resettlement and local integration to refugees, for whom repatriation has become "the preferred durable solution." In relation to IDPs, states are only just beginning to consider what "durable solutions" might mean and how external contributions might go beyond humanitarian relief and peace-building. Yet, there is nevertheless a need to understand the conditions under which states have historically been willing to contribute to working toward sustainable solutions that allow forced migrants to end the cycle of displacement and rebuild their lives. The same applies to understanding the conditions under which states are prepared to engage in addressing the root causes of displacement. When and why, for example, do they contribute in different ways to peace-building, development, and post-conflict reconstruction initiatives?

International Relations and Forced Migration

International Relations is a sub-discipline of political science. It has evolved in order to develop concepts that explain the behavior and interaction of states. These concepts have traditionally been used to explain the big questions relating to war and peace. The distinction between IR and other areas of political science rests upon an assumed distinction between domestic politics and international politics. At the domestic level, there is a government that exercises sovereign authority. At the international level, there is no such sovereign authority. IR has described the absence of a single authority at the international level as "anarchy." Given anarchy, states are able to determine their own behavior subject to the constraints created by the behavior of other states. The field of international relations has therefore focused on attempting to explain how states behave given the existence of anarchy, and when this leads to war and peace. Gradually over time, however, the state-centric approach of IR has been relaxed and the conceptual tools of IR have evolved to explore the role of non-state actors in world politics and to collapse the sharp distinction between the inter-state level and domestic politics. As it has done so, IR has also engaged with the politics of a growing range of empirical areas including human rights, the environment, and trade.

The concepts that have emerged from IR have great relevance for understanding the international politics of forced migration. They can shed light on the relationships that exist between broader global political trends, on the one hand, and the causes and consequences of forced migration, on the other hand. However, perhaps most significantly, they can help to explain the behavior of states and other actors toward forced migration and so offer insights into the conditions under which forced migration can be prevented and its most serious human consequences mitigated.

However, surprisingly, there has been little systematic attempt either from within IR or Forced Migration to explore what IR might offer the study of forced migration. Instead only isolated pockets of literature have emerged on the international politics of forced migration. Some have emerged from within Forced Migration; some from within IR. Depending on which side of this disciplinary fence they have emerged from, the work has had a different character and a different purpose. The work within Forced Migration Studies has used IR Theory to get insights for practice of forced migration; the work within IR has used the empirical area to develop IR Theory. However, the two sub-disciplines have not been systematically integrated to explore the relevance that integrating the concepts of IR Theory with the empirical terrain of forced migration can offer both areas.

The majority of the existing literature on forced migration and global politics relates to refugees and focuses on their relationship to security and conflict. In particular, a significant amount of work has explored the security implications of refugees for host states, whether in the developed or the developing world (Milner 2000; Weiner 1995; Van Selm 2003). This work has varied in the extent to which it has identified the displaced as a direct source of threat to states or an indirect threat that emerges from the way in which forced migrants are perceived particularly by host communities. Meanwhile, more critical work has examined the relationship between forced migration and the human security of those who are displaced (Newman and Van Selm 2004; Poku and Graham 2000). There has also been a growing body of work from mainstream IR scholars examining the empirical relationship between refugee movements and conflict and identifying the conditions under which refugees exacerbate conflict (Lischer 2005; Stedman and Tanner 2003; Salehyan and Gleditsch 2006).

There is also literature on the emergence of the global refugee regime and its relationship to the state system. Much of the work on the emergence of the refugee regime is historical and descriptive, and makes little use of theory (Loescher 2001; Skran 1995; Zolberg et al. 1989). It provides the empirical contours for the study of the institutions that respond to refugees but does little with the material that draws upon IR Theory. Other authors have taken a broader historical perspective in order to explore the dialectical relationship between the emergence of the state system and the historical creation of the category of the refugee (Gibney 2004; Haddad 2008).

Other work attempts to explore the role of UNHCR in promoting international cooperation on refugee protection. Some of this work draws upon wider theories of international cooperation in order to explore the role that power, interests, and norms play in shaping states' responses to refugees, either globally or within a regional context (Betts 2008; Cronin 2003; Suhrke 1998; Thielemann 2003). Meanwhile, some actors examine the role of UNHCR as a partly autonomous international actor, exploring its role in world politics and the lessons it offers for the study of international institutions (Barnett and Finnemore 2004; Betts and Durieux 2007; Loescher et al. 2008; Whitaker 2008).

There is also a critical International Political Economy literature that attempts to examine the way in which the root causes of displacement are underpinned by North–South relations and wider inequalities in the international system. Much of this work argues that an exclusive focus on humanitarian assistance or refugee protection sidelines critical engagement with the power relations that lead to forced migration in the first instance. The work highlights, for example, the roles of structural adjustment policies, Southern states' access to markets, and the international trade in commodities and raw materials as underlying forced migration (Castles 2003; Chimni 1998; Collinson 2003; Duffield 2001).

Beyond these pockets of work, there is little work on the international politics of other aspects of forced migration. The work that exists on IDPs is mainly either descriptive or focuses on analyzing the process of norm creation that has taken place in relation to IDP protection (Phuong 2004; Weiss and Korn 2006). The work that exists on DIDR, meanwhile, largely analyzes domestic politics and has not systematically drawn upon concepts from IR. There is therefore a need to explore more systematically what international relations can offer the study of forced migration and vice versa. A huge range of IR concepts still remain to be applied to examine an array of empirical issues within forced migration. This book therefore represents the first time that the concepts of IR and the empirical context of forced migration have been fully integrated in one volume. It attempts to draw upon and integrate the existing literature on forced migration and international relations, situating it within IR, while also drawing upon a range of IR concepts of relevance to but not yet applied to the analysis of forced migration.

This Book

This book is based on the "International Relations and Forced Migration" course taught at the University of Oxford as part of the graduate studies programme offered by the Refugee Studies Centre. The book stems from the recognition that, despite a growing number of courses being taught at universities that examine the inextricable relationship between forced migration and global politics, there was no single textbook that fully integrates an introduction to IR with an exploration of its application to and relevance for the study of forced migration. The book therefore attempts to fill that gap and to provide a self-contained course that sets out the core concepts of IR in an accessible way and applies them to explore the international politics of forced migration.

Given the expertise of the author and the balance of the existing literature, the main focus of the book is on the international politics of refugees. However, it also integrates into its analysis consideration of the role that IR can play in shedding light on the politics of other areas of forced migration, which have been less widely explored by the existing literature. Each chapter has three main components. Firstly, it introduces a set of concepts and debates from IR. Secondly, it explains their relevance to forced migration. Thirdly, it uses historical or contemporary case studies to integrate the theory with specific empirical examples.

1

International Relations Theories

IR theory provides a set of tools for understanding and explaining the behavior of states and other actors in world politics. It emerges from a concern to theorize why states behave as they do and the conditions under which conflict and cooperation take place between states. Although there is a literature on the international politics of forced migration, there has been very little application of IR theory to understand the politics of forced migration. This is surprising since IR theory and forced migration have potentially great relevance for one another. Forced migration offers a relatively uncharted empirical terrain within which IR theory can test and develop its core concepts, while IR theory can contribute to explaining why states respond to forced migration as they do, while also shedding light on aspects of the causes and consequences of forced migration.

This chapter therefore sets out six of the main groups of IR theories and outlines their relevance for understanding different aspects of forced migration. In doing so it attempts to situate the existing literature on the international politics of forced migration within the main IR theories. The theories that are chosen are not intended to be exhaustive of IR theory but represent the main groups of theories and those with arguably the greatest relevance for interpreting the international politics of forced migration. The six groups of theories that have been chosen are: neo-realism, liberal institutionalism, analytical liberalism, the English School, constructivism, and critical theory.

Each group of theory makes a different set of assumptions about the main actors in global politics and the way in which they can be analyzed. They place different emphasis on which are the most important factors that shape world politics – for example, power, interests, or ideas; they take different levels of analysis as privileged – for example, inter-state relations, domestic politics, or trans-national relations; they make different assumptions about the most relevant actors in world politics – states or non-state-actors; and they make different methodological, ontological, and epistemological assumptions about the study of world politics.

IR theory is useful for explaining and understanding the behavior of states and other global political actors – for example, toward refugees or other forced migrants. Because it can help to explain and understand, it also has relevance for knowing how to influence the behavior of states and other global political actors in a given area of world politics. Many IR theorists claim to "belong to" or to "be part of" a given school of IR theory. This is to miss the point. Although not all of the theories can be used simultaneously because of their incompatible assumptions, no one theory is universally "better" than the others. They simply serve different purposes and one may be better than another in a particular context and for explaining a particular problem.

This chapter suggests that the IR theories represent a set of tools, which can be used in order to explain and understand particular problems and issues from different angles. Theory can be considered to be analogous to a set of torches. Rather like a set of torches, the theories can be used to illuminate different parts of a darkened room. However, it will not be possible to use all of the torches simultaneously or to view all of the room at once. Rather, different torches can be used to shed light on different parts of the room. All of the torches have their uses; which one a person picks up depends upon which part of the room he or she is most interested in viewing. In other words, no one theory is all-explanatory or should be privileged for analyzing all aspects of world politics. Different theories can shed light on some aspects of world politics and are blind to others.

This chapter therefore sets out the theoretical lenses through which IR theory can offer an understanding of the international politics of forced migration. It explains each of the main IR theories, and then suggests how each of these theories would interpret the behavior of states and other political actors in relation to forced migration. Having done this, the chapter applies the different theoretical approaches to a specific case study – the historical emergence and evolution of the global refugee regime – in order to illustrate the different aspects of the case study that the different theories most clearly illuminate.

The Theories

The dominant academic debates in International Relations have evolved since the middle of the twentieth century. The so-called First Debate, which dominated IR until the 1970s, was between realists and idealists, the former believing that the prospects for international cooperation were limited and that states should therefore act in their own self interest; and the latter being more optimistic about the prospects for cooperation, peace, and the development of international institutions. The so-called Second Debate (the "neo-neo debate"), which emerged during the 1980s, was between neo-realism and liberal-institutionalism and revolved around whether states could be conceptualized as acting on the basis of a concern with their relative gains or on the basis of a concern for absolute gains, the latter implying greater prospects for international cooperation than the former. Finally, much of international relations has focused, since the 1990s, on the so-called Third Debate – or the "inter-paradigm debate." This debate relates to the division between rationalist approaches to the study of world politics (mainly drawn from economics) and reflectivist approaches to world politics (mainly drawn from sociology). The former group includes neo-realism and liberal institutionalism and takes states as the main actors in world politics. It regards states as rational, maximizing actors whose identity and preferences are pre-determined and fixed. In contrast, the latter group sees states' and other actors' identities and preferences as constituted through the role of ideas and knowledge.

In explaining IR theories and their relevance to forced migration, it would have been possible to discuss more than a dozen different IR theory labels. However, only six groups of theories are addressed here. The choice of theories addressed by this chapter is not exhaustive. Furthermore, the division of theories is something that could have been done in a variety of ways. For example, "critical theories" could have been divided between neo-Marxism, feminism, and post-structuralism or it could have included post-colonialism. Moreover, classical realism and classical liberalism could have been included as theories in their own right. However, in order to simplify the structure of the chapter, critical theories are dealt with together and classical realism and classical liberalism are addressed briefly as historical antecedents of neo-realism, liberal institutionalism, and analytical liberalism. While the intention of this chapter is to capture the diversity of IR theory it balances this against trying to explain the theories that are most often used within the mainstream of the subject. This section therefore explains each one of the groups of theories and how would they interpret states' responses to forced migration.

Neo-realism

Neo-realism represents the most dominant contemporary theory of international relations. It is most commonly associated with the work of Kenneth

Waltz and John Mearsheimer. It places military power and *realpolitik* at the forefront of the study of world politics. It is the conceptual lens most commonly adopted by academics and policy-makers in the US to understand trends in world politics. Neo-realism has its roots in a long tradition of classical realist thought. The most articulate classical realist proponent was Hans Morgenthau who, in *Politics Among Nations* (1948), argued that all politics is essentially about power. Given that, for Morgenthau and other classical realists, human nature is inherently self-interested and power hungry, the great political challenge is to achieve order. For Morgenthau this represented a significant challenge at the domestic level, even where there is a sovereign authority in the form of a government. Yet, at the international level, this problem of pursuing order was compounded by the absence of a single sovereign authority. For classical realists, because of the absence of a world government – or a Hobbesian "Leviathan" – at the international level, the world could be characterized by "anarchy" – not in the sense of chaos or disorder but simply in the analytical sense of there being no world government.

In the absence of a Leviathan at the international level, Morgenthau argued that states are (analytically) and should (normatively) be self-interested and concerned to maximize their military power. He suggested that order is possible at the international level but that it does not emerge from states being pacifistic or attempting to appease one another. Rather, for Morgenthau, states' pursuit of power is itself the source of stability. Order, for classical realists, comes from the so-called balance of power. By pursuing military power and then informally grouping together with other states until the configurations of military alliances meant that all the potential adversaries had equal power, order could be maintained. So long as a state believes that another state has – independently or through its alliances – roughly equal military strength, it will be deterred from military aggression. Order will therefore follow from the balance of power. So long as the balance of power is not disturbed in some way, stability will endure. For Morgenthau, the logical corollary of this was that the righteous policy-maker should pursue a power maximizing strategy. Attempting to act "morally" through showing consideration for other states will be misguided and be likely to lead to perverse outcomes.

Neo-realism emerges out of Kenneth Waltz's *Theory of International Politics* (1979). It builds upon this classical realist tradition. However, it rejects a number of core elements of classical realism. Firstly, it rejects the normative elements of classical realism, instead attempting to develop a purely analytical, scientific, and rigorous theory of international politics. Secondly, it rejects classical realism's mixing of the domestic level and international level in its explanation of state behavior. For Morgenthau, state behavior is rooted in both human nature and the balance of power at the system level. For Waltz, on the other hand, these levels should not be mixed and neo-realism explains the behavior of states solely on the basis of the "system level." Indeed for Waltz, theories of world politics might be developed at three levels: first-image theories (based on the behavior of individuals), second-image theories (based on politics at the domestic level), and third-image theories (based on the system level). Neo-realism is a distinctly third-image theory of world politics.

Neo-realism draws upon microeconomic theory to build a rigorous and universal theory of state behavior. In order to do so, it makes a number of simplifying assumptions about international politics. Firstly, states are the main actors in world politics. Secondly, states' key concern is survival and self-help and they can be conceived as rational, self-interested power maximizers. Thirdly, states are concerned with *relative gains* vis-à-vis other states. Fourthly, states are only functionally differentiated on the basis of their capabilities. Fifthly, anarchy (as the absence of world government) is the key ordering principle in the international system. In summary, these assumptions create an image of a "black box" state whose identity is fixed and whose interests are pre-defined as being to maximize military power.

Based on these assumptions, neo-realism makes a number of analytical claims about international politics. It suggests, like classical realism, that order comes from the balance of power and that states' primary and exclusive concern should be to maximize military power as a means to maintain their survival and uphold the balance of power. Furthermore, within this account of world politics, the prospects for international cooperation are extremely limited. States are amoral, self-interested power maximizers with very little scope for altruistic or moral behavior. Because they are concerned with maximizing their relative gains vis-à-vis other states, they will not engage in long-run cooperation but will simply engage in temporary alliances that enable them to "balance" against other states.

For neo-realists, the prospects for international cooperation are extremely limited. Because states are self-interested and concerned with their relative gains, international institutions will have little relevance to how states behave unless they are underpinned by power and coercion. The only circumstances under which a situation like international cooperation might arise is when a powerful state has such a significant self-interest in a given form of collective action that it would be prepared to underwrite the entire cost of unilaterally acting at the global level, and tolerate the free-riding of other, smaller states. In other words, for neo-realists, collective action at the global level can only be explained by self-interested hegemony. The view that a powerful state may unilaterally act in the collective interest out of self-interest is referred to as Hegemonic Stability Theory (Gilpin 1975; Kindleberger 1973; Olson and Zeckhauser 1967).

Prescriptively, neo-realists adopt a range of views on how states should behave in order to maximize their interests. Waltz (1979) offers a "defensive realist" perspective, suggesting that states should engage in balancing. So long as the balance of power endures, peace and stability will be preserved. On the contrary, Mearsheimer (2001) offers an "offensive realist" prescription, counseling great powers to aggressively pursue power under all circumstances. Since other states will adopt this strategy, Mearsheimer suggests it would be naïve for any state to engage in power-satisficing behavior. If it were to do so, challenger states would be likely to overtake the preponderant power.

Meanwhile, Walt's (1985) concept of the "balance of threat" offers an alternative neo-realist perspective. It suggests that whether or not a state is a threat is not solely reducible to its military capabilities. Rather, it depends on a range of factors – its aggregate strength, its geographical proximity, its offensive capabilities, and its offensive intentions. For Walt, in contradistinction to Waltz and Mearsheimer, states should balance not against power but rather against threat.

So what can neo-realism offer understanding of the international politics of forced migration? The answer is: not all that much by itself. For neo-realists, forced migration is simply not likely to be a particularly important element of global politics. It is partly for this reason, and given neo-realism's dominance of IR, that there has been so little academic work on forced migration from an IR perspective. Neo-realism's concern is with military power and the politics of war, peace and "hard" security, rather than with areas of "soft security." Furthermore, the fact that neo-realism assumes states to be "black box" entities, and therefore does not look inside the state, excludes a number of important sources of explanation of the causes, consequences, and responses to forced migration. Indeed, in forced migration, the characters of the country of origin, host country, and other third countries clearly matter for explaining variation in outcomes. Similarly, domestic political processes are likely to matter, and the politics of forced migration is not reducible to the analyzing changes in the distribution of military capabilities at the system level.

Nevertheless, this is not to say that a neo-realist perspective has nothing to contribute to understanding the politics of forced migration. Rather, it will simply see the causes, consequences and responses to forced migration as a by-product of states' wider concerns to maximize their military power and relative security. In particular, a neo-realist approach to the politics of forced migration might be based upon four significant claims or hypotheses:

The sources of forced migration may be significantly attributable to changes in the balance of power. For neo-realists, international conflicts are the result of changes in the balance of power. Realist approaches to IR have their origins in attempting to explain how changes in the balance of power in Europe led to conflict in the First and Second World Wars (Carr 1946; Morgenthau 1948). So long as the balance of power holds, there will be stability in the international system; once there is a power vacuum or a shift, conflict will characterize the process of realignment. The process through which international conflict, state partition, and state creation took place in Europe, South Asia, and the Middle East in the first half of the twentieth century, for example, highlights how these processes often lead to significant human displacement – whether internal or external. From a realist perspective the refugee crises that gave rise to the creation of the League of Nations High Commissioner for Refugees and the United Nations High Commissioner for Refugees are a product of the shifts in the balance of power in Europe between 1914 and 1945.

States see forced migration through the lens of security. From a neo-realist perspective, forced migration only matters insofar as it has a relationship to national security. This is one of the reasons why the majority of mainstream IR work on forced migration has examined the relationship between refugees and national security. In particular, it has examined the role of refugees as combatants and refugee camps as sanctuaries for combatants during internal or interstate conflicts (Lischer 2005). In a Southern state context, refugee camps may be sites for wider trafficking in arms or offer succor or refuge to combatants (Crisp 2003). Alternatively, the mere presence of refugees on the territory of another state may indirectly undermine national security by creating tensions or competition for resources between displaced people and the local host population (Milner 2009). Recent work has explored the relationship between refugees and terrorism and whether protracted refugee or IDP situations might represent potential sources of recruitment (Juma and Kagwanja 2008).

States will contribute to providing protection and solutions for forced migrants for exclusively self-interested reasons. From a neo-realist perspective, states are unlikely to engage in altruistic or ethically oriented behavior. Rather, the assumptions of the theory suggest that states will act purely in a way that maximizes their own interests and power. Consequently, neo-realism would predict that states' engagement with forced migration, and their attempts to contribute to protection, solutions, or addressing root causes would not be underpinned by an altruistic concern for the welfare of the displaced. Rather, a neo-realist perspective would expect states' responses to be highly selective and based on wider interests. For example, during the Cold War, refugees were given asylum and resettlement because of strategic Cold War interests (Loescher 2001). Offering asylum to defectors from the USSR and the Warsaw Pact countries was seen as a means to discredit Communism. Throughout the history of UNHCR, states have selectively earmarked their contributions to UNHCR in accordance with their own strategic and security interests. When states do not have an interest in contributing to protection and solutions, international institutions will have little impact on their behavior. They will be purely led by attempting to maximize their wider interests – whether security-based or economic.

International cooperation in relation to forced migration only takes place when there is hegemony. From a neo-realist perspective, the prospects for international cooperation to address the root causes of displacement or to provide protection or solutions are extremely limited. States will act on their own self-interests and will not wish to be constrained by long-term institutionalized cooperation. The only time when collective action will take place is when a hegemon has a sufficiently strong interest in addressing issues related to forced migration that it will either unilaterally underwrite the costs of addressing the problem or enforce compliance from other weaker states. For example, when the US had a strong interest in addressing the refugee crises in Europe after the Second World War and the Indo-Chinese mass exodus after the 1970s it was prepared to underwrite a significant proportion of the resettlement and the financial costs of the burden-sharing initiatives (Suhrke 1998).

Liberal institutionalism

Liberal institutionalism emerged in the late 1970s from the observation that there was increasing international cooperation between states, which neo-realism was simply unable to explain, and which was not reducible to the role of a hegemon. It attributed this increasing cooperation to the proliferation in international institutions, which enabled states to acquire mutual benefits from international cooperation (Keohane 1984). Liberal institutionalism makes the same assumptions as neo-realism except for one crucial difference: states are concerned with *absolute gains* rather than relative gains. Other than this changed assumption, states remain rational, self-interested power maximizers. Yet, this single altered assumption is important because it dramatically alters the prospects for international cooperation. If states are concerned with absolute gains then cooperation can offer opportunities for mutual gain and world politics becomes a positive-sum rather than a zero-sum game.

Given that states can mutually benefit from international cooperation, international institutions can play an important role in facilitating that cooperation. In particular, they overcome collective action failures by creating the regulatory framework within which states can be assured that other states will reciprocate over a longer term time horizon. Where for example, states would be better off acting collectively but do not act collectively because of a suspicion that other states will free-ride or not reciprocate, an institutional framework can change these incentives. For example, Keohane (1984) identifies the role that international institutions can play in reducing the transactions costs of cooperation, reducing the likelihood of states "free-riding" through surveillance and information, and facilitating issue-linkage in bargaining to ensure that cooperation can be mutually beneficial. In other words, institutions can enable states to be better off acting collectively than they would have been acting in isolation.

Liberal institutionalism has particularly been applied to highlight the role that international institutions can play in the provision of so-called global public goods. As with street lighting at the domestic level, global public goods are goods, once provided, the benefits of which are non-excludable and non-rival. In other words, the benefits of global public goods extend to all actors irrespective of whether they contribute to provision and are not diminished by another actor's enjoyment of those benefits. Examples of global public goods include climate-change mitigation, the development of a polio vaccine, and international action to address meteorites (Barrett 2007). The problem with global public goods is that no individual state has an incentive to be the provider and all states have incentives to free-ride. Collectively, states would be better off if they shared the costs of providing; individually their rational response is to shirk responsibility. Institutions can overcome this problem by creating the conditions under which states reciprocate in providing global public goods.

Liberal institutionalism has particular relevance for the international politics of forced migration because it can help to explain the conditions under which international cooperation takes place in relation to different aspects of forced migration. It can offer insights into when and why international regimes such as the global refugee regime have emerged and when they are effective. On the other hand, the main limitation of liberal institutionalism is that, like neo-realism, it takes states as undifferentiated black-boxed actors and also looks at international politics purely at the inter-state level. A liberal institutionalist approach to the international politics of forced migration would have a number of characteristics:

States created and maintain international institutions relating to forced migration for reasons of mutual self-interest. From a liberal institutionalist perspective, states agreed to create the 1951 Refugee Convention because they believed that its existence would serve their own interests. They believed that the regime would: i) offer security by reintegrating the displaced within the state system; and ii) fulfil a humanitarian function. Even though providing asylum imposes a cost on an individual state, the existence of the regime provided these benefits and so states were prepared to cooperate provided others reciprocated. The regime created the conditions for this reciprocity to take place. A similar logic could be applied to analyze why a regime has begun to emerge in relation to IDPs. States recognize the long-run benefits of international cooperation and so have begun to work to create an international regime that can build long-run confidence in reciprocity.

International institutions relating to forced migration can influence states and facilitate international cooperation by creating rational incentives for states to behave differently. The creation of international agreements and international organizations to oversee those agreements generates incentives for rationally acting states to adjust their behavior. For example, even though the refugee regime has no enforcement mechanism, it has an influence on how states respond to refugees. The surveillance and monitoring function of UNHCR in Article 35 of the 1951 Convention means that states can be identified and highlighted as violators if they breach norms such as *non-refoulement*. This international institutional framework means that it is in states' long-run self-interest to comply with the regime because they a) value the existence of the overall regime, and b) know that if they do not comply they will be identified as free-riders and other states may also cease to cooperate.

Analytical liberalism

Most International Relations theories (neo-liberalism, liberal institutionalism, and liberal constructivism) analyze world politics at the "system" or inter-state level. They thereby bracket the role of domestic politics. One of the great challenges for IR has been how to conceptualize the relationship between domestic and international politics. Rationalist approaches have struggled to reintroduce the "unit-level" of analysis into IR without compromising the rigor and parsimony of the system-level theories. The main contribution of analytical liberalism is to reintroduce domestic politics into IR while not undermining the possibility of retaining a theory of inter-state relations.

Analytical liberalism builds on the legacy of idealism and classical liberalism (Angell 1910; Kant 1795). These theories are associated with the

Wilsonian values that led to the creation of the League of Nations. Classical liberals argued, against classical realism, that international cooperation and enduring peace in international relations could be possible. They further argued that one of the main factors that determines how a state behaves in its foreign policy is the character and domestic politics of that state. In particular, classical liberal thought argued that liberal democratic states are less likely to go to war with one another than non-liberal democratic states. This so-called "Democratic Peace Theory" formed the basis of much of liberal theory in the second half of the twentieth century. (Doyle 1997; Russett 1993).

However, one of the main criticisms of classical liberalism is that it was more ideology than theory. In positing the claim that liberal democratic states behave in "more desirable ways" it made strongly normative claims about how the domestic character of states should be, and had less to offer in terms of being a generalizable and analytical theory of world politics. In response to this, the work of Andrew Moravcsik (1997) has attempted to develop an analytical theory based on the legacy of classical liberalism. While abandoning many of the normative and ideological claims of classical liberalism, Moravcsik develops an account of the way in which domestic politics matters for a state's foreign policy.

Moravcsik argues that the "national interest" emerges from the aggregation of domestic preferences. In particular, foreign policy emerges from interest-group formation and lobbying within the state. Meanwhile, events at the system level matter only insofar as they feedback into domestic preferences. Moravcsik argues that his theory is compatible with neo-realism and liberal institutionalism because its analysis of the "unit-level" determines the conditions under which neo-realist or liberal institutionalist assumptions then apply at the "system-level." Where Moravcsik diverges from classical liberalism is that the specifically "liberal" character of a state no longer matters; what is important is the domestic character of the state and domestic politics, irrespective of whether the state is liberal, authoritarian, capitalist, or socialist.

Analytical liberalism has not been applied to analyze the international politics of forced migration. However, it has great potential because of the way it allows international politics to be explored on "two levels" and for domestic politics and preferences to be reintroduced to the analysis. Indeed, when states provide asylum or refugee protection, or take humanitarian action in relation to IDPs, this behavior is significantly influenced by the domestic politics and character of the state. Public opinion, electoral politics, interest groups, the decision-making procedures of the state, and that state's core political values all matter for how it responds to refugees and

IDPs. In particular, an analytical liberal approach to forced migration might make three core claims:

Domestic politics significantly influences states' responses to refugees and other forced migrants. Analytical liberalism sheds light on the fact that the way in which states relate to forced migration, not only within their own territory, but also abroad, is strongly influenced by domestic political process. In liberal democracies, elections, interest groups, and lobbying all matter for how relatively closed and communitarian or open and cosmopolitan a state's policies are at a given time. For example, in the "crisis of asylum" since the 1990s in both North and South, domestic politics, conducted through the media, electoral campaigning, and public information campaigns, has shaped asylum and refugee policies. In the North, the media and politicization have contributed to a backlash against asylum seekers. This has contributed to the development of foreign policies designed to securitize refugees and IDPs by limiting their access to spontaneous-arrival asylum channels (Crisp 2003).

Interest groups in domestic politics shape states' international responses. At various stages, states have adopted more or less generous and open policies toward refugees and asylum seekers on the basis of interest-group formation and lobbying. Where diaspora groups have been particularly active within a country's domestic politics, they have often been able to lobby effectively for greater resettlement or humanitarian assistance for a particular group of displaced people. In the aftermath of the Vietnam War, for example, the Vietnamese diaspora in the US mobilized to influence the US Government to provide significant amounts of resettlement to Vietnamese refugees as part of the international community's response to the so-called Indochinese "boat people" (Robinson 1998).

The character of a state will shape its response to forced migration. Not all states respond to forced migration in the same way. Historically, some states have adopted particularly generous humanitarian responses to refugees and IDPs. Canada and Norway for example have consistently made disproportionately large contributions in humanitarian and development assistance. Meanwhile, during the 1970s and 1980s, Tanzania had a reputation for being one of the most generous asylum states in Africa. From an analytical liberal perspective, the character of a state and its domestic decision-making procedures will matter. For example, liberal, democratic states may have certain values which will make them respond in restrained, pacific, and sometimes humanitarian ways (Steiner 2003). On the other hand, however, an interesting paradox emerges in many developing countries in which liberalization and democratization, in the context of structural adjustment policies, appear to have made states less generous and hospitable toward refugees. Structural adjustment has increased competition for resources between citizens and non-citizens while democratization has enabled citizens to express their grievances about this through the electoral process. In many cases, it seems that African states were able to be more generous toward refugees as authoritarian states than they are as democracies (Crisp 2003; Milner 2009).

English School/international society

The so-called English School of International Relations is closely associated with Hedley Bull's *The Anarchical Society* (1977). In terms of its position along the spectrum of IR theory, it can be situated between classical realism and constructivism. As with (neo-)realism, anarchy and the balance of power are important. As for Waltz, international politics is characterized by anarchy, states are the main actors in world politics, and order emerges as a result of the balance of power. However, unlike for neo-realism, anarchy and the balance of power are social institutions rather than universal, scientific laws. For Bull, international politics can be characterized by an international *society* rather than an international system. In other words, rather than inter-state relations being characterized by strategic interaction between pre-defined units, it is characterized by a social interaction in which norms and institutions emerge and define how states behave.

This means that although international politics may be characterized by anarchy, and order may emerge from the balance of power, these are not inevitable. Order represents the current dominant value of international society, but it is conceivable that justice may, in future, become the dominant value. The English School approach therefore draws attention to the need to place world politics within a broader historical context and to recognize how the institutions of international society shape what states regard to be appropriate conduct for a given identity. For English School theorists, international society is in the process of evolving from a pluralist society, in which sovereign states hold different sets of values, to a solidarist international society in which common cosmopolitan values are emerging in a way that is creating institutions that are increasingly based on not only order but also justice (Wheeler 2000; Wight 1977).

The English School has been largely sidelined from mainstream North American International Relations. However, it offers a useful interpretive approach to understanding world politics because it places international politics within a broader historical context, shedding light on the historical contingency and specificity of particular norms of state behavior and the contexts in which they have emerged. It therefore allows the international politics of forced migration to be situated in broader institutional structures relating to sovereignty, the state system, and the emergence of international law. An English School approach to forced migration might advance two main claims:

Patterns of forced migration and states' responses need to be seen in a broader context of historical change. The English School highlights that states' responses to forced migration are strongly influenced by the institutions that shape state behavior in the international society. In turn, it highlights how these institutions have emerged in a specific historical context. In particular, it suggests that the very concept of a refugee cannot be seen in isolation from the historical creation of the contemporary system of nation-states. For Haddad (2008), it was the creation of the Westphalian state system that brought into existence the notion of the refugee and also created the inevitability of refugees. She argues that there is an important and mutually constitutive relationship between state, citizenship, and refugees. Prior to the creation of the Westphalian system, she argues, refugees could not have existed as a meaningful category in the feudal, religiously divided Europe without clearly delineated nation-states (Haddad 2008). Furthermore, the categories of forced migrants and the international institutional responses to them have evolved within the broader context of changing notions of state sovereignty and emerging institutions relating to human rights.

How states see forced migration is the product of the dominant international institutions. The English School highlights the importance of institutions in shaping how states define their interests. The institutions of the state system, the balance of power, mutual respect for treaties and norms, for example, shape how states behave in all areas of world politics including forced migration. Since states are part of a society of states, their behavior, like that of people in a society, will be shaped by social norms. One of the reasons why states will adhere to social norms is that, like people, they pursue legitimacy. Although states pursue economic and military power, this, by itself, is not particularly useful. A far more efficient means to wield influence in world politics is through holding authority, which can be considered to be "power plus legitimacy" (Hurrell 2007). The English School sheds light on the way in which states pursue legitimacy as a means to acquire authority. One of the main means by which they can do so is through respecting international norms and institutions. From an English School perspective, the pursuit of legitimacy is a central part of explaining why states adhere to, for example, the core principles of the 1951 Refugee Convention. It also contributes to explaining why normative taboos in forced migration such as the non-deportation of citizens are generally upheld in international society (Gibney 2008).

Constructivism

Constructivism is distinct from rationalist approaches to IR in terms of what is often referred to as its "ontology." Ontology relates how actors – whether people or states – are understood to exist. Rationalist theories assume that the identities of states are fixed; they are determined by the assumptions of the model and do not change through states' interactions with one another. In contrast, rather than assuming that states' identities and interests are fixed, as neo-realism and liberal institutionalism do, constructivism recognizes that states' identities are constituted and changed through their interactions with one another. In other words, states' interests are a product of their identities which, in turn, emerge through social interaction. This idea that states' identities and interests are not fixed but can be changed introduces a key role in world politics for norms and ideas. It implies that states can be persuaded, though ideas or argumentation to view issues or problems differently and so change their behavior over time on the basis of holding different perceptions.

In Wendt's *Social Theory of International Politics* (1999) he suggests that "anarchy is what states make of it." In contrast to rationalist approaches to IR, he argues that even though there may be no world government, there is no inevitability to the type of behavior that follows from this. Even if it is analytically correct to identify "anarchy," states can adopt a variety of different behaviors and responses to this. While the structural conditions of the international system may be defined in a certain way, states have agency to respond to those structures and, over time, the interaction between the structure of the international system and the units that comprise it will lead to change in the structures and the identities of the actors.

Wendt's (1992; 1999) approach to world politics has in common with neo-realism and liberal institutionalism that it is a system-level theory of international politics. In other words it does not open up the "black box" of the state to include an account of domestic politics or incorporate analysis on non-state actors. Nevertheless, other constructivist writers have gone beyond these rigid assumptions to apply a constructivist ontology to explore the role of non-state actors and trans-national actors in world politics. For example, constructivism has explored the way in which international human rights norms become embedded within domestic politics and, in turn, feedback and shape international politics (Risse et al. 1999). It has also analyzed the way in which non-state actors have played an important role in shaping norms and ideas in ways that have fundamentally altered the behavior of states over time – in areas such as colonialism, slavery, and human rights (Crawford 2002; Keck and Sikkink 1998).

Constructivism has a great deal to offer the study of the international politics of forced migration. It opens up the possibility that the politics of forced migration is not exclusively defined by interests and power but that ideas and norms also matter. It suggests that non-state actors such as IOs and NGOs can make a difference and that the current practices of states are not inevitable but can be changed through persuasion and argumentation. Two core elements of a constructivist approach to forced migration would be:

The refugee regime and IDP regime have socialized states in a way that shapes their values and interests over time. From a constructivist perspective, norms and institutions matter, not because they constrain rational, self-interested actors but because they constitute and shape how those actors see the world and understand their interests. In other words, they socialize states and other actors into holding certain perceptions about who they are and what they value. Despite having no enforcement mechanism, the basic norms of the 1951 Convention have broadly been upheld. From a constructivist perspective, this can be interpreted as being because states have internalized those norms over time, institutionalizing them within domestic legislation in ways that have then shaped their behavior and interests in relation to asylum and refugee protection. As a result, core norms such as *non-refoulement* have become increasingly established. Furthermore, constructivism would argue that the emergence of norms relating to IDP protection has begun to change states' perceptions of IDPs and led to a gradual acceptance that IDPs have a legal status and states have obligations to engage in the protection of IDPs just as they do refugees.

Non-state actors such as International Organizations can play an important role as actors in world politics. Constructivism opens up the possibility that non-state actors – such as IOs, NGOs, and academics – can exert independent influence on world politics. From this perspective, for example, UNHCR can be viewed as having had an independent influence on state behavior through persuasion and moral authority (Loescher et al. 2008). Its own organizational dynamics have also been important for the international politics of refugee protection, shaping how it has responded to states' interests and how it has used its autonomy to shape the politics of refugee protection

(Barnett and Finnemore 2004). Constructivism also highlights an important role for NGOs in the politics of forced migration. In the area of DIDR, significant normative change has taken place, largely because of the role of trans-national civil society. For example, the resistance of the Narmada Bachao Andolan (NBA) movement to the construction of the Sardar Sarovar Dam in India, and its links to civil society outside India, contributed to changing awareness and understanding about DIDR. Moreover, this contributed to the development of new international norms through changing World Bank lending guidelines and influencing the creation of the World Commission on Dams, created in 1998 to examine the impact of the construction of big dams in developing countries (Khagram 2004).

Critical theory

Critical theory approaches to international relations represent a broad spectrum of different theories. They have in common the view that theory and concepts are not neutral and objective but are themselves political. In Robert Cox's words "all theory is for someone and for some purpose." He distinguishes between "problem-solving theory" which "takes the world as it finds it," and critical theory, which questions how knowledge is created and whose interests it serves (Cox 1981). Critical theories can be divided into neo-Marxist, Frankfurt School, and post-structuralist approaches.

Neo-Marxist approaches to IR identify capitalism as a major driving force in world politics. The starting point for understanding neo-Marxist approaches to IR emerges from the Leninist claim that "imperialism is the highest stage of capitalism." Once capitalists exhausted domestic opportunities to extract surplus value from labor, Lenin claimed, they would need to go abroad to seek alternative sources of labor and raw material to which to apply their capital. Dependency Theory and World-System Theory build on this by arguing that inter-state relations are defined hierarchically according to states' position in the global division of labor. For Wallerstein (2004), the world divides into core countries (the economies of which are mainly based on the service industry), semi-periphery countries (the economies of which are mainly based on creating manufactured and semi-manufactured products to export to the core), and periphery countries (the economies of which are mainly based on primary products that are exported to the semi-periphery). For Wallerstein, this hierarchy shapes how states, as the vehicle for capitalism, relate to one another. Much of critical theory builds on this Marxist foundation. For example, Gramsci (1971) built on Marx's notions of base (as the relationship between capital and labor) and superstructure (as the culture that supports the relationship between capital and labor) to argue that the concepts and ideas that shape people's perceptions of the world themselves reinforce power relations. For Gramsci, hegemonic forms of knowledge emerge which shape how the world is seen. These hegemonic forms of knowledge lead to dominant ways of seeing the world that uphold existing power relations. In other words, knowledge is linked to power and the liberal frameworks through which people interpret the world are themselves part of the prevailing power structures.

Related to this, the Frankfurt School of writers, such as Adorno and Horkheimer (1972), have argued that culture and knowledge shape how people see the world. Concepts and categories are not neutral but contribute to shaping what people regard as possible. The dominant knowledge structures limit the possibilities for reflection and for conceiving alternatives. However, the Frankfurt School attempted to conceive a Critical Theory project designed to emancipate people from the hegemony of dominant forms of knowledge. For example, Habermas's (1993) notion of "discourse ethics" suggests that through dialogue people from different cultural perspectives can dialogically undercover a universalist, cosmopolitan truths. Linklater (1982; 1998) applies the Frankfurt School to IR to argue that the Westphalian state system creates a dominant and totalizing form of knowledge which defines how people see and categorize themselves. However, drawing upon Habermas, he argues that the state system inherently contains contradictions within it that offer possibilities for emancipation. He argues that the fact that citizenship exists at multiple levels – state, regional, local – represents a contradiction that allows opportunities for people to move beyond the communitarian logic of the nation-state and instead realize an international cosmopolitanism.

Post-structuralism has in common with the Gramscian and Frankfurt School approaches that it identifies that there is a relationship between power and knowledge and that categories, concepts, and ideas are not neutral and objective. Where it differs is that it sees these knowledge structures as deeply entrenched and constitutive of social actors. Hence most post-structuralists are more pessimistic about the prospects for an emancipatory project that can liberate people from hegemonic knowledge. Post-structuralist approaches look at the world as made up of "discourses" – or dominant practices – that are internalized by and constitute social actors, their behavior, and world view. The most common post-structuralist approach in IR draws upon the work of Foucault to argue that the concepts and knowledge categories that make up the practice and language of world politics are inextricable from power relations. Because these discourses constitute all social actors, there is no neutral or objective vantage point from which to view or understand the discourse from outside. IR theory for example is far from neutral. Instead, it has a relationship to power and shapes the practice of world politics. Just as Foucault analyzed how social sciences such as criminology, psychology, and psychotherapy shape notions of normal behavior and lead to action to ensure control, conformity, and "normality," so too IR theory or Forced Migration Studies might be seen, from a Foucauldian perspective, as normalizing discourses that shape practice in the real world. For Foucault, the prospects for emancipation lie in using the intellectual tools of archaeology and genealogy to identify and expose how discourses have emerged and been normalized.

The various strands of critical theory invite academics to problematize the dominant categories and concepts that exist in academia and practice, and to explore how, why and for whom such concepts and ideas have emerged and become dominant. The concepts are diverse and differ in terms of their methodological and analytical implications. Nevertheless, a critical theory approach to forced migration might have two core elements:

The labels and categories of forced migration themselves represent and uphold power relations. Forced migration is conventionally divided into policy categories: "asylum seekers," "refugees," "IDPs," "project affected persons" (in the case of DIDR). These labels are often treated as unproblematic and represent the basis on which research and academic analysis are shaped. However, labeling is not neutral but has important practical and political effects (Zetter 1991). When the policy categories lead and guide research they shape it. The labels are not neutral or necessarily based on analytically substantive differences between people's circumstances. Yet, from a critical perspective, they have been created for someone and for some purpose. Critical theory invites exploration of how, why, and for whom the labels and categories of forced migration exist in the ways that they do. From a Gramscian perspective, for example, Chimni (1998) has examined the role of UNHCR in contributing to the creation and dissemination of hegemonic knowledge which works to serve the interests of Northern states rather than those of refugees or developing countries.

The nation-state should not be taken as the unproblematic starting point for analysis. Much of the analysis of forced migration takes the nation-state as an unproblematic starting point for analysis. Concepts such as refugees and IDPs are defined in relation to the nation-states and it is assumed that the Westphalian system is unchangeable and fixed. Within analysis of the international politics of forced migration, this can lead to a tendency to reify the nation-state in ways that exclude from analysis important non-state or trans-national actors. For example, if the state is not disaggregated, important interests and power relations may be excluded from analysis of politics. As neo-Marxist approaches to IR highlight, a purely state-centric approach risks ignoring the role of the international political economy in shaping the politics of forced migration. Similarly, assuming the state system to be immutable may exclude contemplating alternative conceptions of reality that might address or identify some of the underlying causes of forced migration. Critical theory approaches therefore invite post-Westphalian conceptions of the theory and practice of forced migration.

Case Study: The Evolution of the Global Refugee Regime

As was explained in the introduction, an international regime has evolved over time to regulate how states respond to refugees. A "regime" can be defined as the "norms, rules, principles, and decision-making procedures that regulate actor behavior in a given issue-area" (Krasner 1983). The refugee regime has emerged gradually and changed over time. Its historical evolution is something that the different IR theories can help to explain. However, no single IR theory can fully or adequately explain its evolution. Instead, different theories account for it differently and can explain different aspects of the process. This section briefly explains how the refugee regime has emerged and evolved in order to demonstrate what aspects of that process each of the different theories outlined above are able to shed light on (Loescher 2001: Loescher et al. 2008).

The origins of a global refugee regime emerged in the aftermath of the First World War when the League of Nations High Commissioner for Refugees (LNHCR) was created in 1921. The LNHCR did not set out a universal definition of a refugee but worked to achieve situation-specific agreements in relation to specific groups of refugees, initially those fleeing the dissolving Russian and Ottoman empires and by the 1930s those fleeing Germany and Austria. In order to enable people to move across borders, the Office provided refugees with so-called "Nansen Passports" to allow them access to flight to League members. The LNHCR's effectiveness declined as the League lost credibility in the 1930s and the Great Depression led to anti-immigration sentiment in the US and Europe (Loescher et al. 2008; Skran 1995).

The Second World War and the resulting massive displacement in Europe led to the revival of the regime. In order to ensure that repatriation of the displaced under Allied control took place, the US led an initiative to create the United Nations Relief and Rehabilitation Agency (UNRRA) in 1943. It was 70 percent funded by the US and lasted until 1947 before becoming the International Refugee Organization, which the US used as a means to coordinate post-war resettlement for Europe's displaced populations. By 1950, however, the US had little interest in an unlimited multilateral commitment to refugees. It instead wished to focus its political attention and resources on the Cold War, seeing refugee movements and defection as a means to discredit the USSR and channeling financial resources into Marshall Aid and NATO to bolster Western Europe's security as a bulwark against the USSR.

With the end of the IRO in 1950, UNHCR was created by the international community in order to address the plight of the remaining post-War refugees in Europe. Alongside it, the 1951 Convention on the Status of Refugees was negotiated as a means to create an agreed definition of who would be recognized as a refugee and what rights they would be entitled to receive. The initial scope of UNHCR and the 1951 Convention was restricted to Europe and displacement which had its origins prior to 1951, its mandate was temporary, and the Office would have to rely upon annual voluntary contributions for funding. The highly restricted mandate parameters of the 1951 Convention and UNHCR were largely dictated by the interests of the USA. Nevertheless, the enduring core mandate of the Office, to provide protection and solutions for refugees, was formally defined and continues to be the basis of its work today. For the first five years of its work, UNHCR's small staff therefore focused almost exclusively on providing limited legal protection to Europe's post-war refugees.

It was not until 1956 that UNHCR began to establish itself in the eyes of the US. The suppression of the Hungarian Revolution by the Soviet Union, and subsequent exodus of 200,000 Hungarian refugees to Austria and Yugoslavia in 1956, marked the turning point. In this context the Office managed to use its mandate skilfully, interpreting the exodus as having its origins prior to 1951, proving its usefulness to the US in the Cold War context. From the late 1950s, the work of UNHCR therefore began to expand with US support, offering informal support for Chinese refugees in Hong Kong and for Algerian refugees in Tunisia.

In 1967, the international community agreed on a Protocol to the 1951 Convention. The 1967 Protocol removed the time and geographical limitations of the 1951 Convention and was signed by a number of states, including the US, which had not signed the 1951 Convention. Nineteen-sixty-seven, and the US backing for the Protocol, marked the beginning of a truly multilateral refugee regime, in which the international community committed itself to working toward protection and solutions for refugees on a global scale. UNHCR subsequently expanded its work to provide protection to refugees in the post-colonial context and in a number of

Cold War proxy conflicts throughout Africa, Latin America, and Southeast Asia. During the 1980s, as a number of refugee situations became increasingly longstanding, UNHCR's role began to extend beyond simply offering legal protection to engaging in the management of refugee camps and settlements in the developing world. It was financially supported by the US in accordance with its strategic interests in relation to containing and discrediting Communism.

With the end of the Cold War and the "New World Order," UNHCR expanded massively under High Commissioner Sadako Ogata, and its mandate incorporated a growing range of functions including a greater role in repatriation and humanitarian relief. Even though the formal mandate of UNHCR did not change, it began to interpret its mandate in ever broader and more creative ways. One of the primary reasons for this was to try to make the Office more "relevant" to states in the context of the end of the Cold War, given that the US no longer held an obvious geo-strategic interest in refugee protection. With the end of a number of Cold War proxy conflicts and the emergence of new peace deals, UNHCR engaged in major repatriation operations to return refugees to their countries of origin, such as Cambodia, Mozambique, and Afghanistan. Meanwhile, new intra-state conflicts began to emerge, particularly in the Balkans and Sub-Saharan Africa. In this context, UNHCR was called upon by states to provide humanitarian relief, and offer care and maintenance to the displaced, not only in first countries of asylum but increasingly to IDPs within countries of origin (Loescher 2001).

In the early twenty-first century, increasing political concern with migration and security in the context of globalization and the so-called "War on Terror" contributed to an ever-less hospitable climate for refugees. States were more reluctant than ever to provide asylum or resettlement. In this context, states continued to overtly propound the integrity of the 1951 Convention and the basic tenets of the refugee regime but simultaneously worked to circumvent incurring its obligations. The creation of an IDP regime, attempts to develop the basis of international cooperation in relation to migration and human mobility, and a growth of unilateralism all began implicitly to challenge the foundations of the refugee regime. UNHCR once again defined its mandate in ever-broader terms, formalizing its role as the UN agency with responsibility for IDP protection in 2006.

This brief summary illustrates that the evolution of the global refugee regime has taken place in the context of much broader changes in world politics, and has been greatly influenced by the politics of the inter-war, Cold War, post-Cold War, and post-9/11 eras. Different IR theories would offer different accounts of the reasons for the evolution of the refugee regime, placing different degrees of importance on different factors, and telling the story in slightly different ways. Arguably, each of the theories has different strengths and weaknesses in interpreting the evolution of the refugee regime and can shed light on different aspects of the process.

A neo-realist approach would highlight the way in which the refugee regime has evolved according to the strategic interests of the major powers. From a neo-realist perspective, refugees would not have been of particular interest to those powers for their own sake. However, refugees would have been important for states in the context of their broader concern with issues relating to security and the balance of power. A neo-realist account of the regime would need to explain its emergence and endurance in relation to the extent to which it has met the strategic interests of the US. Most neo-realists would be skeptical about the prospects for multilateral cooperation but would interpret the emergence of the regime through the lens of hegemonic stability theory. Insofar as the regime served the interests of the US, it would be prepared to underwrite the costs of maintaining the regime. A neo-realist account therefore sheds light on the centrality of the US's wider geo-strategic interests for the regime. At times when the regime enabled the US to enhance its relative position vis-à-vis the USSR, the regime was strong; at times when it served no obvious strategic interest for the hegemon, the regime was weak.

A liberal institutionalist approach would emphasize that the emergence of institutionalized international cooperation took place because it was mutually beneficial for states. It would suggest that states collectively recognized that they could benefit from mechanisms that ensured that reciprocity would take place to overcome common problems. For example, it would suggest that the ad hoc agreements of the League of Nations era, the creation of UNHCR initially to overcome displacement in Europe, and the global regime created in 1967 were all based on the recognition by states that they would all be better off with international cooperation than with unilateralism, free-riding and shirking responsibility. A liberal institutionalist perspective would suggest that the endurance of the refugee regime is difficult to explain by neo-realism's emphasis on states' short-run interests but once an institutional framework guarantees reciprocity it is in states' long-run interests to continue to comply with the basis of the 1951 Convention and the 1967 Protocol even given changing political circumstances.

An analytical liberal approach would look at the role of domestic politics in shaping how states have defined their evolving interest in the regime. In the post-war context, for example, the Jewish lobby in the US and Europe played an active role in ensuring political commitment to resettlement.

Furthermore, during the Cold War, domestic politics mattered for how refugees fleeing Communism and the "red terror" were perceived and welcomed in the US. Diaspora groups and former colonial links have also influenced the selective engagement of the US and European states in refugee crises in the South. For example, the US commitment to Indochinese refugees, which was a defining feature of the refugee regime between 1975 and 1996, was partly underpinned by the role of the Vietnamese diaspora in the US.

An English School approach would emphasize broader historical trends in the evolution of the refugee regime. It might emphasize that, alongside the emergence of the refugee regime, there has been a broader shift from a pluralist international society toward a more solidarist international society. Where at the start of the twentieth century sovereignty was absolute, states held vastly different values, and there were few international institutions, a different form of international society emerged with the creation of the League of Nations and then the United Nations. A range of cosmopolitan values have emerged in relation to human rights. Although a concern with global order has certainly motivated the emergence and principles of the refugee regime, this has been tempered by values relating to justice.

A constructivist approach would point to the way in which ideas and norms have shaped states' identities and interests. Indeed, ideas have played a central role in the evolution of the regime. At crucial turning points in the regime, states' decisions have been underpinned by a broader ideational framework. In the post-war context, the creation of the UN was influenced by ideas relating to multilateralism. In the aftermath of the Cold War, UNHCR's expansion was aided by a similar ethos that the collapse of the Soviet Union marked "the end of history" and ushered in a New World Order. Similarly ideas relating to security have been central to how states have interpreted their interests in the context of concern with terrorism after 9/11. A constructivist account also draws attention to the reasons why the refugee regime has endured in spite of dramatic changes in the international system. Indeed, from a constructivist perspective, once norms such as the 1951 Convention are created, they socialize states over time. For instance, international norms become domestically internalized and embedded on how states respond at the international level. A constructivist approach also draws attention to the role that UNHCR has played as an autonomous actor in world politics. For example, how at different stages, under Lindt in 1956 and Ogata in the 1990s, UNHCR has taken advantage of wider political contexts in order to make itself "more relevant" and ensure either its institutional survival or expansion.

A critical theory approach would highlight how the regime has evolved to serve the interests of the powerful. With each change in the regime, it would ask "whose interests did it serve?" For example, it might explain the evolution and expansion of UNHCR's mandate since the 1990s in the context of the security and "containment" agenda of UNHCR's powerful Northern donor states. During the 1990s, UNHCR took on a growing "humanitarian" role in countries like Bosnia and Zaire. From a critical theory perspective, one might argue that these operations did not have exclusively positive outcomes for the displaced but they did serve to contain the effects of insecurity and conflict and to divert attention from the international community's failure to engage in addressing the underlying causes of conflict and displacement.

Conclusion

IR theory offers a range of different lenses for viewing and interpreting world politics. The theories explained in this chapter are not exhaustive of the range of IR theories but offer a starting point for thinking through different problems relating to forced migration and its relationship to global politics. Each one sheds light on different aspects of the international politics of forced migration. Which theoretical framework is most relevant depends on what questions one is asking and what aspect of the politics of forced migration one is looking at. Different questions and different problems will require a different theoretical framework.

The theories outlined in this chapter set the groundwork for the book's subsequent chapters. The remaining chapters in the book address specific themes in forced migration. Each one draws upon and explains a range of conceptual tools that are relevant to those specific themes. However, many of the concepts that are explained and illustrated have their intellectual roots within the main bodies of IR theory that are outlined in this chapter.

2

Sovereignty and the State System

Since the seventeenth century, the idea of the nation-state has become a central feature of world politics. The world has been gradually divided into abstract territorial entities in which governments are internally and externally recognized as exercising authority over their territory and population. The creation of the modern state system has been based on an assumed congruence between the nation, as cultural community, and the state as a political-territorial entity. Over time, international society has expanded beyond its European origins to incorporate an ever-growing number of states such that, by the end of the twentieth century, the political division of the globe into territorially delineated states had become the dominant universal mode of political organization (Bull and Watson 1984; Österud 1997).

The legitimacy of the state system has been supported by the concept of state sovereignty, which describes the legitimate exercise of power of the state over a given area of territory or a people. For example, it implies that states have authority to make the rules and to exercise the monopoly of coercive violence for the given population and territory. The legitimacy for this sovereignty is generally assumed to derive from both internal sources, being based on either the consent of the population or the state's ability to maintain order, and external sources, being based on mutual recognition by other states (Hinsley 1966; Jackson 1990). Since the seventeenth century, the notion of state sovereignty has become the foundational principle of international law and the basis of inter-state relations.

Analytically, International Relations has therefore tended to take sovereignty as given and to analyze international politics as the interaction of discretely defined nation-states (Donnelly 2000). Mainstream IR theories such as neo-realism and liberal institutionalism focus almost exclusively on inter-state relations and assume the sovereign state to be a pre-existing, pre-defined entity. In contrast, however, other alternative theoretical approaches have challenged the assumption that state sovereignty need be seen as universal and ahistorical. The English School and constructivism, for example, have questioned the historical contingency of the idea of the nation-state, examining where it has come from, and how it has historically and culturally come to be the dominant form of political organization. Meanwhile, many critical theorists examine the negative consequences of absolute sovereignty, and the implications it has for human rights.

Understanding the relationship between state sovereignty and forced migration is crucial for understanding the international politics of forced migration. Concepts such as "refugee" and "IDP" exist in relation to sovereignty and the state. Their legal definitions are entirely relational to the state system. The notions of a "refugee" or "IDP" only make sense insofar as they describe a relationship between the concepts of citizen, state, and territory that comprise the nation-state. Indeed the state system is premised upon an unproblematic nexus between state, citizen, and territory. However, the existence of refugees and IDPs represent anomalies to this. The concept of a "refugee" exists as a manifestation of both the breakdown of the state–citizen and citizen–territory relationship upon which the sovereign state is premised. Meanwhile, the "IDP" concept is distinct from the refugee insofar as there is no breakdown of the citizen-territory relationship but there is a breakdown of the state-citizen relationship.

On the one hand, the concepts of refugee and IDP therefore serve to reinforce the state system. They entrench the insider/outsider relationship between citizens and non-citizens by giving it legal and conceptual status. They also serve to normalize the relationship between territory, state, and citizen by clearly defining exceptions to it as anomalous. On the other hand, they challenge the unconditional nature of state sovereignty, highlighting the way in which the citizen–state–territory relationship frequently is not as it is implied by the ideal-type of the nation-state. Indeed, international recognition of the plight of refugees and IDPs has been at the heart of the gradual shift away from absolute and unconditional state sovereignty toward recognition of the need for states to earn sovereignty through their respect for human rights.

This chapter attempts to unpack the complex relationship between state sovereignty and forced migration. It provides an historical perspective that highlights the evolving and mutually constitutive relationship between them. The chapter begins by explaining the concept of state sovereignty in historical perspective. It then explains how sovereignty and statehood are dealt with by different theoretical perspectives in International Relations. Having set out the conceptual groundwork, the chapter applies the concepts to explore the relationship between sovereignty and refugees, sovereignty and human rights, and sovereignty and IDPs.

Sovereignty in Historical Perspective

States have a long history. In the ancient world clearly defined political institutions exerted control over city-states. In *The Peloponnesian Wars*, for example, Thucydides describes the conflicts that took place between the ancient Greek city-states of Athens and Sparta. However, these types of ancient structures differ from the modern state. They were generally confined to the city and had no clearly defined territory, and lacked the highly institutionalized bureaucracies of the modern state. Indeed, the citizen–territory–state nexus of the modern state system, defined by both its internal authority vis-à-vis the population and its external authority, defined by states' mutual recognition, is a creation of the seventeenth century and emerged within a European context.

Medieval Europe was characterized by feudalism, which in its most basic form can be understood as the granting of land in return for military service. The land-owning nobility would provide land and property rights to people in exchange for allegiance and security. In this context, different monarchs or aristocrats would control different areas of land and society. Within the Holy Roman Empire, religion played an important role in maintaining these structures. Each prince or nobleman would have the right to determine the religion of his own domain, defining its own religious denomination, and often basing its alliances with other territories mainly upon commonality of this denomination.

Over time, the rise of powerful monarchies with central bureaucracies gave a number of countries the characteristics of the modern state. The monarchies of England, France, the Netherlands, and Spain, for example, grew powerful enough to raise armies and to exercise internal authority through the nobility that they controled. In 1555, the Peace of Augsburg allowed the monarchies in different areas to define themselves as Catholic, Lutheran, or Calvinist. This laid the groundwork for the subsequent Peace of Westphalia in 1648, which is commonly regarded as heralding the birth of the modern sovereign state. The Peace of Westphalia initiated a new order in Europe based on the concept of national sovereignty. For the first time, it created clearly defined internal political boundaries within Europe and brought about the mutual recognition of different monarchies' right to define their own religious and political choices within their territory, superseding the feudal society of the Middle Ages.

Gradually, the idea of the nation-state evolved. In a European context, centralized states began to develop the bureaucratic mechanisms for identifying their populations, raising taxation, raising armies through conscription, and holding the monopoly of violence on their territories (Scott 1998). Ideologically, nationalism began to emerge as a means to legitimate the modern nation-state. The emergence of inventions such as the flag and the printing press raised awareness of the nation-state, enabling people to develop a sense of shared identity and allegiance (Anderson 1983). With the rise of nationalism, new states were created through the process of unification that took place in states such as Germany and Italy (Hobsbawm 1990). By the early twentieth century, the insider/outsider relationships of the modern state system were clearly defined within Europe and had spread elsewhere through the overseas empires of the European states. Authors such as Gong (1984) and Keene (2002) have highlighted the relationship between this spread of sovereignty and power. Until the twentieth century, large proportions of the world were either under dominion or only had quasi-sovereignty. Sovereignty represented a reward for states and was conditional upon their adoption of certain sets of values that were indicative of moving from the "uncivilized world" and adopting the "civilized" values of international society (Keene 2002: 147).

During the twentieth century, sovereignty became entrenched as the foundational principle of international law. In 1933 the Montevideo Convention on the Rights and Duties of States defined the state as a person of international law, offering a definition of a state possessing four main qualifications: a permanent population; a defined territory; a government; and the capacity to enter into relations with the other states. Furthermore, in the aftermath of the Second World War, the UN Charter made state sovereignty and the mutual recognition of states the constitutive norm of world politics. Article 2(4) of the Charter states that "All Members shall refrain in their international relations from the threat or use of force against the territorial integrity or political independence of any state, or in any other manner inconsistent with the Purposes of the United Nations"; meanwhile Article 2(7) states that "Nothing contained in the present Charter shall authorize the United Nations to intervene in matters which are essentially within the domestic jurisdiction of any state or shall require the Members to submit such matters to settlement under the present Charter."

In the second half of the twentieth century, international society expanded dramatically with decolonization and independence (Bull and Watson 1984). The number of states has expanded from 69 in 1945 to 193 in 2008. The new states adopted the Westphalian state system that the European colonialists left behind. Internally, the colonial powers left behind the apparatus of the European state system. Externally, membership of the international community brought with it the necessity to accept the framework of mutual recognition of the existing members. As Jackson (1990) highlights, one of the challenges that this adoption of the European state system posed for the post-colonial world was that while many achieved external recognition, they often lacked internal authority and were therefore put into a position of having only "quasi-sovereignty."

Alongside this trend, however, the twentieth century also witnessed a counter-veiling tendency. The major shift in international law was in its focus not only on the relationship between states but also on that between the state and the individual. Indeed, while most of public international law had previously been about the rights and duties of states toward one another, international human rights law, international humanitarian law, and international refugee law signaled a shift in the balance between state sovereignty and human rights. By the end of the twentieth century there was a growing consensus that sovereignty was no longer absolute but was conditional or "contingent" upon states behaving in a certain way, particularly vis-à-vis their own populations. Following the Cold War, there was growing jurisprudence on the conditions under which sovereignty was violable. Article 42 of the UN Charter, which allows derogation of the principle of non-intervention when there is a threat to international peace and security and authorization from the UN Security Council, was interpreted in increasingly broad ways including circumstances relating to crimes against humanity and genocide. Out of this emerging jurisprudence, states agreed upon the concept of the *Responsibility to Protect* which sets out the notion that the international community as a whole has responsibility for ensuring human rights and argues that there are circumstances in which external intervention in another sovereign state may be justified (Bellamy 2009). In the early twentieth century, then, state sovereignty remains a core principle in world politics; however, it is no longer absolute.

International Relations Perspectives on Sovereignty

Over recent years, International Relations has shown increasing interest in issues relating to state sovereignty and its relationship to the states system. Different theoretical approaches to IR view sovereignty in different ways. For most mainstream approaches to IR, sovereignty is assumed. Most rationalist approaches – notably neo-realism and liberal institutionalism – take sovereignty as given. This is because, in taking their level of analysis as the inter-state (or system) level, they assume the nation-state to be the irreducible unit of analysis. Sovereignty is therefore not treated as historically contingent or as socially constructed, but as a fact that is prior to analysis. In contrast, a range of alternative approaches have attempted to take a more nuanced approach to sovereignty and to problematize its relationship to the state system. Moving beyond rationalism's view of sovereignty as merely an analytic assumption, a number of alternative approaches have examined sovereignty as a norm based upon a set of practices which shape and constitute states' behavior in complex ways. Among these, Krasner's "organized hypocrisy" model, the English School, and Constructivism offer particularly useful accounts of state sovereignty. This section therefore sets out these alternative approaches to sovereignty with a view to applying them to forced migration in the following section.

Rationalist approaches

Rationalist approaches – notably neo-realism and liberal institutionalism – take sovereignty as given. For most rationalists, sovereignty is taken merely as an analytic assumption. It represents the unproblematic ontological starting point on which their account of international politics is based. As Biersteker and Weber (1996: 5) highlight, "Neorealists tend to combine population, territory, authority, and recognition – the principal constitutive elements of sovereignty – into a single, unproblematic actor: the sovereign state." This logic follows from rationalist approaches' concern to analyze anarchy as a constraint on state behavior. The advantage that this assumption provides is that it offers a parsimonious framework within which to understand inter-state relations.

However, the problem with assuming state sovereignty as given is that, analytically, it may miss some of the nuances and contingencies relating to sovereignty. Firstly, it is unable to recognize that sovereignty is not always absolute and that it is historically contingent. As classical realists such as Carr (1946) and Morgenthau (1948) recognized, there is no inevitability that sovereignty represents the only conceivable form of political organization at the international level. Indeed, other norms – such as human rights – may compete with sovereignty and, at times, be privileged over and above sovereignty. Secondly, by "black boxing" the state, rationalist approaches cannot account for the domestic dimensions of sovereignty, whereas sovereignty can only be fully understood by examining both its internal and external dimensions. By failing to recognize these two aspects of sovereignty, rationalist approaches may also miss many of the contradictions within sovereignty that are important for understanding world politics. In the forced migration context, for example, rationalist approaches would struggle to account for how refugees emerge from contradictions in sovereignty. As Haddad (2008), for example, highlights, refugees may result from a breakdown between the assumption of negative sovereignty in international society and positive sovereignty at the domestic level. Where states are externally recognized but there is an internal breakdown of the assumed state–citizen nexus, refugees may be an inevitable outcome.

These limitations make it difficult for rationalist approaches to engage with issues such as human rights, humanitarian intervention, and forced migration, the understanding of which rely upon recognizing the nuanced, historically contingent, and conditional nature of sovereignty (Donnelly 2000). On a practical level, as some critical theorists have argued, taking sovereignty as given may also risk reifying the notion of sovereignty in ways that may contribute to legitimating states' claims to absolute sovereignty. There are therefore sound academic and practical reasons for exploring alternative analytical frameworks for understanding sovereignty.

"Organized hypocrisy"

In his book, *Sovereignty: Organized Hypocrisy*, Krasner (1999) responds to claims within international relations that states' authority is being eroded by "new" influences such as globalization and human rights and that sovereignty is shifting from a previously absolute and inviolable principle to one which is challenged by new norms and practices. Instead, he suggests that state sovereignty has historically never been the absolute and inviolable international norm that it is frequently perceived to be. On the contrary, states have often violated or created exceptions to sovereignty, especially when it has been in the interests of powerful states to do so. For Krasner, sovereignty represents "organized hypocrisy" insofar as it is a longstanding norm that is nevertheless frequently violated.

His starting point for analysis is to try to clearly define "four meanings" of sovereignty, a concept which he rightly argues has often been muddled and confused within IR. Firstly, he defines "international legal sovereignty" as the practices of mutual recognition between territories. Secondly, he defines "Westphalian sovereignty" as political organization based on the exclusion of external actors from authority structures within a given territory. Thirdly, he defines "domestic sovereignty" as the formal organization of political authority within the states and the ability of public authority to exercise effective control. Fourthly, he defines "interdependence sovereignty" as the ability of public authorities to regulate the flow of transboundary movements. The first two concepts relate to authority and legitimacy and the latter two to control. Krasner focuses mainly on the first two as norms of sovereignty and he tries to explain the conditions under which international legal sovereignty and Westphalian sovereignty have been upheld and violated.

He argues that state rulers base their decision-making on two different logics of action: logics of consequences (essentially, interests) and logics of appropriateness (essentially, norms). The first logic involves rational preference maximization based on cost-benefit analysis, the second logic involves following rules that correspond to particular roles. Krasner argues that the international system has generally been dominated by the logic of consequences. Where there are unambiguous rules and norms these may be followed; however, where there are multiple and contradictory roles and rules, the logic of consequences will prevail. International rules are often contradictory. For example, norms of non-intervention contradict rules on human rights. Consequently, even though international legal sovereignty and Westphalian sovereignty are defined by clear rules, both have been historically violated both by voluntary agreement and by coercion. As Krasner (1999: 7) explains, "rulers have found that it is in their interests to break the rules." This has been particularly the case in the context of power asymmetries between states, whereby "stronger states can pick and choose among different rules selecting the one that best suits their instrumental objectives" (p. 6).

He looks at various issue-areas in which sovereignty is a central component – minority rights, human rights, sovereign lending, and state creation. In each of these areas, he suggests that differences in national power and interests, not international norms, have been and continue to be the most powerful explanation for the behavior of states. Organized hypocrisy is a useful idea for analyzing the politics of forced migration because it highlights how focusing too much on sovereignty as the principal barrier to international action obscures the diverse range of responses to different groups of forced migrants, within different regions, categories, and historical contexts. Sovereignty is often used to justify inaction but is frequently violated or circumvented when doing so is in the interests of the powerful. Chomsky (1999) makes a similar argument from a critical perspective in *New Military Humanism* in which he highlights how "consistency has underlied the inconsistency" of international humanitarian responses – contrasting the response of the international community to internal displacement in Chechnya in the late 1990s with the active (but self-interested) response in Bosnia and Kosovo.

English School

The English School also provides a more nuanced view of sovereignty than that provided by rationalist approaches. It suggests that there are competing values in international society – on the one hand, order and, on the other hand, justice. Historically, states have privileged order over justice, and the principles of sovereignty and non-intervention have been an important source of global order (Bull 1977; Vincent 1974). However, as Bull (1977) argued, although international society may currently privilege values of order over values of justice, there is no inevitability to this. It is conceivable that international society might develop alternative norms that privilege justice, whether between states or toward human beings. Building on Bull, other English School authors conceived the idea that there could be alternative, competing forms of international society, at different historical junctures and within different issue-areas (Wheeler 2000; Wight 1977).

Firstly, a "pluralist" account of international society sees world politics as characterized by only a minimum set of norms of co-existence such as the balance of power, diplomacy, and respect for international agreements (Bull 1977; Vincent 1974). From a "pluralist" perspective, states hold different values and world politics is defined by a communitarian logic within which there is little international cooperation and little prospect for justice to be privileged above order. Here international society is a society of sovereign states. Secondly, a "solidarist" account of international society regards world politics to be characterized by a denser framework of international institutions within which states have developed significant international cooperation. From this perspective, states can and have developed common cosmopolitan values which are enshrined in international norms (Linklater and Suganami 2002). Finally, Hurrell (2007) suggests that one may also take an alternative "complex governance" perspective on international society, in which the basis of international order and justice is increasingly defined by non-state actors – including the private sector, transnational civil society, and supranational organizations.

These three frames offer a historical sociological means to view the evolution of state sovereignty in international society. They highlight the degree to which norms and rules beyond a pluralist normative framework have emerged in different issue-areas. For example, Hurrell (2007) applies the three conceptual frameworks to examine the emergence and role of norms in relation to nationalism and identity politics, human rights, economic globalization and trade, violence and collective security, and the environment. In the context of forced migration, the frames are potentially useful for analyzing the way in which international society has gradually and historically moved from a pluralist – based on norms sovereignty and non-intervention – to a solidarist framework, and the tensions that exist between these logics. As Haddad (2008: 3) has argued, "the refugee brings to the fore the clash between pluralism and solidarism, communitarianism and cosmopolitanism, sovereign rights and human rights," which are dominant themes in the English School. New rules and norms relating to human rights, refugees, and internally displaced people have emerged since the Second World War, moving international society beyond a range of thin norms focused exclusively on maintaining order to a set of norms that focus on values of justice, particularly toward the individual. However, as Hurrell (2007) highlights, even with the emergence of new and denser norms, the conflict between order and justice has remained and norms that are ostensibly about justice have been used by powerful actors to legitimate certain forms of global order. In the case of the refugee and IDP regimes, Hurrell's observation is particularly useful because it highlights the way in which derogations to sovereignty and to the pluralist international order have often been driven not only by values of justice and morality but also by structures of liberal order driven by powerful actors (Alderson and Hurrell 2000; Hurrell 2007).

Constructivism

Constructivism also provides a nuanced conceptual framework for understanding state sovereignty. Biersteker and Weber (1996) identify state sovereignty as a social construct, criticizing the ahistorical and asocial way it is viewed by much of International Relations. They argue (p. 3) that "the modern state system is not based on some timeless principle of sovereignty, but on the production of a normative conception that links authority, territory, population, and recognition ... in a particular place (the state)." For them, state sovereignty is an "inherently social concept." They analytically separate the state – as "a geographically contained structure whose agents claim political authority within their domain" – from sovereignty – as a "political entity's externally recognized right to exercise final authority over its affairs." They take the former to be an identity and the latter to be an institution that is constructed and reinforced through a set of practices. The practices of state sovereignty are important because they socially construct the identity of the state. For Biersteker and Weber, there are four practices in particular which construct and reproduce state sovereignty: recognition, territory, population, and authority.

Each of these practices has historically constituted state sovereignty and the states system. Firstly, state sovereignty is socially constructed through territory by, for example, boundaries, exclusionary practices, and the creation of racial, ethnic, or cultural "others." Secondly, state sovereignty is socially constructed through populations by, for example, nationalism, the creation of national and political community, and citizenship. This notion draws upon Benedict Anderson's (1983) work on the way in which national identity is constituted through practices such as the flag, the printing press, national anthems, and historical narratives. Thirdly, state sovereignty is socially constructed through authority by forms of political organization which may privilege the singular Westphalian state to different degrees. For example, trans-national or federal structures may exist as alternative forms of political organization which reinforce the Westphalian model to greater or lesser extents. Fourthly, state sovereignty is socially constructed through recognition by, for example, the degree to which states conform to the perceived ideal of the Eurocentric Westphalian ideal. Strang (1996), Inayatullah (1996), and Jackson (1990) all highlight how non-Western states face particular challenges of recognition linked to the perception of the sovereign ideal held by powerful actors.

These four practices which contribute to the social construction of sovereignty have particular relevance for understanding the politics of forced migration. They shed light on the mutually constitutive relationship between sovereignty and forced migration. On the one hand, categories of forced migration – such as refugee and IDP – exist in relation to sovereignty. On the other hand, Biersteker and Weber's analysis also highlights how states' responses to forced migration construct, reproduce, reconstruct, and deconstruct state sovereignty. In particular, they facilitate the practices relating to territory and population described by Biersteker and Weber. From a constructivist perspective, how states categorize and respond to forced migration is part of the process through which state sovereignty is constituted through boundaries, practices of inclusion and exclusion, and the creation of an external "other" in opposition to the national political community.

Sovereignty and Refugees

It is often recognized that human rights and sovereignty exist in a contradictory relationship. On the one hand, human rights imply that states have universal obligations toward their citizens; on the other hand, sovereignty implies that states have unambiguous authority within their own territory. It has therefore been common to assert that there is a trade-off between the two and that a gradual movement has taken place since the Second World War, in which the creation of a global human rights regime has led to a move away from absolute sovereignty toward contingent sovereignty. Indeed, a growing number of states have been socialized into adopting international human rights norms (Risse et al. 1999). States have universal obligations toward their own citizens and mechanisms exist for ensuring compliance. In the terms of the English School, the post-Second World War era has therefore witnessed a move from a pluralist to solidarist international society, from communitarianism to cosmopolitanism, and from values of order to values of justice in the area of human rights (Dunne and Wheeler 1999). This shift is clearly illustrated by the emergence of international human rights law, international humanitarian law, humanitarian intervention, and the creation of the "Responsibility to Protect," for example.

Within this context, it is tempting to cast refugees within this broader human rights analysis and to regard the concept of the refugee and international responses to the problem of the refugee as part of this broader trend – as a move away from pluralism toward solidarism. However, in practice, this characterization would be misleading and only captures one dimension of the relationship between sovereignty and refugees. The nature of the relationship between the refugee and the system of sovereign states is far more nuanced and cannot be adequately captured as part of the broader relationship between sovereignty and human rights. Although refugees are often regarded as "human rights abuses made visible" and international protection is about according human rights to people who are unable to access them within their country of origin, their direct conceptual relationship to the international state system means that their relationship to sovereignty is analytically distinct from the broader relationship between human rights and sovereignty. Rather than representing a necessary challenge to the state system, the "refugee" is both a manifestation of state sovereignty and exists in a mutually constitutive relationship to the international state system.

In her pioneering work, Emma Haddad (2008) explores the relationship between the refugee, sovereignty, and the state system. She critically engages with the commonly held assumption that the "refugee" represents a product of the international state system "going wrong." Most of "refugee studies," she observes, implies that the problem of the refugee results from a breakdown in the "normal" citizen–state relationship. In contrast, Haddad (p. 1) argues that the existence of refugees is "an inevitable if unintended consequence of the international states system," and that this recognition is a crucial part of understanding the position of the existence of the refugee and developing responses to refugee protection.

Drawing upon a predominantly English School approach, she argues that the refugee exists as a figure that falls outside of the citizen–state–territory nexus. This situation arises not because of an aberration in the international state system but because of contradictions that are inherent to and inevitably arise from the nation-state system. She suggests that there is a discrepancy between the practice of the state system and the ideal-type concept of sovereignty. In particular, there is frequently a gap between the negative sovereignty of international society and the positive sovereignty of the individual state. On the one hand, the Westphalian state system upholds non-intervention and mutual recognition. On the other hand, within some states, the assumed relationship between citizen and state breaks down such that some people face a well-founded fear of persecution by their own state. In Haddad's (2008: 4) words, "what in fact is 'going wrong' when refugees appear is that the theory and practice of the international state system and the concept of sovereignty on which it relies are failing to coincide."

Historically, Haddad argues that the "problem" of the refugee is not one of the post-Second World War era, as is often assumed. Rather, it is an historical problem that emerges with, and as an inevitable consequence of, the creation of the international states system in the seventeenth century. Refugees become an important concept with the creation of the Westphalian system. Prior to the Peace of Westphalia, she argues, the concept could not exist in its present form. The feudal system which existed in medieval Europe precluded the type of citizen–state–territory nexus on which the existence of the refugee is based. Although other groups – such as the expulsion of the Jews from Spain in 1492 or the Huguenots – are often cited as earlier examples of refugee movements, Haddad argues that there is a qualitative distinction between modern refugees and pre-modern forced migration. The earlier movements were not characterized by the crossing of a well-defined jurisdictional border and were not addressed through international cooperation in the same way as contemporary movements. For Haddad (2008: 63), the historical emergence of the concept of the refugee coincides with the historical emergence of the Westphalian state system: "The (modern) refugee is only fully intelligible within the context of a pluralist system of states in which individual political communities fail to guarantee the content of substantive sovereignty."

Furthermore, for Haddad, there is a mutually constitutive link between the refugee concept and international society. Not only is the refugee an inevitable consequence of the sovereign state system but it also serves to reinforce the state system. She highlights how during the twentieth century the development of the refugee regime has evolved with and constituted the evolution and development of the modern states system, claiming (p. 115): "The identity of international society was in part formulated by the refugee issue, and the refugee question itself in part constructed by the evolving identity of international society and its constituent parts, sovereign states."

For example, as anthropologists such as Malkki (1995) have argued, "solutions" to the "problem" of refugees have been premised upon the ideas of reinserting refugees within the Westphalian state system in order to correct the aberration to the citizen–state–territory nexus. Furthermore, the refugee has contributed to reinforcing and legitimating the sovereign state system by creating clear notions of insider and outsider and creating the refugee as an "other," which can be offered a form of quasi-citizenship prior to being reintegrated within the "normal" logic of the state system (Haddad 2008: 113–27). On the one hand, therefore, refugees represent an anomaly or failure of the state system, which the refugee regime was created to correct. On the other hand, the insider/outsider relationship created by refugees reinforces the social construction of the nation-state. Haddad's work therefore usefully highlights the complex and mutually constitutive relationship between the concept of the refugee and the international state system. Although upholding refugees' rights may represent a challenge to sovereignty, the concept of the refugee and states' responses to refugees have generally worked to reinforce rather than undermine sovereignty and the state system.

Sovereignty and IDPs

Sovereignty has been the traditional basis for the distinction between refugees and IDPs. While an international regime for refugees began to emerge in the first half of the twentieth century, it took until the 1990s for anything resembling an IDP regime to emerge. States agreed to cooperate to provide protection for refugees but not to cooperate to protect those in a "refugee-like situation" who had not crossed an international border. Similarly, UNHCR had a mandate to protect refugees but only a very limited role in protecting IDPs. Where the international community did play a role in protecting IDPs it was only with the explicit permission of the host government. The basis of this distinction between refugee and IDP protection was the argument that states and the international community could not interfere in the affairs of a sovereign state. So long as people fleeing persecution or conflict remained on the territory of their country of origin, they were considered the responsibility of that state and not that of the international community. In other words, there was no IDP regime because the border mattered. The very conception of an IDP emerged in contradistinction to refugees. It was not until the 1990s and the aftermath of the Cold War that international negotiation began on the basis of an IDP regime. The *Guiding Principles on Internal Displacement* established a "soft law" framework based on the application of existing human rights and international humanitarian law standards, and international agencies developed a collaborative framework within which to share responsibility for the protection of IDPs (Bagshaw 2005; Phuong 2004; Weiss and Korn 2006).

A challenge is to explain the emergence of the IDP regime and its relationship to sovereignty. On the one hand, one might consider the development of the Guiding Principles to represent a norm that compromises the inviolability of sovereignty. At first glance it appears to be a part of the broader trend in the normative relationship between human rights and sovereignty in the post-Cold War era. The Guiding Principles appear to erode sovereignty and to privilege the human rights of citizens, legitimating external intervention in order to ensure the protection of displaced people. This characterization diverges from the argument presented above that the refugee regime serves to reinforce rather than undermine state sovereignty. On the other hand, however, one might argue that far from undermining sovereignty, the creation of an IDP regime helps to reinforce sovereignty, albeit the sovereignty of powerful states. Indeed, the context in which the IDP regime was created was one in which many Northern states were concerned with international migration and were seeking ways to reinforce their border control through intervention in Southern states in order to "contain" the onward movement of people (Castles 2003; Duffield 2001). This "containment" logic would suggest that, far from representing a compromise to sovereignty, the IDP regime serves to uphold sovereignty, albeit on a selective basis.

The different theoretical perspectives on sovereignty outlined above shed light on different aspects of these competing interpretations of the relationship between IDP protection and sovereignty. Krasner's *Organized Hypocrisy* suggests that states will selectively violate the norms of sovereignty when it is in the interests of powerful. This interpretation of the development of an IDP regime would suggest that state representatives choose to derogate sovereignty because the logic of consequences supports their interests. Indeed, the development of the Guiding Principles and the circumstances under which powerful states have historically supported IDP protection has been when they have had broader interests. These interests have been in areas such as controlling and containing the outward flow of migrants and refugees, and limiting the external spill-over of the effects of conflict, for example. Prior to the development of the Guiding Principles, for example, UNHCR was invited to provide protection to IDPs in post-Cold War conflicts such as Iraq, Somalia, and Bosnia, in which the aim of the states supporting the derogation of sovereignty was to contain refugee movements or other trans-boundary spill-overs (Barutciski 2002; Chimni 1998; Dubernet 2001).

Drawing upon Krasner's four meanings of sovereignty, one could also nuance the effects of the IDP regime on sovereignty by disaggregating sovereignty into its component parts. On the one hand, the Westphalian sovereignty of Southern host states is eroded since the regime allocates a degree of authority over the domestic affairs of the state to outside actors. On the other hand, the regime arguably reinforces the interdependence sovereignty of Northern states who are able to use the regime as a means to limit the onward movement of people as asylum seekers, refugees, or migrants.

From an English School perspective, one can derive a complementary reading of the development of the IDP regime. A simplistic reading of the development of the IDP regime would regard it as a shift from a pluralist to a solidarist international society and as a shift in the values of states from order to justice. However, a more complex reading, might suggest that the development of rules that appear to be grounded in principles of justice actually have a different function of maintaining order (Alderson and Hurrell 2000; Hurrell 2007; Reus-Smit 2001). Indeed, one could argue that norms of justice have been created in order to uphold global order on the terms of the powerful. Indeed, by developing the norms within the framework of justice, they serve to legitimate forms of liberal global order. The English School perspective highlights the tension between order and justice that underpins the IDP regime and the way in which a normative framework ostensibly based on justice has been instrumentally used to legitimate and develop a particular form of global order. This analysis would be fully consistent with the notion, drawn from Krasner, that different aspects of sovereignty are reinforced and other aspects are undermined by the IDP regime in ways that serve the interests of the powerful.

Conclusion

Understanding the relationship between forced migration, sovereignty, and the state system is important because the labels and concepts on which forced migration is based – in policy and analysis – are themselves defined by sovereignty and the state system. Both the refugee and IDP categories are defined in relation to the state system and could not exist without the concept of sovereignty and the state–citizen–territory relationship that it confers. It would therefore be impossible to understand forced migration unless one critically analyzes its relationship to the state system. The main categories of forced migration – refugee and IDP – have a mutually constitutive relationship to sovereignty. On the one hand, the existence of the state system and sovereignty are what bring into existence and make intelligible the concept of a refugee or an IDP. On the other hand, the practice of protecting, resolving, excluding, and including the refugee or IDP contribute to reifying and reconstructing sovereignty and the state system. In other words, the categories of forced migration and the state system are two sides of the same coin.

Nevertheless, there are important differences in the relationship between refugees and sovereignty and between IDPs and sovereignty. As Haddad argues, refugees are an inevitable consequence of sovereignty and the state system. So long as the ideal-type relationship between state, citizen, and territory is upheld as the basis of international society, there will be people who fall outside of that framework and are in need of international protection. Furthermore, the existence and category of the refugee serve to reinforce the state system by reifying the boundary and identifying the refugee as an aberration from the "normal" citizen–state relationship. The relationship between the category of IDP and the state system is arguably more nuanced. On the one hand, the notion of IDP protection appears to privilege human rights norms in a manner that erodes and compromises absolute sovereignty. On the other hand, the category of IDP only exists in relation to the border. Furthermore, rather than arguing the IDP regime has either eroded or reinforced state sovereignty, a more realistic interpretation would be that it has altered different aspects of sovereignty in different ways. In Krasner's terms, the IDP regime might be considered to erode the "Westphalian sovereignty" (i.e. the exclusion of external actors from authority structures within a given territory) of Southern states in order to reinforce the "interdependence sovereignty" (i.e. the ability to control trans-boundary flows) of Northern states.

IR offers a range of tools for understanding the relationship between forced migration and the state system. Although they have uses in other areas, rationalist approaches such as neo-realism and liberal institutionalism are insufficient for analyzing this relationship because of their analytical assumptions. In particular, by assuming sovereignty and the state as given they cannot account for the historical construction of sovereignty and its relationship to the historical emergence of the categories and norms relating to forced migration. In order to understand this relationship, a deeper level of analysis is required than the problem-solving theory that dominates much academic work on world politics. A range of alternative approaches may have more to offer. Krasner's organized hypocrisy model highlights the role of power and interest in determining violation and compliance with norms. The English School sheds light on the historical emergence and development of norms. Constructivism highlights the role of practice in shaping norms. Each of these tools has potential to shed light on aspects of how and why the concepts of refugee and IDP have emerged and their inextricable relationship to the state system. The next chapter builds on this analysis of the relationship between forced migration and state sovereignty in a more applied context: that of the relationship between security and forced migration.

3

Security

Security is one of the central concepts of International Relations. It can be defined as an object's degree of vulnerability to a threat. Following this definition, any notion of security has two main elements: firstly, a threat; secondly, a referent object (i.e. something or someone that is vulnerable to that threat). Because of the diverse range of ways in which these two elements can be defined, limited, and expanded, security has been argued to be an "essentially contested concept" (Buzan 1991). Traditionally, following realist and neo-realist assumptions, IR has tended to take the referent object to be the nation-state and the source of threat to be the military capability of other states. Recently, however, a range of alternative approaches to security have argued that there may be referent objects other than the state – for example, the individual, identities, or groups – and there may be a wider range of threats beyond military threats – for example, economic or environmental threats.

Both the traditional and more recent approaches to security studies have been applied to address aspects of forced migration. Indeed, of the existing work on forced migration and global politics, the relationship between displacement and security is perhaps the most researched. It has been explored from both a traditional state-centric perspective and a more critical perspective. On the one hand, there has been a range of literature examining the empirical relationship between forced migration and security-related issues such as conflict and terrorism. This work has examined the conditions under which immigration and asylum, refugees and IDPs represent a threat to national security. On the other hand, critical approaches have explored how immigration, asylum, refugees, and IDPs have come to be perceived as a threat, and whether it may be more appropriate to see the displaced as the referent object and the state as the source of threat, rather than vice versa.

How one interprets the relationship between forced migration and security depends upon what theoretical lens one uses to interpret that relationship. Security studies offers a range of different tools for looking at security in different ways. This chapter explains the main approaches to security that emerge from IR: Traditional Security Studies (TSS), Human Security, Critical Security Studies (CSS), the Third World Security Predicament, and Biopower. The chapter outlines each of these approaches. In each case it explains how they have been applied to understand world politics and what they offer for understanding the politics of forced migration. Finally, the chapter applies the concepts to two case studies relating to security and forced migration: the securitization of asylum since 9/11 and protracted refugee situations in the developing world.

Traditional Security Studies

Conventional approaches to security have their origins in realist approaches to world politics. From this perspective, the nation-state is the most important actor in world politics. Nation-states maximize the welfare of their own citizens through upholding "national security." Following Morgenthau (1948), individual states must prioritize their own survival and national security. Since other states will behave in this way, a failure of one state to prioritize national security will jeopardize its existence. Furthermore, from a realist perspective, if all individual states focus on "self-help" and uphold national security, then humanity will also be better off than if states attempted to uphold other values such as justice or had regard for the welfare of other states and their citizens. This is because, through the pursuit of national security, the balance of power will emerge at the inter-state level and lead to order and the absence of conflict. For Morgenthau, it would therefore be irresponsible for a state to focus on any other priority beyond national security.

A realist approach to security consequently takes the state as the key referent object and regards the military power of other states as the main source of threat. From these underlying assumptions, a body of theory referred to as Strategic Studies has emerged, which focuses on how states can and do behave in relation to the military threat posed by other states. Strategic studies' core focus in the Cold War era was on analyzing how states could ensure that other states would be deterred from military aggression. This approach to security was particularly applied in the context of analyzing the bipolar relationship between the US and the USSR and the role of nuclear deterrence in the Cold War. However, despite the end of the Cold War, TSS and the notion of "national security" remain central to the mainstream of IR theory and state policy-making.

Much of contemporary security studies does not follow this caricature of TSS but nevertheless retains important elements of it. In practice, for example, most post-Cold War security studies acknowledges that non-state actors such as guerrilla movements and terrorists can represent a threat to the state. It is also often prepared to acknowledge that intra-state conflicts are an important part of post-Cold War international affairs. However, it continues to focus mainly on military threats such as conflict and terrorism, and generally regard them as important insofar as they represent potential sources of instability at the international system level.

Much of the literature on the relationship between forced migration and security (and much policy-making on immigration and asylum) implicitly adopts elements of a TSS approach. It takes the state as the principal referent object and examines the relationship between forced migration and high-order military threats to the state. In other words, forced migration is seen through the lens of national security. This is partly because forced migration is generally only considered of relevance to mainstream IR in North America insofar as it has a relationship to national security. In order for forced migration to register on the radar of foreign policy in the US, it has generally needed to have a connection to "national security." Methodologically, much of the literature on forced migration and security examines the empirical relationship between displacement and military threats to the state, generally taking refugees as an independent variable in relation to sources of insecurity.

Stedman and Tanner (2003) identify the way in which refugees, and the refugee regime, have been manipulated, as resources of war, by both states and non-state actors. In *Refugee Manipulation*, they suggest that refugees and the refugee regime have been instrumentally used in conflicts by great powers and by groups in exile. Both of these, they suggest, have had significant implications for international security.

Following authors such as Weiner (1995) and Loescher (1993), Stedman and Tanner (2003) argue that refugees have often been instrumentally manipulated by great powers for strategic purposes. This was most notably the case during the Cold War when the US, in particular, selectively supported refugee groups as a means to support "refugee warriors" engaged in the fight against Communism in the developing world. The US had an interest in refugees in the developing world insofar as they were related to the proxy conflicts of the developing world. Refugee warriors were seen as a crucial tool for engaging in proxy conflicts, being both a resource and a threat. Their presence could be used to support military bases or to provide sanctuary and support to combatants. Guerrillas in exile were selectively supported or not, through ostensibly "humanitarian" assistance in the proxy conflicts of Central America and Sub-Saharan Africa during the 1970s and 1980s. For example, the US selectively supported the Nicaraguan Contras in exile in Honduras, while withholding support for Salvadoran refugees in Honduras who had fled the right wing government in El Salvador. Meanwhile, it also supported exiles who had fled socialist Ethiopia in the Horn of Africa, and aided and abetted the Khmer Rouge in Cambodian refugee camps on the Thai border as a means to oppose the Vietnamese-backed regime in Phnom Penh.

They further argue that refugees have often been used as resources of war by groups in exile. For exiled rebel groups, refugees have provided international legitimacy, a pool of potential recruits, sources of food and medicine, and a shield against external attacks. For example, the refugee regime for Palestinians in Jordan and Lebanon and the refugee regime in Zaire, which provided protection to those fleeing the Rwandan genocide, have both been used by combatants to fulfil these purposes. In both cases, the structures of the refugee regime – including camps and international assistance, have been instrumentally used by parties to the conflicts – such as Hamas and the Interahamwe militias – in ways that have sustained and perpetuated international conflict.

In *Dangerous Sanctuaries*, Lischer (2005) explores the conditions under which refugee crises represent a catalyst for conflict – both internal and inter-state. She rejects the type of socioeconomic explanations relating to poor living conditions, large camps, bored young men, and the border location of camps, which she claims represent the conventional wisdom on the relationship between refugees and conflict (e.g. Crisp 2003). Instead, she claims that variation in the relationship between refugee crises and the exacerbation of conflict can be found in political explanations. She identifies three important factors that shape the relationship. Firstly, the origin of the refugee crisis matters. She divides refugees as either being situational refugees (fleeing generalized violence), persecuted refugees (fleeing group-based persecution), or state-in-exile refugees (fleeing defeat in civil war). She argues that because of the degree of grievance and group cohesion, the latter is likely to be most pre-disposed to violence and the former the least. Secondly, the policy of the receiving state matters. She argues that the greater is the willingness and the ability of the host states to secure its borders and engage in demobilization the lower will be the likelihood that refugee crises will exacerbate conflict. Thirdly, the influence of external state and non-state actors matters. Through aid, pressure, and practical assistance, external actors, including humanitarian agencies, can encourage or prevent the spread of violence. For example, humanitarian aid in refugee crises can often exacerbate conflict through feeding militants, sustaining and protecting militants' dependents, supporting a war economy, and providing legitimacy to combatants.

In post-conflict situations, refugees and IDPs have also been identified as potential "spoilers" in attempts to develop peace-building initiatives (Stedman 2008). They may disrupt post-conflict reconstruction and peace-building as returnees with property and rights-based claims, through remaining militarized groups in exile, by remaining outside of peace negotiations, postponing possibilities for repatriation, or refusing to renounce violence, for example. This recognition has been used to highlight the need to include a focus on refugees both in analysis of conflict and within policy initiatives relating to peace-building.

As well as conflict and peace-building, TSS-based approaches to forced migration have explored the relationship between displacement and terrorism. Immigration has been increasingly seen in security terms since September 11th 2001 in both the developed and the developing world and asylum channels have been identified as a means through which terrorists might acquire access to the territory of intended target states. In both the Madrid and London bombings, for example, asylum seekers were implicated in the planning and execution of the attacks. Given that many refugee populations in the developing world are Muslim, and much terrorist concern focuses on Islamic terrorism, the Palestinian, Somali, and Afghan refugee populations, for example, have been perceived as potential sources of threat to regional and international security. A particular concern focuses on the possibilities for radicalization and recruitment in the refugee and IDP camp environment. The protracted situations in the Middle East, Sub-Saharan Africa, and South-Central Asia, in which large number for young men are left with few opportunities and future prospects, represent fertile ground for terrorist recruitment.

While not all of these approaches are entirely state-centric or realist in approach, they serve to illustrate elements of the TSS approach's application to forced migration; in particular, the way in which forced migration relates to conflict and national security. A TSS approach to forced migration is useful insofar as it can be used to highlight empirically the relationship between forced migration and high-order military threats to the state – such as conflict and terrorism, and so highlights when forced migration is likely to "matter" for a self-interested and security focused state. However, TSS has difficulty accounting for a number of important aspects of the relationship between security and forced migration.

Firstly, TSS has difficulty accounting for non-military threats to security. Even if one assumes, as TSS does, that the most important referent object for security is the state, threats do not necessarily have to have a connection to military security in order to matter. Forced migration is important for state security for reasons that go beyond the nexus to military threats. Questions relating to asylum, refugees, and IDPs are important because they relate to societal security, involving questions of identity and community. They also have implications for a state's economic security often leading to competition for scarce resources between host communities and the displaced populations. TSS struggles to account for these sources of insecurity which are important for understanding forced migration and which may have an indirect impact upon the broader "national interest" at the international system level.

Secondly, TSS often assumes that national security is synonymous with individual security. In practice, forced migration illustrates that this is not always the case. Frequently, states may be unwilling or unable to ensure the security of individuals, and states may even be the greatest source of threat to individuals. Displacement is itself a manifestation of the disjuncture between the interests of a state and the interests of its citizens. For example, refugees and IDPs usually result from a state persecuting its own citizens. Similarly, destination countries may often behave toward refugees and asylum seekers in ways that suggest the former is more of a threat to the latter than vice versa.

Thirdly, it depoliticizes the concept of security, assuming that a given threat is objectively and uniformly a threat to an entire society. In practice, "security" is used for political purposes in order to legitimate action that may benefit certain groups and disadvantage others. Assuming a single "national interest" masks these differences and implicitly serves to privilege a given group's own interests. For example, in the case of forced migration, asylum seekers, refugees, and IDPs do not always objectively represent a threat to the state, but are frequently constructed as such by politicians and the media for electoral gain or to sell newspapers. A more critical approach would seek to ask how an issue comes to be seen as a "security" issue and whose interests this "securitization" serves.

Fourthly, it sidelines the role of perception. In practice, security and insecurity do not exist as purely objective standards. Rather, they are subjective and inter-subjective concepts. Threats are important and have political consequences insofar as they are perceived and believed to be threats. This is especially important in forced migration, in which the securitization of human displacement is often not based on empirical fact but on perception. Public discourse and the language used to describe refugees, asylum seekers, and IDPs shape how they are perceived and their relationship to security.

These limitations of TSS are to some extent addressed by the alternative, critical concepts of security that have emerged since the end of the Cold War. The next sections therefore explain these approaches and what they can offer an understanding of the relationship between forced migration and security.

Human Security

In the immediate post-Cold War era, "national security" was recognized to be less relevant to explain sources of threat than it had been in the context of bipolarity. The old focus on strategic deterrence and the fear of nuclear conflict between the superpowers was no longer considered the most salient aspect of security. By the 1990s, intra-state conflicts and complex humanitarian emergencies in Iraq, Somalia, Bosnia, and Rwanda dominated the attention of international policy-makers. Threats were no longer considered to be solely from other states but also from internal conflicts, poverty and inequality, communicable disease, climate change, and natural disasters. Furthermore, these threats were no longer considered to be exclusively to the state – but to "people."

The label of "human security" emerged as a policy category rather than an academic concept in the 1990s, as a corrective to the state-centric and military focus of TSS. It was first given substance in UNDP's 1994 UN Human Development Report and was later given further substance by the 2003 Commission on Human Security, which was chaired by Sadako Ogata and Amartya Sen. MacFarlane and Khong (2006: 11) outline the two ways in which human security was defined in the policy world:

> Most people instinctively understand what security means. It means safety from the constant threats of hunger, disease, crime and repression. It also means protection from sudden and hurtful disruption in the pattern of our daily lives – whether in our homes, in our jobs, in our communities or in our environment. (UNDP, 1994)

> In essence, human security means safety for people from both violent and non-violent threats. It is a condition or state of being characterized by freedom from pervasive threats to people's rights, their safety, or even their lives. From a foreign policy perspective, human security is perhaps best understood as a shift in perspective or orientation. It is an alternative way of seeing the world, taking people as its point of reference, rather than focusing exclusively on the security of territory or governments. (Commission on Human Security, 2003)

The concept has two central elements. Firstly, it takes the individual, rather than the state, as the referent object of security. This is based on the recognition that the security of people is not always synonymous with that of the state. Given that the purpose of national security is to ensure individual security, it was argued to make more analytical sense to be concerned simply with human security rather than working via the referent object of the state. Secondly, it broadens the scope of security to include a range of non-military threats. The UNDP report in 1994 set out seven such sources of threat: economic, food, health, environment, personal, community, and political.

In other words, human security entails a horizontal expansion ("widening") in the concept of security beyond the military realm to include a wide range of other threats and a vertical expansion ("deepening") to include referent objects beyond the state, upwards to include regional and global actors and downwards to include regional and global identities. It posits that the individual human being is the only irreducible focus for discourse in security. Claims to other referent objects therefore derive from the sovereignty of the individual and his or her right to dignity.

MacFarlane and Khong (2006) explore the archaeology of the concept of human security. They suggest that it represents an idea with an intellectual history which predates the post-Cold War era. For them it is part of a broader set of ideas about the relationship between the individual and the states, which have evolved over time. They suggest that the state became the most significant referent object after the Peace of Westphalia for normatively sound reasons. The primacy of the state reflected the problems faced by individuals in seventeenth-century Europe. As individual nations emerged, there was a need for the state to preserve internal order and to limit threats from external aggression. Any cost to individual human rights represented an acceptable cost in the context. However, MacFarlane and Khong argue that a number of changes occurred during the late nineteenth and early twentieth centuries which led to the individual's security gradually becoming a priority. Increasing civilian casualty rates in war, the killing of civilians in genocide and conflict in the twentieth century, the end of the USSR and bipolarity, the role of globalization in creating new sources of transboundary threats such as communicable disease and environmental change all contributed toward a changing perception of the relationship between the states and the individual.

However, MacFarlane and Khong also suggest that although the hegemonic understanding of security has gradually shifted from state to individual it has always been contested. Throughout much of modern history, the hegemonic interpretation of security has been statist and military. However, there has been a persistent historical tendency to view the purpose of the polity as the protection of the welfare of the individual human subject and to question the absolute right of the state where its actions have conflicted with its subjects' interests and core values.

The relationship between the state and the individual posited by the concept of human security is central to forced migration. Protection emerges from a recognition that the security of the state is not always synonymous with that of the individual and that sometimes there is a need to ensure that individuals are protected outside of the framework provided by the states system. As Newman (2003: 7) highlights, orthodox definitions of security put human displacement at the periphery of politics because they ignore non-military sources of threat and also situations in which the security of the state and the wellbeing of the individual citizen conflict.

Newman (2003: 16) argues that human security is essentially a normative concept which can play an important political role in ensuring that refugees and IDPs are privileged within policy. He suggests that the concept can be used to highlight the plight of refugees, to attract more resources, and to push displacement up the policy agenda. Indeed, the policy category was picked up and used by UNHCR during the 1990s and used it as a central part of its policy discourse during Sadako Ogata's term as High Commissioner. There were also arguments to suggest that human security might represent a better analytical basis for assessing protection needs than the arbitrary notions of exile and political persecution inherent to the refugee definition. It was seen as a powerful way of mobilizing state support for refugee protection and durable solutions.

Indeed, the emergence and evolution of the international normative and legal framework addressing forced migration is in many ways indicative of the historical trend toward reprioritizing the security of the individual. The post-Cold War era has opened up the political space within which state sovereignty has been increasingly viewed as contingent rather than absolute. The Guiding Principles on IDPs (Phuong 2004), the use of refugee movements as a justification for military intervention under Chapter VII of the UN Charter (Loescher 2003), and the emergence of the notion of "Responsibility to Protect" (Bellamy 2009) all highlight elements of a shift away from viewing the sovereign state as the essential and exclusive referent object of security.

Poku and Graham (2000) also highlight the way in which human security is of value for understanding forced migration because of the way in which it "widens" the sources of threat. Human mobility is becoming increasingly complex and it affects both moving and hosting communities. Population movements are particularly security-sensitive because they change societies. For example, it can lead to environmental damage by putting pressure on finite resources, have implications for health, and even lead to the exacerbation of conflict in contexts such as the Arab–Israeli context in which population, mobility, and refugees are a significant aspect of the conflict.

However, Suhrke (2003) is skeptical about the value of applying human security to forced migration. She argues (p. 101) that it is "too inclusive to be useful." Because of its wide ranging definition of security, human security means everything and yet nothing (Paris 2000). It implies that threats to the individual can come from almost any source and offers no basis on which to prioritize different threats or to reconcile conflicts between competing interests. One problem is the question of who should define the core values of the individual that are being secured, especially given that there are possible trade-offs? For example, environmental security may conflict with development; human rights may conflict with religious values (MacFarlane and Khong 2006: 11). In the context of forced migration, these types of conflicts are extremely evident. For example, the host community's interests may conflict with those of the displaced; environmental preservation may conflict with the need to host and protect large numbers of people during a mass influx; immediate humanitarian imperatives may clash with long-term development objectives.

Human security is also difficult to distinguish from concepts such as human rights and human development. Because of human security's wide-ranging scope and the difficulty of knowing which elements should take priority, one of its limitations is therefore that it is extremely difficult to operationalize in any meaningful way. Suhrke suggests that since the movement of refugee populations is very rarely on a magnitude that would constitute a significant threat to a community and that the security threat is mainly focused on small groups, it makes more sense to talk about "vulnerability" than human security.

Critical Security Studies

CSS has a close relationship to HS. It has in common with human security that it, firstly, changes the referent object of security from the state to the individual (Krause and Williams 1997), and secondly, that it broadens the scope of security beyond the military to include economic, cultural, and societal security, for example (Buzan et al. 1998). However, unlike human security, CSS has emerged from an academic rather than a policy context. It emerges from an intellectual critique of realist approaches to security. It attempts to highlight many of the consequences that stem from a state-centric view of security. Consequently, CSS is more explicit about the idea that the state can be the main source of threat to individuals. It highlights how even when the security of the state is synonymous with the security of some citizens, this usually comes at a cost which is borne by others who are rendered insecure (Wyn Jones 1999). Much of CSS therefore has an explicit normative focus on emancipation of marginalized, poor, and unrepresented and attempts to place their security at the core of its agenda (Booth 1991). It attempts to repoliticize the process by which the security of some individuals is privileged to the detriment of others.

CSS represents a diverse group of perspectives on security. Two schools of thought offer different CSS perspectives: the Welsh School and the Copenhagen School. The approach of the Welsh School is mainly material, drawing upon neo-Marxism and critical theory. It examines the range of interests and power relations that lead the security of some to be privileged over that of others. Meanwhile, the Copenhagen School is mainly ideational, drawing upon constructivism. It examines how certain issues come to be seen in security terms and how certain values within a society come to be seen as needing to be protected from external threats.

The Welsh School is based upon the work of a group of academics based at the University of Wales in Aberystwyth during the 1990s. It draws particularly upon the work of Ken Booth (1991; 1997; 2004). The approach is based upon a critique of realism. It has its roots in the Coxian critical theory dictum that "all theory is for someone and for some purpose." It suggests that TSS, with its realist underpinnings, is not politically neutral and that what is in the "national security" interest does not uniformly serve the collective interest. Rather, it serves to uphold the security of privileged elites, in ways that often render the politically and economically marginalized insecure. From the Welsh School perspective, CSS is an intellectual project intended to make transparent and uncover the way in which states' security policies render the politically marginalized insecure. However, it is also a normative project which explicitly aims to place marginalized people at the core of its research agenda and to reveal how "national security" agendas serve political purposes.

A Welsh School perspective can be applied to analyze the disjuncture between national security and the security of forced migrants. Dubernet (2001) uses a CSS perspective to examine IDP protection in the 1990s. She looks at the creation of "safe havens" and "humanitarian corridors" by the international community for IDPs in Iraq, Somalia, and Bosnia. Although they were ostensibly created for humanitarian purposes, they did little to enhance the security of the displaced. In practice, they served the security interests of would-be asylum states by "containing" the displaced within the country of origin. Meanwhile, the "safe havens" were not at all safe, and undermined the security of the displaced. They prevented IDPs from crossing borders to become refugees, while offering no meaningful protection. The Srebrenica massacre of 1995, in which around 30,000 Bosnian Muslims were killed by Serb militias within a "safe haven" overseen by UN peacekeepers, illustrates the lack of security for the displaced.

Meanwhile, DIDR can also be explored from a Welsh School perspective. In India, for example, the construction of large dams is frequently justified as being in the "common good" or the "national interest" (Roy 1999). Since the Nehruvian era, big dams have been seen as part of "national security," underpinning the nation's national development strategy and playing a symbolic role. However, in practice dam building has had significant redistributive consequences. The benefits have predominantly accrued to relatively small groups of economic and political elites in urban areas, while the costs have mainly been borne by politically under-represented minority groups such as tribal "adivasis" (Khagram 2004). In other words, dam building has served to privilege elites, to the detriment of the vulnerable and politically marginalized. A CSS perspective would highlight the way in which the "national interest" depoliticizes these unequal distributive outcomes.

The Copenhagen School is based mainly on the work of Ole Waever. It examines security more at the ideational than material level. Waever's main work is based on the two related concepts of "societal security" and "securitization." The concept of societal security emphasizes that external threats are often to values and identities rather than material entities. In particular, threats are frequently perceived to exist in relation to cultural identity – for example, to language, ethnicity, or religion. Consequently, many threats are constructed in relation to a social group, that defines itself as a "we," in opposition to "others." Waever (1993) has explored how this notion of societal security usefully explains how migration has come to be seen as a security issue in the EU because the cultural values of a group come to be perceived as threatened.

Building upon this idea, the Copenhagen School has developed the notion of "securitization," which refers to the way in which an issue comes to be inter-subjectively perceived as related to security (Buzan et al. 1998). "Securitization" represents a "speech act" with real, political effects. Labeling something as "security" is not a politically neutral act. It gives it a special status and legitimates action that would otherwise not be legitimate. For example, when an issue – such as climate change or migration is related to security, it becomes a greater political priority and is pushed further up the policy agenda. Because security is seen as urgent and fundamental, "securitizing" an issue justifies immediate and exceptional action that might otherwise be considered disproportionate.

For example, as asylum and immigration have come to be linked to security, so extraordinary measures have been justified in the name of security. In government departments, asylum has been a component of security. For example, in the US asylum is a function of Homeland Security and in the EU, asylum is part of Justice and Home Affairs. Meanwhile, the media and political rhetoric have reinforced the commonly held association between asylum seekers and refugees on the one hand, and terrorism and threats to economic and societal security on the other hand. This has contributed, for example, to the legitimation of practices involving derogations of human rights, the suspension of civil liberties, extra-judicial detention, military interception at sea, reinforced border control, forcible deportation, and *refoulement*, practices which would generally be associated with addressing military threats to national security.

Third World Security Predicament

Security has often been studied from a Eurocentric perspective. The majority of academic approaches to security relate the concept to liberal democratic Western states which have internal authority and external legitimacy. This view of the fully sovereign, liberal democratic state does not adequately capture the nature of "threats" and how governments respond to these threats in a developing world context. A number of authors have attempted to address this gap in the literature in ways that have relevance for understanding the relationship between forced migration and security in the developing world.

Ayoob (1995) describes the idea of the "Third World Security Predicament." As relative latecomers to the Westphalian system, developing states face additional challenges in establishing internal and external authority. While they may have external legitimacy, they frequently lack internal legitimacy. The absence of internal cohesion, the lack of internal recognition for state boundaries and institutions may exacerbate vulnerability to both external and internal threats. One consequence of this incomplete state-building process is that developing country governments may not always be concerned with the security and survival of the nation-state. Rather, they are often more concerned with the security and survival of the incumbent regime. Security policies may be designed to safeguard the concerns of the ruling elite and its support base rather than those of the entire population.

Similarly, Jackson (1990) argues that many developing countries have "quasi-sovereignty." On the one hand, they have external authority. Their external borders and territorial integrity are respected and the ruling government is recognized in inter-state negotiations. On the other hand, they often have little internal sovereignty. They may not be seen as legitimate by the entire population or even have control over the entire territory of the state. Regimes are therefore focused on survival and manipulate the international system to do so. Leaders use external authority to advance internal legitimacy.

Clapham (1996) builds on this argument, exploring the encounter between African states and the Western state system. He highlights the way in which African states often lack internal sovereignty but hold external legitimacy. Many regimes use the latter in order to enhance the former, drawing upon their connections to the internal system as a means to secure their own position as the ruling elite. In particular, African states have used the norms and conventions of international relations to serve the private ends of elites. African states therefore need to be understood in this context. International assistance, trade relations, and compliance and non-compliance with international institutions are often used as a means to develop and maintain domestic patron–client relationships.

Ayoob, Clapham, and Jackson offer compatible and mutually supportive perspectives on how Southern states respond to security issues. They highlight how many developing states are not concerned with the security of the nation-state *per se*, but with the survival of the regime, using external legitimacy as a means to build internal authority. Collectively, they suggest that many developing states are likely to regard issues to be relevant for security insofar as they threaten the incumbent regime's survival. These perspectives contribute to explaining the conditions under which developing states view refugees and IDPs as a "threat" rather than an opportunity.

Milner (2009), for example, has drawn upon these perspectives in order to explore the relationship between asylum and security in Africa. He examines how this relationship has evolved in Tanzania, Guinea, and Kenya. In each case, the state's response to asylum has been historically shaped partly by how the incumbent regime has interpreted its own security and survival. In Tanzania, for example, the government adopted particularly generous policies toward refugees during the 1970s and 1980s, which contributed to the regime's international legitimacy. However, by the mid-1990s, democratization and structural adjustment contributed to removing the government's ability to provide social services to its own population and created a mechanism which made it even less possible to prioritize non-citizens over voting citizens. In Kenya, the government has been historically hostile toward hosting Somali refugees. This is partly because they have been perceived as a threat to the regime, being associated with irredentism, the spill-over of conflict, and competition for resources.

Biopower

The concept of biopower introduces a post-structuralist perspective to the study of security and forced migration. It can be defined as the practice of modern states in exercising control over their population. Work on biopower focuses on analyzing the techniques (beyond the use of violence) that are used by states in order to exercise power over the population. The concept draws upon the work of Michel Foucault who explored the techniques through which the state has historically controlled human sexuality, health, and criminality, for example.

Foucault analyzed the way in which discourses (dominant ideas and social practices) define "normality" in human behavior and define deviance and "abnormality" in ways that legitimate intervention by the state. Through the creation of discourses that constitute collective understanding of "normality" and define "abnormality," Foucault highlights how the state has used techniques including surveillance, measurement, statistics, and knowledge to ensure that deviance is corrected and control is maintained. Foucault explores the way in which the state used techniques including surveillance, measurement, statistics, and knowledge to ensure that deviance was corrected and control maintained. For Foucault, power and knowledge are very closely related. In the case of sexuality, psychiatry was used to identify and correct deviance. In the case of mental health, psychology was used to identify and correct madness. In the case of criminality, criminology was used to identify and correct delinquency. In each case, the dominant discourses have defined people who comply with the norm and enabled action that intervenes to correct aberrations.

Nyers (2006) applies the concept of biopower to explore how states respond to refugees, the techniques that states use and the consequences they have for refugees and the discourses of refugee policy. In particular, he examines what he calls "states of the exception" – the creation of exceptions that legitimate and underpin dominant norms. He argues that the category of the refugee serves to reinforce the sovereign states system. Refugees represent an aberration to the state system but through selective inclusion and the categorization of the exception as a "refugee," states legitimate exclusion. Nyers therefore looks at asylum and refugee protection as institutions that themselves perpetuate practices of exclusion. In his words (p. 22): "all solutions are deeply implicated in the conditions that make the problem possible in the first place." For Nyers, many of the structures that exist to "help" refugees are therefore structures that perpetuate the existence of refugees as what Arendt called "bare life" and leads to what he refers to as "humanitarian violence."

Hyndman (2000) adopts a similar perspective in her analysis of UNHCR's refugee camp management. She argues that rather than simply serving a humanitarian function, camps also serve a control function for the host state and the international community. Their geographical location, structure, and layout ensure regularity, order, and control. They use space in a way that enables surveillance, control, and a clear division between the violent and insecure areas in which refugees reside and the highly securitized compounds in which humanitarian workers and UNHCR reside. A structure which is ostensibly for the benefit and security of refugees thereby serves control functions for the state and UNHCR.

Case Study 1: Securitization of Asylum Since 9/11

Based upon the work of the Copenhagen School, the concept of "securitization" has become increasingly used in International Relations. It offers a useful means through which to explore the process through which an issue comes to be linked to security and the political effects this has on that issue. Indeed, the issue of asylum and immigration is an area which has become increasingly connected to security in the media and politics in ways that have had profound effects on the policy and practice of refugee and IDP protection.

Following the terrorist attacks on the US on September 11th 2001, Western liberal democracies have adopted a range of new restrictions on asylum and immigration. These have been implemented as part of a wide range of homeland security policies adopted to reduce the likelihood that terrorists will acquire access to their territories (Hampshire 2008). States have adopted a range of restrictionist policies on asylum including the increased use of interdiction, extraterritorial processing of asylum claims, carrier sanctions, and detention, for example. These policies have had in common that they have tried to limit the spontaneous arrival of asylum seekers on states' territories. Since 9/11, there have been a growing number of attempts by Western states to deport or extradite terrorist suspects who have claimed asylum and attempts by states to avoid incurring obligations to *non-refoulement* that might apply to terrorists.

However, this begs the question of how and why asylum seekers have become associated with terrorism and securitized since 9/11. As Newman (2003: 9) observes, the link between terrorism and asylum is empirically weak. Yet, asylum seekers and refugees have been increasingly seen as a "threat." For example, the refugee admission quota for the USA was set at 70,000 for 2002 but only 30,000 were admitted. This was because new INS checks stalled admissions and resettlement was temporarily suspended. In the aftermath of the attacks, policy and the media in the US and Europe focused on asylum and refugees even though the 9/11 attackers had entered the country on student visas rather than as asylum seekers.

As Van Selm (2003: 71) explains, in a number of developed countries, particularly the US, an association was made between the "asylum seeker" and the "terrorist," such that the two became inextricable in policy and media debates. Even though the 9/11 attacks had not been carried out by asylum seekers, the earlier 1993 attempt to bomb the World Trade Centre had been carried out by an asylum seeker. The popular view of many asylum seekers as Muslims and Arabs contributed to enabling refugees as potential source of threat. Furthermore, the later 7/7 attacks in London directly implicated Somali asylum seekers in ways that reinforced popular perception of the relationship between asylum and terrorism. These perceptions have arguably contributed to policies relating to asylum and forced migration that "securitize" displaced people. For example, since 9/11 a number of European states have attempted to move away from spontaneous-arrival asylum to find ways to either process asylum claims or ensure protection on the territory of another state. The range of European proposals focusing on extra-territorial processing of asylum claims in North Africa and Eastern Europe, and on "protection in the region of origin" emerged in the context of concern with terrorism (Noll 2003).

Mares (2003) analyzes how the process of securitization of asylum seekers has taken place in the Australian context. He highlights the dialectical process through which the media and political debate have been mutually reinforcing and created the dominant perception of asylum seekers and refugees as a threat. In the Australian case, Mares implies that the process of securitization precedes 9/11 and the pervasive international concern with terrorism. In the Australian case he identifies it as stemming from post-1999 public concern with spontaneous-arrival asylum seekers coming from Afghanistan. In media and policy debates during John Howard's term as Prime Minister, spontaneous-arrival asylum seekers were associated with "infectious disease," "illegal immigrants," "queue jumpers," and seen as "bogus" and "phoney." Meanwhile, the opposition Labour Party was viewed as "soft on illegal immigrants." The popular debates created binaries of citizens/non-citizens, and divided asylum seekers into analytically meaningless categories of bogus/genuine, legal/illegal, or good/bad refugees.

Case Study 2: Protracted Refugee Situations and Critical Security Studies

Protracted refugee situations (PRSs) have been defined by UNHCR as situations in which more than 25,000 refugees have been in an "intractable state of limbo" for more than five years. Indeed, in many refugee crises in the developing world, refugees find themselves confined to camps and enclosed settlements for extremely long periods of time. In situations in which conflict or repression have been ongoing in the country of origin, and there has been little prospect of a durable solution such as repatriation, resettlement, or local integration, refugees have found themselves effectively "warehoused" in insecure camps and settlements in remote border areas. In 2006, around six million refugees (ten million including Palestinians) were in PRSs, with the average length of exile being around 17 years. Examples of PRSs include Afghans in Pakistan and Iran, Palestinians in Jordan and Lebanon, Burundians in Tanzania, Somalis in Kenya, Burmese in Thailand, and Nepalese in Bangladesh (Loescher et al. 2008; Loescher and Milner 2005). PRSs have implications for both state security and human security. They represent a situation in which state security frequently conflicts with and even undermines the security of individual refugees.

PRSs are frequently seen by host states of asylum as a security threat. Milner (2000) highlights how they can be seen as a security threat on two levels. Firstly, they may represent a *direct* security threat through the spill-over of conflict. PRSs are frequently in insecure border locations. Many refugee camps are militarized or offer sanctuary to combatants in ways that way represent a perceived threat to the security of the host state. Secondly, PRSs may represent an *indirect* security threat. They may lead to grievances amongst the local population. In situations in which there are scarce resources, and the refugee population is seen to be privileged in the provision of services, social conflict may arise between local people and refugees. Furthermore, if a given refugee population upsets the demographic balance in a region by introducing a large number of people of a certain ethnicity or nationality it may be perceived as a threat.

The situation of Somali refugees in Kenya illustrates some of these sources of perceived threat to the state. Since the collapse of the Siad Barre regime and the outbreak of civil war in Somalia in 1991, there has been a significant Somali refugee population hosted in the Dadaab camps of Northern Kenya. By 2006, there were around 150,000 refugees in the camps. In terms of direct security, the camps are located close to the Somali border and have been seen as a source of small arms trafficking, the spill-over of conflict, and sanctuary for combatants. A series of cross-border incursions and violent incidents have reinforced this perception of the refugees as representing a direct security threat. In terms of indirect security, the camps are located in relatively deprived areas of the country in which the local host populations have little access to resources. There have therefore been some grievances about competition for resources – including the refugee population's access to service provided by the international community and its use of natural resources. Meanwhile, the historical perception of Somalis in Kenya as being associated with irredentism and past inter-state conflicts has contributed to generalized anti-Somali sentiment in the country.

These perceptions of direct and indirect threats to state security have led to the securitization of the Somali refugee population by the Kenyan government. Since the 1990s, the government has used the claim that the Somali population represents a threat to justify and legitimate a range of measures. It has used the notion of threat to justify confinement of the refugees to the camps and to deny refugees who leave the camps access to social services. This deprivation of freedom of movement and livelihood opportunities has been justified in security terms. Fear of demographic imbalance and past inter-state conflicts between Somalia and Kenya have been used to perpetuate xenophobic attitudes toward the Somali population. Meanwhile, at various stages the Kenyan Government has used the language of terrorism, and the Western association of "Somalis" and "terrorism" to justify ever greater rights restrictions (Juma and Kagwanja 2008).

The securitization of the Somali refugee population by the Kenyan government has had significant implications for human security. It has legitimated what has been described as refugee "warehousing," enabling the Kenyan government to justify the confinement of refugees to closed camps in a highly insecure border region. The refugees who have been in the Dadaab camps since 1991 have had few opportunities to earn a livelihood or have freedom of movement. Access to basic services such education and health services have often been inadequate. Furthermore, although the situation has improved, the camps have often been violent, and there were regular reports of rape and gender-based violence during the 1990s (Helton 2002). The levels of violence and access to human security in the Dadaab camps have often contrasted with the better quality of refugee protection provided to Sudanese refugees in, for example, the Kakuma camps in the northwest of the country.

Indeed, PRSs represent a threat to human security that is often justified on the grounds of state security. Long-term confinement to camps in insecure border regions and inadequate access to 1951 Convention rights such as freedom of movement and recourse to law are features of PRSs around the world. Host states of first asylum frequently argue that in situations of mass influx they have no choice but to suspend access to certain rights given their limited resources. Meanwhile, the international community has historically done little to overcome the world's PRSs. It has contributed only modestly and selectively to enhancing refugee protection in PRSs or to identifying possibilities for durable solutions. Instead, it has used humanitarian assistance in order to confine the refugee problem to a designated geographical area, using international organizations to manage and oversee those refugee populations (Hyndman 2000).

Conclusion

Security is an essentially contested concept. There is no single, neutral, and objective definition of security. How it is defined and understood has political and practical consequences. Depending on what referent object, which sources of threat, and what analytical lens one uses to understand security, the wellbeing of different groups of people will be privileged in radically different ways. States, regions, groups, values and identities, regimes, and individuals represent possible referent objects for security. Meanwhile, existential threats emerge not only from external military threats but also a range of other economic, social, and environmental sources. Moreover, security can be understood from a range of theoretical perspectives, which may be informed by realism, critical theory, constructivism, or poststructuralism, for example.

It is clear that no single definition of security can fully capture the contested rights and interests involved in forced migration. Development-induced displacement, internal displacement, protracted refugee situations, and asylum and immigration all involve the contestation of rights and values between different groups of people. In each case, different groups will be threatened or be perceived to be threatened in different ways, and the language of security may be invoked by different actors to justify and privilege certain forms of behavior and action, or claims to rights. The analytical tools provided by security studies cannot arbitrate between the competing interests and claims to security. However, they can be used to make transparent the basis of normative claims to security and the interests and power relations that underlie those claims.

4

International Cooperation

International cooperation is necessary for overcoming the most serious negative consequences of forced migration. No one state acting in isolation is likely to be able or willing to address a large scale refugee or IDP situation by itself. The costs of addressing mass influx situations, overcoming protracted refugee situations, or tackling humanitarian emergencies are often higher than a single state is prepared to bear, and the benefits of addressing such situations are often so diffuse that states will only contribute to overcoming crises when they are supported by other states. Protection, durable solutions, and addressing root causes rely upon states collaborating and coordinating their behavior. It is therefore crucial for theory and practice to understand the conditions under which international cooperation takes place.

International cooperation is commonly defined as occurring "when actors adjust their behavior to the actual or anticipated preferences of others" (Keohane 1984). According to this definition, it does not necessarily involve states changing their underlying preferences but strategically adjusting their behavior in order to achieve a more preferable outcome than would have been possible acting in isolation. International cooperation is commonly divided into two sets of problems: coordination and collaboration problems. The former relates to a situation in which states adjust the means by which they achieve a given end – how they do something collectively; the latter relates to a situation in which states adjust the ends that they are working toward – what they do collectively.

International cooperation is especially important in relation to so-called global public goods. These are goods that (like street lighting in domestic politics) have benefits that are, firstly, non-excludable and, secondly, non-rival between actors. In other words, once provided, the benefits will be available to all states, irrespective of who has actually contributed to providing the good, and one state's enjoyment of those benefits will not diminish the benefits available to another state. The problem with global public goods is that, based on these characteristics, there will be little incentive for individual states to be the provider. Consequently, without a binding institutional framework, the good would be under-provided in comparison to what states would have collectively provided had they collaborated. Examples of global public goods include the creation of a vaccine to combat polio, action to address HIV/AIDS, and climate change mitigation (Barrett 2007). The challenge with global public goods is therefore to ensure that international institutions are designed and created that overcome collective action failure and ensure the provision of global public goods.

To some extent, refugee and IDP protection might be considered to be global or regional public goods insofar as the provision of protection benefits a number of states, irrespective of whether they themselves contribute to providing protection. Similarly, durable solutions and action to address the underlying causes of displacement might also be regarded to confer non-excludable benefits to states. This is because, once provided, they will benefit a number of states – in terms of providing security and fulfilling humanitarian goals – irrespective of whether those states actually contribute to provision. This means that, in the absence of a binding institutional framework, states are likely to free-ride on other states' contributions to protection, and protection will be under-provided in comparison to what would have been collectively desirable (Betts 2003; Suhrke 1998).

Regime theory represents the area of IR theory that focuses on international cooperation and the provision of global public goods. It examines the role of international institutions (as formal and informal rules) in enabling states to cooperate. In particular, it explores how regimes – as "principles, norms, rules, and decision-making procedures" overcome coordination and collaboration problems and facilitate international cooperation (Krasner 1983). Regime theory examines the negotiation, monitoring, implementation, and enforcement of regimes, and their effectiveness in leading to cooperation (Hasenclever et al. 1997). It attempts to identify the conditions under which regimes can facilitate collective action.

The insights of regime theory have relevance for the refugee regime and the emerging IDP regime. Both refugee protection and, to an increasing extent, IDP protection are governed by international regimes. Regime theory has rarely been applied to either in order to explore when, how, and under what conditions the UN and other actors are able to facilitate cooperative outcomes. Yet it has real practical insights to offer in terms of identifying what, for example, UNHCR can do to facilitate mutually beneficial international cooperation between states that can simultaneously lead to better protection or durable solutions or address the underlying causes of displacement.

This chapter therefore provides the tools and concepts for understanding the conditions under which international cooperation takes place in relation to forced migration. It attempts to highlight the role that actors such as UNHCR can play in facilitating international cooperation. The chapter divides into three parts. Firstly, it explains the competing theoretical perspectives on international cooperation, drawn from neo-realism, liberal institutionalism, and constructivism. Secondly, it applies these to explore their relevance to forced migration by looking at burden-sharing in the global refugee regime. Thirdly, it explores two empirical case studies of successful international cooperation in the refugee regime – the Comprehensive Plan of Action on Indochinese Refugees (CPA) and the International Conference of Refugees in Central America (CIREFCA), both of 1989 – in order to assess the conditions under which international cooperation has taken place in the refugee regime.

Theoretical Perspectives on Cooperation

International relations in general, and regime theory in particular, offer three broad approaches to understanding international cooperation. Each one makes different assumptions about states and the state system and so derives different conclusions about the prospects for international cooperation and the conditions under which it is possible. Broadly speaking, neo-realism offers a power-based approach to international cooperation; liberal institutionalism offers an interest-based approach to international cooperation; constructivism offers a knowledge-based approach to international cooperation.

Neo-realism

Neo-realism is skeptical about the prospects for international cooperation and the role of international institutions in facilitating cooperation. Because states are primarily concerned with relative gains, international cooperation, which is generally oriented toward the pursuit of mutual gain, is of little interest to states. States may engage in temporary alliances in order to maintain the balance of power; however, these alliances will fall short of enduring cooperation (Grieco 1988). Neo-realists also doubt that institutions can play an independent role in facilitating cooperation. Mearsheimer (1995) argues that institutions are basically reflections of the distribution of power in the world. They are created on the basis of the self-interested calculations of the great powers and exert no independent effect on state behavior. For Mearsheimer, there is little empirical evidence of cooperation that would not have occurred in the absence of institutions, and which cannot be explained simply by the self-interested choices of the powerful.

From a neo-realist perspective, cooperation can only be explained by Hegemonic Stability Theory (HST). HST implies that the provision of a global public good depends upon one state being powerful enough to be able and willing to either provide the good unilaterally or coerce others into doing so (Hasenclever et al. 1997). In other words, what at first glance appears to be international cooperation will, in reality, be the self-interested actions of a great power. Hasenclever et al. describe two circumstances in which a hegemon will provide an international public good where there would otherwise be collective action failure: the "benevolent leadership model" and the "coercive leadership model."

In the benevolent HST model, a large state bears the cost of providing a global public good because it has a sufficiently large unilateral interest to provide the good. It draws upon the notion of "exploitation of the big by the small" (Olson and Zeckhauser 1967). Here, if the dominant power places a higher absolute valuation on the public good than the smaller powers, it will provide that non-excludable good irrespective of free-riding. In other words its valuation of the public good is sufficiently high that it will be prepared to bear a disproportionately high cost for its provision. Kindleberger (1973) describes how the United States has played this role in the international monetary system, disproportionately contributing to maintaining the fixed exchange rate system and using the dollar as a vehicle currency at different times in its history. It has also often been argued from this perspective that the UN is only effective at times when the US, as the global hegemon, has had a sufficiently large self-interest in a given course of action to be willing to underwrite the costs of that action.

In the coercive HST model, the hegemon will use its power to coercively induce other states to undertake a given action or to contribute to the provision of a global public good (Calleo 1987: 104; Gilpin 1975). Rather than underwriting the costs of a public good itself, the US, for example, may be able to use its superior military or economic power to induce compliance from weaker states. This form of "cooperation" has been evident during the Cold War and post-Cold War contexts in which the US has often used military or economic inducements to persuade client states to ally with it in various international and regional conflicts. As with the benevolent HST model, it is doubtful that this type of behavior can really be described as cooperation.

Liberal institutionalism

Liberal institutionalists criticize neo-realism for failing to explain the extent of international cooperation, particularly in non-security areas. In *After Hegemony*, Robert Keohane (1984) highlighted how, by the 1970s, there was significant international cooperation particularly in the economic sphere, which neo-realism had great difficulty explaining. Simultaneously, there was a proliferation in the number of international institutions. The former trend, Keohane suggested, could be explained by the latter trend. In other words, even in the absence of hegemony, cooperation could be facilitated by international institutions.

From a liberal institutionalist perspective, states are assumed to be interested in absolute gains rather than relative gains. This means that they can benefit from the joint gains that stem from long-run cooperation. However, there are nevertheless practical barriers to cooperation. Acting in isolation, states are likely to act differently from how they would act collectively. If there is no guarantee that cooperation will endure in the long-run, an individual state's rational strategy is likely to be to free-ride on others or to avoid contributing out of suspicion that others may "cheat." The fear of free-riding and "cheating" lead to what is known as "collective action failure" (Olson 1965). States may not necessarily collaborate or coordinate their behavior even though they would be collectively better off if they did so. Acting in isolation, states will free ride or "cheat" even though cooperation would be in their long-run interests.

This disjuncture between individual and collective rationality is commonly illustrated by liberal institutionalists using the game theoretical analogy of Prisoner's Dilemma. In a two-actor model with two states, each state may prefer mutual cooperation (CC) to mutual defection (DD), yet is even better off when the state can benefit from the unrequited cooperation of the other actor (DC). However, being the state which behaves cooperatively without a reciprocal response (CD) is the least desirable outcome. Consequently, the states' preference ordering will be DC>CC>DD>CD. In a single interaction, each state will find it rational not to cooperate, and will receive a higher payoff through defection. Consequently, even though both states have a common interest in achieving the CC outcome, acting individually, they will end up at the suboptimal DD outcome.

Actor B

	C	D
C	3,3	1,4
D	4,1	2,2

Actor A

Figure 4.1 Prisoner's Dilemma. Number left (right) of comma refers to A's (B's) preference ordering (1 = worst outcome; 4 = best outcome)

Liberal institutionalism has argued that international institutions may play a role in overcoming the type of collective action failure illustrated by the Prisoner's Dilemma, and enabling states to move from box DD to box CC.

This is because international institutions enable states to take a longer-term perspective of their interests and thereby change their incentives to cooperate. The liberal institutionalist literature identifies a number of ways in which they can do this. Firstly, institutions may create repeated interaction between states over time. Rather than cooperation being based on "one-shot interaction" as the Prisoner's Dilemma implies, institutions ensure that interaction is repeated over time or "iterated." This reduces the incentives for a state to free-ride or defect because it means that it will be forfeiting potential longer-term gains. Secondly, institutions can provide information through surveillance that identifies free-riding states, thereby reducing the incentives for "cheating." Thirdly, institutions have been argued to have a role to play in terms of reducing the transaction costs of cooperation. By institutionalizing states' coordination of activities, cooperation becomes "cheaper" and so the practical obstacles to cooperation are reduced. Fourthly, institutions may facilitate issue-linkage, combining issues within international bargaining in a way that facilitated side-payments across issues. By including more issues and so state interests in bargaining, the possibilities for mutual gain become greater (Axelrod 1984). Other roles that institutions can play in facilitating cooperation include creating the stable conditions for international negotiations and helping to increase the value of reputation (Hurrell 2007: 68).

Constructivism

Constructivism criticizes the neo-neo debate for failing to explain the source of states' preferences, which are exogenously given. Instead, for constructivism, states' preferences are endogenously defined through their interactions. Constructivism can therefore explore the mechanisms through which states' preferences are constituted through, for example, norms, ideas, and the role of argument and persuasion. By questioning where preferences come from, constructivism opens up the possibility of facilitating international cooperation by changing the perceptions that underlie states' interests. For neo-realism and liberal institutionalism, states will act on the basis of a rational cost-benefit analysis. From a constructivist perspective, what is perceived as a "cost" or a "benefit" is itself subject to contestation and change.

For constructivism, institutions matter but for different reasons than those identified by liberal institutionalism. For liberal institutionalism, institutions matter because they constrain the behavior of states, incentivizing certain forms of action. The identities and underlying preferences of states remain fixed but the institutions make certain strategies a more or less desirable means to meet those ends. For constructivism, institutions matter not only because they are constraining but also because they constitute and change the identities and therefore the preferences of states. They contribute to the creation, dissemination, and diffusion of norms, in ways that socialize states over time. In other words, institutions contribute to interest convergence by transforming states' identities and hence their perceived interests (Checkel 1999; Risse et al. 1999).

A constructivist approach introduces a role for other actors involved in norm creation and diffusion. International cooperation is no longer simply an inter-state game. The importance of ideas, knowledge, argument, and persuasion means that non-state actors matter. They have a significant role in influencing the prospects for and nature of international cooperation. International organizations, academics, firms, NGOs, and individuals all become relevant to determining the normative and ideational context within which states cooperate.

Epistemic communities such as academics and think-tanks have a role to play in developing new forms of knowledge and ideas that define the context in which states define their interests (Haas 1989). In international debates which require scientific and technical expertise such as those on the international regulation of the environment or new technologies, such groups can play a highly influential role in agenda setting, determining how problems are understood, and which solutions are considered within international debates. Even where scientific expertise is not required, academic input can influence the ideational context within which states define their interests.

Constructivism also opens up the possibility of seeing international organizations (IOs) as autonomous actors in world politics. Rather than automatically implementing the pre-defined preferences of states, they may have their own interests and play a role in independently influencing the prospects for cooperation. Barnett and Finnemore (2004), for example, identify IOs such as UNHCR as being autonomous actors that significantly influence the trajectory of inter-state cooperation. They often have their own organizational sociologies which mean that the process of translating states' collective interests into action is mediated by the range of institutional interests found within the IO. Many IOs also have a normative basis for their work and may therefore be able to draw upon this as a means to resist the prevailing realpolitik of a given era. They may be able to use persuasion (Risse 2004) or moral authority (Hall 1997) in order to exert independent influence over the behavior of states.

Constructivism also opens up the possibility that other non-state actors may influence international cooperation through developing and disseminating new norms and ideas, or through persuasion. Keck and Sikkink (1998) highlight the role that NGOs and trans-national advocacy networks have played in disseminating and diffusing norms in areas such as human rights and the environment in ways that have influenced inter-state cooperation in these issue-areas. Moreover, although IR lacks an adequate theory of the role of the individual in world politics, there has been a growing recognition that individuals matter in determining the prospects for international cooperation. They may, for example, serve as important norm entrepreneurs especially if they have the necessary attributes for leadership (Nye 2008; Power 2008).

Burden-Sharing in the Refugee Regime

There are two ways in which a given state can contribute to refugee protection: either by providing protection to refugees who reach its territory (asylum) or by contributing – through resettlement or financial contributions – to the protection of refugees who are on the territory of another state (burden-sharing). In the case of asylum, the refugee regime sets out a strong normative and legal framework, underpinned by the principle of *non-refoulement*, whereby states must refrain from sending a refugee back to a state in which he or she faces a well-founded fear of persecution. In contrast, in the case of burden-sharing, the regime provides a very weak normative and legal framework, setting out few clear norms, rules, principles, or decision-making procedures. Burden-sharing (in terms of resettlement and financial contributions) is often taken to be the most clear representation of the degree of international cooperation in the global refugee regime. Different theoretical approaches offer different explanations for the conditions under which burden-sharing

takes place within the global refugee regime. This section integrates the existing Forced Migration literature on burden-sharing with the International
Relations literature on international cooperation, situating some of the forced
migration literature within the broader theoretical debates.

Suhrke (1998) offers a neo-realist perspective on burden-sharing. She
argues that the prospects for international cooperation in the refugee
regime have been extremely limited. This is because, for Suhrke, refugee
protection represents a global public good. Once provided, its benefits are
non-excludable and so, in the absence of a binding institutional framework,
states will have little incentive to contribute to burden-sharing. Instead, they
are more likely to engage in free-riding, shirking or shifting the burden of
responsibility on to other states. She consequently suggests that the refugee
regime can be analogously represented by the analogy of Prisoner's Dilemma,
whereby states acting in isolation will under-contribute to burden-sharing in
comparison to the level that would have been collectively optimal. Suhrke's
argument is neo-realist insofar as she argues that the only way in which
Prisoner's Dilemma has historically been overcome is in situations in which
a global hegemon has underwritten the costs of refugee protection on the
basis of its own self-interest.

She suggests that the two examples of successful multilateral cooperation – refugee resettlement in Europe after the Second World War and the
resettlement of Vietnamese refugees after 1975 – had their own underlying
and, implicitly realist logic. Both depended on hegemonic power. In the
former case, she argues that participating states shared a sense of values and
obligation toward victims of the war, creating an "instrumental-communitarian"
interest in resettlement. Although not explicitly stated, this argument can be
incorporated within the notion of "benevolent leadership model." The
United States, for example, unilaterally established the International Refugee
Organization and resettled over 30 percent of the refugees, while Australia
and Israel were also major contributors. This high level of commitment,
Suhrke argues, stemmed from the states' sufficiently high valuation of the
need to provide protection such that they were prepared to resettle outside
of an institutional framework, irrespective of the non-excludability of the
benefits. In the latter case, Suhrke explicitly makes the case that "coercive
hegemony" was required, with states needing "to be persuaded or pressured
by the hegemon," which was again the United States. Her argument, then,
is that multilateral cooperation is only possible where either a benevolent or
coercive hegemon is present.

In contrast, other authors take a broader view of burden-sharing, which
might be considered to draw upon liberal institutionalist underpinnings.
They identify ways, other than hegemony, in which collective action failure

and the Prisoner's Dilemma may be overcome. Thielemann (2003), for example, explores the factors that motivate states' contributions to burden-sharing within the EU context. He looks at European contributions to UNHCR's Humanitarian Evacuation Programme (HEP) for refugees fleeing Kosovo in the late 1990s. He suggests that states were motivated by a combination of interests and norms. In terms of interests, geographical proximity, historical and economic ties, and the stock of Yugoslavs already in the country provide a partial explanation for states' willingness to contribute. However, solely interest-based accounts fall short and norms are also needed to explain the contributions. In particular, states' wider commitment to norms of solidarity, represented by proxies such as commitment to overseas development aid and the welfare state correlated with contributions to the HEP.

Furthermore, authors who have looked at global rather than regional burden-sharing identify the role of international institutions as important in facilitating burden-sharing. In particular, UNHCR has sometimes been able to create an institutional framework within which burden-sharing has taken place. It has done so by fulfilling many of the roles that liberal institutionalism identifies as important variables in international cooperation – such as engaging in issue-linkage, monitoring and surveillance, reducing transaction costs, and enhancing states' concern with reputation. Whether through its regular Geneva-based meetings such as the Standing Committee or the Executive Committee, through the work of its Division of External Relations or through convening ad hoc initiatives and conferences, UNHCR has sometimes been able to facilitate overcoming states' concerns with cheating and free-riding and been able to facilitate international burden-sharing (Betts 2005; Loescher 2001; Loescher et al. 2008). Notable examples of successful international cooperation that have taken place in the absence of a global hegemon include the International Conference on Refugees in Central America (CIREFCA), within which UNHCR played a central facilitating role while the USA was largely absent from the initiative.

Betts and Durieux (2007) provide a constructivist perspective on international burden-sharing. They explore the role of UNHCR in trying to create and disseminate norms relating to burden-sharing. They argue that UNHCR is capable of autonomously influencing processes of norm-creation that over time may lead states to change their commitment to burden-sharing. In particular, they set out two ideal-type models through which IOs such as UNHCR can engage in the creation and dissemination of new norms: a "top-down" model and a "bottom-up" model of norm-creation, which they describe as the institutional bargaining model and the good practice model.

In the first case, norms can be created through a UNHCR-led institutional bargaining process within which states negotiate formal agreements, which are either "hard law" or "soft law" agreements. UNHCR can facilitate such agreements in three stages: appealing directly to state interests; channeling those interests into commitments; formulating agreements on the basis of the resulting convergence of interests, which become accepted norms. Once agreed, these norms are gradually internalized by states and shape their behavior over time. UNHCR has fulfilled this role in, for example, the negotiation of Executive Committee Resolutions.

In the second case, norms can be created through a good practice model. Rather than crafting "generic" legal frameworks, IOs such as UNHCR can also work toward the development of what might be called "practical facilitation tools" i.e. sets of criteria, guidelines, mechanisms or modalities of international cooperation, and even "model agreements" where feasible, that make it gradually easier for states and international organizations to share responsibilities. In particular, UNHCR can, firstly, recognize examples of existing "good practice" by states; secondly, analyze, evaluate, and compile these examples of good practice; thirdly, develop further pilot projects to demonstrate the value of these practices; and, finally, consolidate norms of "good practice" in formal agreements. UNHCR has fulfilled this role in, for example, developing norms of good practice in areas such as refugee status determination, the provision of self-sufficiency for refugees, and many aspects of protection.

Two Case Studies: Comprehensive Plans of Action

This section explores the conditions under which cooperation has taken place in practice by assessing two successful attempts by UNHCR to facilitate international burden-sharing. It examines the Comprehensive Plan of Action on Indochinese Refugees and the International Conference of Refugees in Central America (CIREFCA), both of 1989. Both were conceived as "Comprehensive Plans of Action" to address longstanding refugee situations in the global South. They are useful for exploring the conditions under which international cooperation has taken place in the refugee regime because they represent the most successful examples of international cooperation in the modern history of the global refugee regime elements (Betts 2008). Broadly speaking, Comprehensive Plans of Action (CPAs) represent multilateral approaches to ensure access to durable solutions for refugees within a given regional context. Such approaches can be regarded as CPAs insofar as they were comprehensive in terms of drawing on a range of durable solutions simultaneously, cooperative in terms of involving additional burden- or responsibility-sharing between countries of origin and asylum, and third countries acting as donors or resettlement countries, and collaborative in terms of working across UN agencies and with NGOs.

The Indochinese CPA (1988–96)

The aim of the Indo-Chinese Comprehensive Plan of Action (CPA), which was based on a Geneva-based conference in 1989, was to provide a long-term solution to the mass influx of refugees fleeing mainly by boat from the Socialist Republic of Vietnam (SRV) to Southeast Asian states and Hong Kong (Robinson 1998; 2004). The CPA was conceived in the aftermath of the breakdown of a previous 1979 agreement in which, faced with a mass exodus of "boat people" from Indochina to Southeast Asian states and Hong Kong, and the reluctance of the first countries of asylum to admit the predominantly Vietnamese, the US had stepped in and offered to resettle all the Indochinese boat people who arrived in neighboring states. By the late 1980s, however, the agreement had collapsed, the US had reduced its resettlement rate, and the ASEAN states – such as Malaysia and Indonesia – and Hong Kong were increasingly "pushing back" arriving boats. However, a new possibility for international cooperation emerged because, with the collapse of the USSR, the main country of origin, Vietnam, had become a viable partner in international cooperation (Towle 2006).

UNHCR was able to facilitate a three-way agreement between the resettlement states led by the US, the countries of first asylum, and Vietnam to overcome the mass exodus. Firstly, the ASEAN states and Hong Kong agreed to refrain from "pushing back" the arriving boats and to host the screening process for asylum seekers. Secondly, the United States, along with a number of European states, Canada, and Australia committed to resettle all of those Indochinese asylum seekers who were recognized as refugees in the countries of first asylum. Thirdly, Vietnam agreed to accept and facilitate the humane return of all those asylum seekers who were not recognized as refugees, while allowing other non-refugees to apply to move abroad through the so-called "Orderly Departure Procedure." Each of these three sets of commitments was taken to be inter-locking and conditional upon one another. If any one state failed to meet its share of the bargain, the deal would collapse.

All three groups of states had interests in finding an overall solution. The ASEAN states and Hong Kong wanted to end the mass influx of refugees.

The US wanted to ensure regional security and resolve the humanitarian legacy of the Vietnam War. Vietnam hoped to use the CPA to rehabilitate itself in the eyes of the international community having lost its main ally, the USSR. However, UNHCR nevertheless needed to facilitate agreement and ensure the commitment of these states. A significant part of the success of the initiative rested upon UNHCR and Sergio Vieira de Mello, as convenor of the conference, bringing states together around the negotiating table, facilitating ongoing discussions, and convincing states that fulfilling their obligations was the only way to meet their own interests.

Although the CPA was criticized on human rights grounds, it was a success in terms of promoting international cooperation and resolving a longstanding refugee problem. By 1996, it had successfully overcome a 20-year-long refugee exodus from Vietnam and found solutions for the hundreds of thousands of so-called "boat people" who had fled to other parts of the region in the aftermath of the formation of the SRV in 1976.

CIREFCA (1987–95)

The aim of the International Conference of Refugees in Central America (CIREFCA), which was a multi-year process based around a conference held in Guatemala City in 1989, was to provide long-term solutions for refugees displaced by civil conflicts in Central America and to improve protection standards throughout the region. It represents the single most successful example of UNHCR-facilitated international cooperation in the recent history of the refugee regime. In the aftermath of the civil conflicts in the region during the 1980s, two million people were left displaced, of which around 150,000 were recognized by UNHCR as refugees.

In 1987, the Central American states agreed to a peace deal referred to as the Esquipulas II peace deal and, in response, the UN developed a process for regional post-conflict reconstruction and development, the Programme of Economic Cooperation and Development for Central America (PEC). Within this context, UNHCR recognized the need and opportunity to address the region's refugee situations, developing CIREFCA as a means to provide durable solutions to the refugees who had been in exile as a result of being displaced by the often extreme right and left wing governments that had been in power during the Cold War.

CIREFCA adopted an approach known as "Refugee Aid and Development," in which it developed a series of projects and programmes that attempted to target development assistance to facilitate improved protection and durable solutions for refugees, while simultaneously providing assistance to local host populations. The development projects gave refugees in exile access to self-sufficiency and local integration and gave returning refugees opportunities to reintegrate through establishing development projects that made social services and infrastructure available to both the displaced and the host communities.

CIREFCA received almost full funding for its projects and programmes and ensured that by the mid-1990s the majority of the region's refugees were no longer reliant upon humanitarian assistance and had received access to durable solutions either in their host state or in their country of origin. The success of the initiative relied upon the commitment of both its mainly European donors and the Central American states. Both the European donors and the Central American hosts were prepared to commit to the initiative because they had a strong interest in ensuring the wider security and development of the region, and viewed CIREFCA as an important component of that wider process. Nevertheless, UNHCR played an important role in enabling cooperation to take place. It conceived CIREFCA as part of the wider process. It also ensured leadership, coherence, and technical guidance and support. Consequently, CIREFCA enabled the Central American states to implement a range of development projects that simultaneously helped to integrate and reintegrate refugees while supporting national development.

Lessons for International Cooperation

The two CPAs provide particular insights for the conditions under which UNHCR has been able to facilitate international burden-sharing to overcome longstanding refugee situations. On a political level, they require interests, linkages, and leadership. On a practical level, it appears important that a number of further conditions are met by UNHCR and the wider UN system: country of origin involvement, ownership, inter-agency collaboration, and a strong UN regional presence. These conditions can be explained in turn.

Interests

Firstly, both CIREFCA and the Indo-Chinese CPA relied upon the existence of state interests in resolving the long-standing refugee situation. In neither case did the main stakeholders have significant interests in altruistically resolving the "refugee issue" for its own sake. They did, however, have perceived interests in issue-areas that related to the wider context within which the refugee situation was more broadly embedded. In particular, both the states within the region and the donor and resettlement states outside of the region had perceived interests in related issues such as security, migration, peace-building, and development. In the case of CIREFCA, the interests of the main European donors lay in the wider concern to promote security, democracy, and human rights in Central America, partly for ideological reasons and partly as a means to promote inter-regional trade. In the case of Indo-China, the interests of the US lay mainly in supporting regional security and promoting political change within the SRV, the interests of the ASEAN states mainly related to migration control, and the interests of the SRV related to attracting development assistance and political recognition.

Issue-linkage

Secondly, though, the existence and recognition of these underlying interests was not by itself a sufficient condition for inter-state agreement. Rather, the CPAs relied upon UNHCR facilitating the creation of a perceived linkage between the "refugee issue" on the one hand, and these wider interests on the other. This was particularly effectively achieved in the case of CIREFCA, in which UNHCR contributed to institutionalizing a number of these "linkages." A direct relationship was formed between CIREFCA and UNDP's development initiatives such as PEC and PRODERE which created an association between development assistance and durable solutions. Similarly, a clear link was formed with the Esquipulas II Peace Accords as a result of their direct reference to displacement. Developing such linkages brought not only state commitment but also wider support from across the UN system, notably from the UN Secretary-General.

Leadership

In both cases, UNHCR committed high-level staff to work on the CPAs. In particular, the directors of the relevant regional bureaux – namely Sergio Vieira de Mello and Leonardo Franco – were highly committed and led the processes both internally and externally. They were also able to draw on significant support from the High Commissioner, and high-level staff throughout headquarters. Although it is rarely argued in grand theories of international politics, the role of individual personalities was crucial, as it has been throughout the history of the refugee regime (Skran 1995). However, what is also crucial to recognize is that UNHCR created an enabling environment which allowed such leadership to emerge. Political momentum was particularly important in both cases and this relied upon having a clear vision that could be conveyed to states and a message that the end goal was achievable and in the interests of all stakeholders. Perhaps most notably, the two main conferences in Geneva and Guatemala City and the CPA documents did not address every detail of implementation. Rather they were used as political focal points upon which the wider process could build. They were consciously conceived as politically focused commitments, rather than pledging conferences and were used primarily to build momentum and credibility for the process.

Country of origin involvement

In both CIREFCA and the CPA, the countries of origin were active partners within the negotiations, making the promotion of voluntary repatriation or return a viable component of each comprehensive approach. There is no practical reason why a CPA need necessarily have to include return. However, in practice, given that states tend to regard repatriation as "the preferred durable solution" and approaches to the asylum–migration nexus are only likely to be meaningful if non-refugees are returned, the viability of the country of origin, as a negotiating partner and a recipient of returnees, would appear to be an important pre-condition for a successful CPA. In the case of Indochina, the SRV's role was what made resolution of the impasse on the 1979 agreement possible. In the case of CIREFCA, the positive impact of the change of government in Nicaragua and the evolving role of the Guatemalan government, for example, show the importance of the countries of origin as partners in the process.

Ownership

Rather than being passive recipients of external support, the countries in the region were active participants throughout the two processes. The active involvement of not only the countries of origin but also the countries of asylum ensured that there was "buy-in" by all of the relevant actors. In both cases the states had an identifiable stake in the success of the process and were vocal in promoting the initiatives and engaging the donor and resettlement countries. In CIREFCA the projects were compiled by the Central American states themselves with the technical support of UNHCR, ensuring that they had clear interests in implementation. Similarly, the availability of additional development assistance created an incentive for them to drive the process. In the case of Indochina, the "countries of temporary refuge" were directly involved in identifying their own "cut-off" date and developing their own reception and status determination procedures in consultation with UNHCR. This, and their collective bargaining position through ASEAN, gave them a central role throughout the process. The notion of "ownership" was therefore significant inasmuch as it meant that UNHCR did not have to provide all of the political momentum for the initiative in isolation.

Inter-agency collaboration

In both initiatives the scope of the comprehensive approach necessarily went beyond the bounds of UNHCR's mandate. In order to address these concerns, inter-agency collaboration was required. During CIREFCA, UNDP's role allowed an integrated development approach that could simultaneously provide for the needs of groups who fell outside of UNHCR's mandate; notably IDPs, the "externally displaced," and local populations. The Indochinese CPA was one of the first examples of UNHCR–IOM partnership. IOM's role was important in relation to the logistical aspects of resettlement and providing alternative migratory channels for non-refugees. Although no clear division of labor was established, the debates within UNHCR at the time reveal that a role for IOM was considered to be important so that UNHCR would not be directly implicated in the deportation of non-refugees. Although IOM ultimately refused to play a role in return, meaning that UNHCR largely had to renounce the role to states, the organization assumed a significant role particularly with respect to the Orderly Departure Procedure, providing an alternative migration channel for non-refugees wishing to leave Vietnam. Together the Indochinese and Central American cases therefore show the importance of UNHCR partnership with development actors when a CPA focuses on integrated development, and the importance of IOM partnership in cases related to addressing an asylum-migration nexus. The CIREFCA experience in particular also highlights how important it is not to see UN approaches to resolving protracted refugee situations in purely UNHCR-centric terms. Rather, by seeing responses to protracted refugee situations as part of a broader context, the Office of the Secretary-General and the New York-based UN system can play a significant leadership role and facilitate inter-agency collaboration.

Strong regional presence

An important element of both initiatives was the strong UNHCR presence within the region, supported by frequent and high-level visits to the region by headquarters staff. Part of CIREFCA's success has been attributed to the presence of much of the process in Central America. A so-called Joint Support Unit – comprising UNHCR and UNDP – was present in San José, the representatives were particularly strong, and Spanish provided a common working language. During the Indochinese CPA, the majority of the intergovernmental meetings were held in the region. As with CIREFCA, this allowed high-level participation by, for example, the region's foreign ministers.

Conclusion

Different theoretical perspectives offer different insights into the conditions under which international cooperation is likely to take place in a given issue-area. Those different perspectives can be applied to understand when and under what conditions states are likely to cooperate in providing protection, durable solutions, or overcoming the root causes of displacement in relation to refugees and IDPs. This chapter has explored what insights those different perspectives offer understanding the conditions under which inter-state burden-sharing has taken place in the global refugee regime. The case studies of UNHCR's attempts to facilitate burden-sharing suggest that each of the neo-realist, liberal institutionalist, and constructivist approaches to burden-sharing have something to offer. Each highlights different factors which have contributing to facilitating international cooperation in the refugee regime.

The two case studies – the Indochinese CPA and CIREFCA – suggest that in the short-run, states' interests are important. In order for international cooperation to take place, states need to have an underlying interest in protection, durable solutions, or addressing root causes. However, notably, these interests have not needed to be based on the welfare of the displaced per se but have generally related to interests in linked issue-areas such as migration, development, or security. As neo-realism and liberal institutionalism suggest, without states having some underlying set of interests, cooperation would not have taken place. In the case of the Indochinese CPA, a hegemon also played a crucial role, with the US playing the role of a benevolent hegemon by underwriting the resettlement and financial costs of the initiative. In contrast, however, CIREFCA belies the assumptions of neo-realism because international cooperation took place largely in the absence of a hegemon, with the US initially refusing to support the initiative because of its backing for Nicaraguan refugees in Honduras.

In both initiatives, UNHCR's success relied upon a number of the factors identified by liberal institutionalism. In the Indochinese CPA, it worked to create trust and overcome states' suspicion that other states would free-ride or cheat, convincing all three groups of states that other states' commitment to contributing relied upon them fulfilling their end of the bargain. Furthermore, the institutional design of both initiatives enabled UNHCR to use issue-linkage, to engage in monitoring and surveillance of states' implementation of the agreements, and to reduce the transactions costs of cooperation.

However, in both case studies, constructivism also sheds light on some of the factors that enabled cooperation to take place. UNHCR needs to be seen partly as an autonomous actor. It played a key role of persuasion in influencing how states saw and acted on the basis of their interests, and individuals such as Sergio Vieira de Mello and Leonardo Franco served an important role as norm entrepreneurs. Meanwhile, the wider normative and ideational context in which the two initiatives took place – at the end of Cold War – created an auspicious historical juncture for reasserting international human rights norms.

All three theoretical perspectives on international cooperation therefore have something different to offer understanding cooperation in relation to forced migration. In the short-run, the rationalist approaches are useful because this is the time horizon over which interests and power are most likely to shape the prospects for cooperation. In the long-run, constructivist approaches are useful because they highlight how norms shape states' preferences and expectations over time. IOs such as UNHCR have a role to play in relation to both. In the short-run they may be able to draw upon realism and liberal institutionalism to facilitate interest convergence; over the long-run, they may be able to engage in the creation and dissemination of norms and ideas that shape states' interests.

5

Global Governance

Introduction

In recent years the study of global governance has become a major focus of International Relations, spawning an enormous amount of literature (Barnett and Duvall 2005; Wilkinson 2005; Woods 2002). Consideration of global governance emerges from one of International Relations' central observations: that there is a distinction between domestic politics and international politics. In domestic politics there is a sovereign that can uphold order within a state. In international politics there is no sovereign and international politics has therefore been characterized by "anarchy" – not in the sense of chaos but in the sense of the absence of world government (Morgenthau 1948). It is essentially this distinction between domestic and international, and the pursuit of order in the absence of world government that defines International Relations as a distinct discipline. Global governance emerges as a response to that problem. Where government exists at the domestic level, global governance has emerged at the international level.

Global governance is often poorly defined. Its simultaneous emergence within both a policy and academic context has led to it being used in a range of ways that are rarely precise or rigorously defined. For some, it represents a policy category with, at best, little substantive meaning and, at worst, a strongly normative and even imperialist agenda (Eagleton-Pierce 2008; Wilkinson and Hughes 2002). Nevertheless, in order to posit a working definition, one might consider it to be regulation that exists over and above the level of the nation-state, whether at the international, supranational, or trans-national level. Governance distinguishes itself from government insofar as there is no single authoritative rule-maker. Rather, governance is a negotiated and contested process involving multiple actors, often with different interests and power. Analytically, global governance can be understood as a process which has a number of different stages: negotiation, implementation, monitoring, and enforcement (Rosenau 1992). In order to understand global governance, each of these elements needs to be analyzed and understood.

There has been a proliferation of global governance since the Second World War. A range of international institutions have emerged to regulate the behavior of states and other actors. In the immediate aftermath of the Second World War, the most obvious form of global governance focused on the development of public international law. The UN system, the Bretton Woods Institutions, and a host of new agreements in areas such as human rights and the environment created the basis of a rule-based framework for inter-state relations. Gradually, this picture has become ever more complex with the emergence regional institutions such as the EU and supranational organizations with independent authority such as the WTO and the ICC. There has also been a growing role of non-state actors such as MNCs and civil society in setting international standards through standards-developing organizations such as the International Standards Organization and a range of voluntary agreements such as the Extractive Industries Transparency Initiative (EITI) and the Global Compact (Hall and Biersteker 2002; Mattli and Buthe 2003; Ruggie 2004; Sell 2003).

The logic underlying the creation of multilateral institutions has been to overcome so-called collective action problems, in which there is a disjuncture between a course of action that would be collectively rational, on the one hand, and how actors behave when they consider their interests in isolation from one another on the other hand (Olson 1965). To take the example of climate change, the reasoning underlying the creation of international institutions is that cooperation to reduce greenhouse gas emissions is in states' collective interest but, acting in isolation, it would be individually rational for one state to free-ride on the emissions reductions of other states. International institutions contribute to overcoming collective-action failure and enable joint gains to be derived from cooperation because they reduce the costs and increase the benefits of international cooperation. For example, by providing information, reducing the transaction costs of cooperation, providing surveillance, creating stable conditions for multilateral negotiations, increasing the value of reputation, and creating a context within which mutually beneficial issue-linkage can take place, institutions facilitate cooperation (Axelrod 1984; Hurrell 2007: 68; Keohane 1984).

Since the first half of the twentieth century, a framework for the global governance of forced migration has gradually emerged. On a formal level, it is easy to identify the relevant institutions that regulate the behavior of states. The global refugee regime emerged during the inter-war years with the creation of the LNHCR. In the post-war era, UNHCR and the 1951

Convention represent the main elements of the regime. Over time, these have been complemented by a range of regional arrangements such as the 1969 OAU Convention, the 1984 Cartagena Declaration, and the 2004 EC Directive. There has also been growing recognition that international human rights standards can be applied to the situation of refugees to offer a form of "complementary protection" (McAdam 2007). In the case of internal displacement, an embryonic IDP regime has emerged, initially through the creation of a "soft law" framework in the 1990s, drawing upon international human rights and international humanitarian law which has been implemented through a collaborative institutional arrangement, in which responsibility for overseeing the regime has been shared among different agencies. In the case of DIDR, there are also a number of soft law instruments that shape how states should respond to people displaced by development projects. These include the standards and lending guidelines of the World Bank and regional development organizations, and relevant sources of international human rights law (Barutciski 2006; Cernea 1997).

However, analyzing the global governance of forced migration is more complex than simply identifying the formal institutions that explicitly regulate the issue-area. For example, the behavior of states toward refugees and IDPs is affected by the global governance of a range of other issue-areas. Since the 1990s there has been a gradual proliferation in global migration governance, which has implications for how states respond to issues relating to forced migration. New informal migration-governance structures have emerged on a regional and bilateral level, which affect states' responses to, for example, the spontaneous arrival of asylum seekers. The global governance of peace and security also have significant implications for forced migration; the work of the Peace-Building Commission in post-conflict settings, and the use of Chapter VII of the UN Charter to legitimate intervention on the grounds of refugee flows, for example, highlight these broader institutional links (Roberts 1998). This illustrates the fact that understanding the global governance of forced migration is about much more than simply identifying the formal institutions that regulate states' responses to forced migration. There are a number of debates within the wider global governance literature which have enormous potential relevance for understanding the international politics of forced migration.

This chapter introduces the main debates and analytical tools within the study of global governance and demonstrates how they can be applied to the study of forced migration. Firstly, the chapter begins with an overview of global governance. It defines global governance, explains the genesis of the idea of "global governance," and identifies some of the conceptual challenges inherent to analyzing global governance. Secondly, it then outlines some of the main debates and conceptual tools in global governance and their relevance to forced migration: on the creation and evolution of global governance, the effectiveness of global governance, normative debates on global governance, and the role of international organizations, the relationship between power and global governance, and the role of regime complexity. Finally, the chapter concludes with a case study, in which it looks at the impact of institutional proliferation and regime complexity on the politics of refugee protection.

An Overview of Global Governance

Definition

"Global governance" is a murky and often poorly defined term. However, one can create a working definition based on a number of elements. It is generally used to refer to regulation that exists over and above the level of the nation-state, whether at the international (*between* states), supranational (*above* states), or trans-national (*across* states) level. In other words, global governance includes but is not reducible to agreements between states such as treaties and conventions. It includes regulation that is supranational in the sense of an authoritative body existing independently of states – such as that exercised by the WTO, the European Commission, or the ICC. It also includes regulation that is trans-national in the sense of involving a range of actors and levels of governance. For example, in practice, most "global" governance has connections to domestic politics, being adopted and enshrined within municipal law (Deere 2008).

Governance distinguishes itself from government insofar as there is no single authoritative rule-maker. In the absence of world government or the type of sovereign that exists at the domestic level, global governance is a negotiated and contested process. It is subject to the interests, ideas, and power of the range of state and non-state actors involved in the process of governance. Analytically, global governance can be understood as a process that might be disaggregated into a number parts. One way of dividing and analyzing the process of governance would be to divide it into the negotiation, implementation, monitoring, and enforcement phases of governance (Rosenau 1992).

In contrast to "international cooperation," which was analyzed in the previous chapter, the focus of global governance is not on the states, so much as on the *institutions* (regimes and organizations) as independent variables (i.e. a factor in explaining something), and as dependent variables (i.e. what is being explained). Indeed, this focus begs the question of how one should define institutions. Keohane (1989: 3) defines institutions as "rules (formal and informal) that prescribe behavioural roles, constrain activity and shape expectations." More broadly, one might simply think of institutions as *rules that define appropriate behavior for a given identity.* They may influence the behavior of states and non-state actors either by *constraining* (i.e. creating incentives for behavior based on a given identity) or by *constituting* the identity of states and non-state actors and thereby shaping their behavior.

The genesis of "global governance"

The notion of "global governance" is frequently taken for granted but it is important to critically engage with its origins. "Governance" itself has a long history, implying control and direction, which has been used in a range of controversial policy contexts (Eagleton-Pierce 2008). However, global governance did not emerge as a commonly used term until the 1990s. One of the reasons why the concept has often been used in an imprecise and muddled way is that it has two very different genealogies which are often mixed and intertwined.

The policy-level genealogy of global governance can be found in the Global Commission on Global Governance, convened during the 1990s. Its role was to reflect on the emerging challenges stemming from an increasingly interconnected world in which trans-boundary issues cannot be adequately addressed by individual sovereign states acting in isolation. The 1994 report of the Commission, *Our Global Neighbourhood*, set out a an agenda for how states might cooperate in order to address a range of new threats and challenges in areas such as the environment, trade, trans-national crime, finance, and conflict. Building on this report, "global governance" has subsequently become part of the mainstream policy-level vocabulary used to describe the whole range of roles that international institutions and international organizations play in regulating processes that transcend the jurisdiction of the nation-state.

The academic-level genealogy of global governance emerges from attempts within International Relations to understand the role of international institutions in world politics. In particular, regime theory represents a branch of International Relations that attempted to understand the role that regimes – as norms, rules, principles, and decision-making procedures – play in influencing the behavior of states in particular issue-areas (Hasenclever et al. 1997; Krasner 1983). It tried to explore questions relating to the emergence and effectiveness of regimes, and how they are negotiated, implemented, monitored, and enforced. However, from the late 1990s, dissatisfaction with the explanatory power of regime theory and its rationalist origins led to a focus on the broader concept of "global governance," within which specific research topics have emerged focusing on issues such as the role of international organizations (Barnett and Finnemore 2004), compliance (Raustiala and Slaughter 2002), global public goods theory (Barrett 2007; Kaul et al. 1999), the rational design of institutions (Koremenos et al. 2003), and the role of international law in world politics (Chayes and Chayes 1996; Goldstein et al. 2001).

The use of the phrase global governance is not unproblematic. In contemporary International Relations, the policy and academic origins of the term have increasingly merged. The definition of global governance, the levels of governance and what it regulates, and how, are not always explicit in the burgeoning literature on the subject. The term also frequently carries with it an implicit normative bias, often assuming that "more" governance is both necessary and desirable. These caveats highlight the need for analytical rigor in understanding what global migration governance is, and where it can be found, and what normative claims are implicit in making a case for particular types of governance (Wilkinson and Hughes 2002). Nevertheless, the concept of global governance is useful insofar as it highlights the move away from individual nation-states having absolute authority over policy-making toward a situation in which the behavior of states and other actors is constrained and shaped by a range of institutions which exist beyond the nation-state.

Challenges in the study of global governance

The concept of global governance has emerged with a number of ambiguities relating to the boundaries of the concept. In particular, two related issues, which require clarification, are often left unresolved by the existing global governance literature. Firstly, what does the "global" include? To what extent does it include, for example, regional governance, standards set by private actors, and even elements of domestic regulation? Secondly, what does "governance" include? Is it just abstract, formal agreements that regulate a specific issue-area? Or can it take into account the important issues of informal norms and practices?

What levels of governance are "global"?

The word "global" is neither precise nor helpful in pinpointing exactly what regulation is being discussed. The most indisputable form of global governance is public international law, which is identifiable by the concept of *jus inter pares* – or law between states. However, it has been increasingly recognized that global governance goes far beyond formal treaties negotiated between states at the multilateral level. The notion of the "public" has expanded beyond the state to include a range of non-state actors, both who are involved in the creation of regulation and to whom regulation applies. Regulation does not simply exist at a formal level but also comprises a significant number of informal norms that nevertheless shape the behavior of states and other actors. Furthermore, global governance is often multi-level, existing not only at the multilateral level but also the regional and bilateral level, and often penetrating into domestic politics and municipal law.

Although the most obvious source of global governance is multilateral institutions (Ruggie 1993), a range of other levels of governance have also emerged. The concept of "multi-level governance" is often used to describe the co-existence of multilateral, regional, bilateral, and national forms of regulation (Bache and Flinders 2005). States have created a range of multilateral institutions to regulate a host of issue-areas. Within the framework of the United Nations, for example, a dense tapestry of international agreements comprising public international law have been negotiated and implemented in areas ranging from security to human rights to trade. It has also been increasingly recognized that the scope of global governance goes far beyond the formal multilateral institutions that exist within the structures of the United Nations. On a regional level, institutions have emerged to facilitate cooperation inside the regions and to enhance bargaining power outside. While the European Union represents the most obvious example of regional integration, regionalism is an emerging phenomenon throughout the world, with NAFTA, APEC, ASEAN, IGAD, the African Union, MERCOSUR, and COMESA being amongst the range of regional institutions with a wide range of functions and degrees of policy integration (Fawcett and Hurrell 1995; Mattli 1999).

Yet, it is also important to be aware that global governance is not confined to inter-state cooperation. While some issue-areas are predominantly statist, being negotiated and implemented by states, an increasing range of issue-areas are characterized by what Scholte (2004) describes as a "polycentric" mode of governance. In other words, they involve a growing range of non-state actors in negotiation, implementation, monitoring, and enforcement. For example, as well as NGOs, private sector actors such as multinational companies are increasingly active political actors within global governance. The Global Compact, the Extractive Industries Transparency Initiative (EITI), and the TRIPS negotiations, for example, all significantly involved the role of private actors within global governance

(Falkner 2007; Haufler 2006; Ruggie 2004; Sell 2003). Within this context, International Administrative Law is increasingly being used to describe standard-setting at the international level that falls short of the definition of pubic international law but nevertheless serves as a significant form of regulation at the global level (Kingsbury 2007). An example of this type of standard setting is the work of International Standards Organization (ISO) (Mattli 2003).

Under certain conditions, even regulation found at the domestic level may be either a manifestation or a source of global governance. Firstly, agreements made between states may often be incorporated and adopted within municipal law or may have an influence on shaping domestic politics or domestic bureaucracies (Deere 2008; Risse at al. 1999). Secondly, one state's domestic policies may also represent an implicit form of global governance. This will be the case when policy interdependence means the behavior of one state serves to constrain the behavior or policy choices of another state (Moravcsik 1997). Thirdly, the explanation for the effectiveness of regimes as the international level may be found in the degree of support they receive from powerful constituencies in domestic politics (Drezner 2007). Consequently, even the division between "global" and "national" is not as clearcut as is often implied (Milner 1992).

Does "governance" include informal norms and practices?
Another key challenge in empirically identifying "global governance" is how to take into account forms of regulation which go beyond formal agreements. A significant amount of governance is informal in terms of being based on unwritten norms of behavior or commonly accepted practices of behavior that nevertheless have a profound influence on shaping the behavior of states. Most of the international relations literature on global governance has tended to analyze institutions in terms of abstract formal entities. It tends to take these abstract formal institutions as an independent variable and the behavior of states as a dependent variable. However, it is important to be aware that global governance far more than just abstract formal entities that regulate behavior. The problem, though, is how to identify informal norms. Since they are often only identifiable in the behavior of states, this makes it difficult to clearly separate independent and dependent variables. Consequently, the study of informal norms has largely been shunned.

Even in relation to formal norms, it is not always clear that global governance is best analyzed through simply taking the abstract formal agreements that exist at the global level to be the most appropriate signifier of "global governance." In particular, it is important to look at the ways in which the practice of regimes is not captured by simply looking at the formal, abstract institutions that regulate a given issue-area. Indeed, forced migration is useful for highlighting the ways in which practice matters for global governance. Analytically, one might distinguish between two important dimensions of regimes as practice which are not adequately captured by reducing global governance to the abstract, formal institutions that exist at the "global" level: the vertical and horizontal dimensions of practice (Betts and Schmidt 2009).

The *vertical* level of practice relates to the way in which abstract, formal institutions are transformed as they shift from the global level to their local context, and the way in which this feeds back to affect the global regime. The global refugee regime, for example, changes as it is translated from the global level to specific local contexts and "the regime" is not the same thing in one regional context as it is in another. Schmidt (2008), for example, has analyzed the "global refugee regime" in Uganda and Tanzania. She argues that this matters for how we understand regimes, firstly, because the regime is its practice and, secondly, because the local manifestations of the regime feed back to affect the abstract, global level. Building on this analysis, Bradley (2008) has highlighted how the notion of "protection" within three different regimes changes from the global to the local level. She examines how the abstract notion of "protection" defined by the ICRC, UNHCR, and R2P regimes changed in their application to the specific context of refugees and IDPs displaced from Darfur. Recognizing the vertical dimensions of practice begs the question of whether these issues should be most appropriately seen as merely issues of "implementation" of the abstract, global regime or whether, instead, they call into question the way in which regimes are commonly understood.

The *horizontal* level of practice relates to the way in which regulation in one issue-area often affects the politics of another issue-area, and vice-versa. In most of the literature on global governance, regimes are taken to be, by definition, issue-area specific. However, the politics of forced migration, for example, is affected by regulation in other issue-areas such as migration, development, human rights, security, and peace-building. Furthermore, states' preferences in other areas shape the negotiation and creation of regulation in relation to forced migration. It is impossible to analyze the politics and global governance of forced migration in isolation from the broader set of regimes and issue-areas that influence the politics and global governance of forced migration (Betts 2008). Both the vertical and horizontal dimensions of practice therefore illustrate some of the limitations of analytically reducing regimes to formal institutions that discretely regulate a given issue-area.

The Main Debates in Global Governance

Aside from raising a range of important issues of definition and scope, academic debates on global governance has given rise to a number of important theoretical debates. Many of these debates offer a set of useful conceptual tools that can contribute to explaining the role of international institutions in world politics. This section explains the main debate within global governance and highlights their relevance for understanding the international politics of forced migration. It explains six important debates, gradually moving from some of the traditional debates in global governance toward newer, emerging debates: the creation and persistence of regimes, effectiveness and compliance, normative issues, and the role of international organizations, the relationship between power and global governance, and regime complexity.

Creation and persistence

The main focus of regime theory during the 1980s and 1990s was to explain the creation and persistence of regimes (as norms, rule, principles, and decision-making procedures regulating a given issue-area). Regimes were generally seen to emerge from a bargaining process between states. The core academic challenge was therefore to explain the conditions under which states cooperate in the creation of international regimes. For neo-realists, the creation of regime was explained by hegemony. Either a benevolent hegemon would value a global public good sufficiently to tolerate free-riding by smaller actors or a coercive hegemon would induce other actors to contribute to the global public good (Gilpin 1975; Kindleberger 1973). For liberal institutionalists, regimes are created when it is in states' interests to develop institutionalized forms of cooperation. Institutions are valued by states insofar as they enable actors to coordinate their behavior in mutually beneficial ways; when, for example, they reduce the transaction costs of cooperation or allow actors to demonstrate their credibility through repeated interaction (Hasenclever et al. 1997; Keohane 1984). Insofar as international institutions fulfill these purposes and thereby contribute to states more efficiently meeting their interest, mainstream regime theory would predict that they will continue to exist. Insofar as they no longer yield efficiency gains and cease to enable states to cooperate to achieve their mutual interests, they are unlikely to persist.

In a variation on these traditional debates, Goldstein et al. (2001) have explored the question of "legalization," as a particular form of institutionalization characterized by three components – obligation, precision, and delegation. They define "obligation" as when states are legally bound by a rule of commitment, "precision" as when rules are unambiguously defined, and "delegation" as when third parties have been granted authority to implement, interpret, and apply those rules. For Goldstein et al. (2001), when all three of these elements exist, the creation of a norm or international agreement will reach the threshold of "law" – although each one of the characteristics is subject to variability, existing along a spectrum (Abbott et al. 2001). For example, obligation can vary between non-legal norms and binding rules; precision can vary from vague to precise norms; delegation can vary from diplomacy to international court oversight and domestic adoption. The work on legalization is useful because it highlights the range of forms of institutionalization and begs the questions of "under what conditions do states choose to bind themselves to international legal agreements?" and "under what conditions do states choose to create institutions with strong or weak degrees of legalization"? Goldstein et al. (2001) identify a number of factors that explain these choices including a functionalist analysis of the extent to which different institutional arrangements lead to efficiency gains in relation to specific problems, the role of domestic politics in limiting or enabling the scope for binding norms, and the role of power asymmetries in limiting or enabling the scope for binding norms.

Building on this, Jupille et al. (2008) examine the question of "institutional choice" in order to examine when and why states choose to create or sign up to different forms of institutional arrangements. Based on a bounded rational choice framework, they examine why states choose between the competing options of unilateralism, bilateralism, and multilateralism to address a specific international problem, and why they choose between different degrees of institutionalized cooperation at these different levels. They use this framework as a means to explain the historical evolution of the global trade regime, highlighting how at different historical junctures, states have developed different preferences and have chosen between competing institutional alternatives. For example, they examine how states engaged in institutional choices between the various trade regimes that pre-dated the WTO and how a set of choices between competing institutional alternatives led the present day WTO to become the dominant institutional framework regulating international trade.

These different frameworks are useful for explaining emergence and change in the global governance of forced migration. During the inter-war years, the refugee regime was based on a relatively low degree of legalization. Although the LNHCR was created, its work was ad hoc and situation-specific, and there was no overarching international treaty defining states' obligations toward refugees. In other words, there were low levels of obligation, precision, and delegation. In contrast, the post-war era led to the creation of a UN refugee regime with a high degree obligation, precision, delegation. Initially, the 1951 Convention was limited in its temporal and geographical mandate. Its mandate focused exclusively on addressing the situation of Europe's Second-World-War refugees, and its creation can be easily explained by a combination of European states' mutual interest in developing institutionalized cooperation and the US's role as an external hegemon with an interest in the reconstruction of Europe. In 1967, the scope of the regime was extended in the Cold War context, largely because institutionalized cooperation favored the interests of powerful actors. A high degree of legalization enabled the US, in particular, to use the refugee regime to discredit Communism, while devolving many of the costs to other states.

Since the end of the 1980s, the costs of the regime have increased for powerful states in the context of growing South–North migration, while the benefits, many of which were specific to the Cold War era, have declined. To some extent, it is therefore surprising that the refugee regime has continued to exist. On the other hand, however, states have increasingly engaged in the type of "institutional choice" described by Jupille et al. (2008). They have created a range of alternative institutions – such as new regional cooperative agreements in the area of migration and the emerging IDP regime – to address their concerns with the spontaneous arrival of asylum seekers through, for example, enabling them to bypass UNHCR and the global refugee regime.

Effectiveness and compliance

Aside from exploring regimes as dependent variables (i.e. the conditions under which they are created and change), global governance has also explored regimes as independent variables (i.e. the conditions under which states' international commitments have an effect on the behavior of states). A large amount of literature has attempted to explore the issue of "compliance," which can be defined as a state of conformity between an actor's behavior and a specified rule. Compliance can be distinguished from "effectiveness," which is harder to operationalize, and can be defined as the degree to which a rule induces changes in behavior that further the rule's goals or achieves its policy objectives (Raustiala and Slaughter 2002: 539). A range of theories of compliance have emerged and are summarized by Raustiala and Slaughter (2002) in an excellent overview of the existing literature.

On the one hand, rationalist theories of compliance assume states to be rational and self-interested actors which will respond to rational institutional incentives. Chayes and Chayes (1996) set out a "managerial theory" of compliance in which they argue that states generally comply with their legal commitments partly because of the bureaucratic context in which commitments are negotiated and implemented. For them, states have a propensity to comply with commitments because of three factors: firstly, states sign up to rules and are therefore likely to respect these because these become endogenous to their process of reflection; secondly, once complex domestic bureaucracy is directed to compliance, it becomes costly to change those bureaucratic structures; and thirdly, norms create a sense of obligation over time. Meanwhile, Downs et al. (1996) set out an "enforcement theory" of compliance. According to them, deeper regimes with greater levels of commitments are likely to yield greater the gains from cooperation. However, the greater the depth of commitments, the greater too will be the incentives to opportunistically violate the agreement and the higher the level of enforcement that will be needed to deter free-riding and cheating. This finding suggests that much of the evidence of high compliance with international law is simply a result of the "shallowness" of many international agreements.

On the other hand, constructivist theories of compliance take a different view. As Raustiala and Slaughter (2002: 540) suggest, for constructivists, "compliance is less a matter of rational calculation or imposed constraints than internalized norms of appropriate behavior." They highlight two different strands of this approach. Franck (1990) sets out a "legitimacy theory" of compliance, whereby the perception of a rule as legitimate by those to whom it is addressed significantly determines the likelihood of compliance. For Franck there are four elements of legitimacy that contribute to "compliance-pull": firstly, textual determinacy (i.e. the clarity and transparency of the commitment itself); secondly, symbolic validation (i.e. the communication of authority through ritual and regularized practice); thirdly, coherence (i.e. the consistency in application and in context with other rules); and fourthly, adherence (i.e. the degree to which a rule fits with the normative hierarchy of rules about rule-making). Collectively, fulfilling these conditions leads to a perception of what Franck describes as "right process." Koh (1997), meanwhile, sets out a "norm-oriented theory" of compliance. For Koh, "obedience" can be understood as rule-induced behavior caused by internalizing norms. This approach sees compliance as an element of a normative socialization process in which actors internalize norms over time (Keck and Sikkink 1998; Risse et al. 1999).

Drawing upon these wide-ranging theories, Raustiala and Slaughter (2002) elaborate six clusters of explanatory variable that may underlie compliance: firstly, the problem structure (coordination or collaboration problem; the transparency of behavior; the number of states involved); secondly, the solution structure (what is the specific institutional design in terms of the nature and content of rules? does the agreement use punitive measures? does it use capacity-building measures?); thirdly, the solution process (the methods by which cooperative solutions are developed: inclusiveness, fairness, and perceived legitimacy); fourthly, norms (strength and quality of norms); fifthly, domestic linkages (structural links to domestic actors: incentives among certain domestic actors, the ability to alter preferences/power at the domestic level; incorporation into the domestic legal system); and sixthly, the international structure (bipolarity or multipolarity; hegemony; embeddedness in broader areas of international cooperation).

Within the global refugee regime, there has generally been state compliance with the basic norm of providing asylum in conformity with the 1951 Convention. However, at times, states have sought to minimize their commitments to refugee protection insofar as it has been possible to do so without openly transgressing international rules. The clusters of factors outlined by Raustiala and Slaughter are useful for highlighting some of the features of the global refugee regime that increase the likelihood of compliance and those that make compliance less probable. Indeed they highlight how certain aspects of the refugee regime make it predisposed to state compliance and others to non-compliance (see table below).

In particular, the "rationalist" factors that rely upon creating rational incentives for compliance – the problem structure, solution structure, and solution process – suggest that compliance in the refugee regime would be unlikely. Meanwhile, the overall international structure has arguably become less favorable to compliance over time, with the end of bipolarity and the decline in US hegemony undermining one of the bases of Cold War compliance. On the other hand, however, the "constructivist" factors – norms, capacity-building, and domestic linkages – which rely upon the internalization of norms by states over time, appear to favor compliance. Overall, then, the application of Raustiala and Slaughter's framework to the question of state compliance with the 1951 refugee convention suggests that the compliance which has taken place within the regime has rested far more upon "constructivist" factors than the creation of rational incentives for compliance.

Factor	Manifestation within the refugee regime	Predicted effect on compliance
Problem Structure	Challenging collaboration problem (Prisoner's Dilemma regionally, Suasion Game globally); Large no. of states (near universal)	Negative
Solution Structure	No punitive measures for non-compliance (only surveillance by UNHCR); Some capacity-building measures by UNHCR	Negative – but partly mitigated by capacity-building
Solution Process	Northern bias – norms originally conceived in a European context	Negative
Norms	Relatively widely accepted. Some *jus cogens* norms – e.g. *non-refoulement*	Positive
Domestic Linkages	Often part of domestic legal framework – adopted within domestic law and bureaucratic structures	Positive
International Structure	Variation over time. Bipolarity was a more stable context for the regime than post-CW multipolarity. Hegemony, especially in the Cold War context, favored compliance	Less favorable with the end of the Cold War

Normative debates

Global governance is highly normative. Arguments about "improving" global governance or "making international institutions work better" are commonly made by academics; yet, they contain normative assumptions that are not always made explicit. Much of the liberal institutionalist work on the "rational design of institutions" takes the normative ends of an institutional framework as given by states' existing preferences in order to avoid having to engage in normative debate. Nevertheless, any institutional framework will work to achieve certain ends and it is important to be able to critically assess the normative basis of international institutions. Three core concepts are particularly useful in order to analyze the normative basis of a regime: legitimacy, efficiency, equity. Whether global governance is legitimate, efficient, or equitable matters for its own sake and may also matter instrumentally for the effectiveness of regime in meeting its goals.

Legitimacy

Buchanan and Keohane (2006) analyze the challenges of defining legitimacy in relation to global governance. For them, legitimacy can be seen in two ways. It has a *normative sense* – in terms of having "the right to rule" – and a *sociological sense* – in terms of being "widely believed to have the right to rule." Both of these rely on criteria – the former on objective standards and the latter upon the judgment of an audience. At the national level, legitimacy is generally understood to rely upon public consent, the principal manifestation of which is democratic institutions. In global governance, democracy does not exist in the same way and it is less obvious who the polity is and who the audience should be. Legitimacy is therefore more challenging to define.

For Buchanan and Keohane, three basic options stand out as possible sources of legitimacy: state consent; democratic state consent; and global democracy. The important thing, though, they argue (p. 417) is that global governance fulfils six basic minimum standards: 1) its existence must have a reasonable public basis; 2) it must not allow that extremely unjust institutions are legitimate; 3) it must be based on the ongoing consent of democratic states; 4) it should promote the values that underlie democracy; 5) it should reflect the dynamic character of global governance by allowing for change and renegotiation; 6) it must overcome two key problems: i) the problem of bureaucratic discretion; and ii) the tendency that democracies have to disregard the legitimate interests of outsider, which is all the more problematic at the global level.

Indeed, legitimacy is a particularly important concept in the context of the global governance of forced migration. International organizations engaged in humanitarian work such as UNHCR or ICRC rely upon having moral authority in order to be able to influence states. They have no material power and so rely upon being regarded as legitimate (and hence authoritative) by the states that they are trying to influence. For both UNHCR and ICRC this moral authority comes from their adherence to humanitarian principles such as impartiality, independence, and neutrality. To a large extent upholding these principles involves a trade-off with political pragmatism. While ICRC has chosen to avoid compromising its humanitarian principles in order to preserve its moral authority, UNHCR has frequently compromised its principles in order to pragmatically respond to the realpolitik of humanitarian situations. Any analysis of moral authority needs to be based on a clear understanding of the concept of legitimacy.

Efficiency

The main criteria on which regime theory tends to judge international institutions is in terms of whether they yield efficiency gains. Reflecting regime theory's origins in microeconomics, regimes are commonly understood to be useful for correcting situations analogous to "market failure" in domestic politics. When a group of states is collectively worse-off acting in isolation than they would be within an institutional framework that facilitates collective action, there is a case to be made for the creation of international institutions, just as there would be a case for government intervention at the national level. Whether or not an international institution is regarded as "successful" is commonly judged on the basis of whether it contributes to an "efficiency gain" – in other words, whether it leads to a net welfare gain.

It is important to have a clear understanding of what "efficiency" means. In relation to international institutions, there are at least two possible definitions of efficiency. Firstly, *allocative efficiency* refers to the optimum allocation of resources within a society. It is linked to a concept known as "Pareto optimality," which arises when it is no longer possible to make any actor better off without making another actor worse off. Pareto optimality arises when, within a society, resources (both in terms of production and consumption) are allocated such that overall social utility is maximized. Secondly, *productive efficiency* refers to a ratio of inputs to outputs. In other words, it is about ensuring that for any given input, the yield is as great as possible. This involves using the least-cost method to produce a given output.

Within the context of the global refugee regime, there has been a growing degree of discussion about the extent to which it is "efficient" (Betts 2006). In 2003, for example, one British MP argued in parliament that, "Western states spend annually around $10 billion on less than half a million asylum seekers, most of whom are not in need of international protection. By contrast, the UNHCR supports 12 million refugees and five million internally displaced persons in some of the poorest countries in the world on a budget of only $900 million" (Betts 2006: 148). The difficulty with many of these public debates is that they often implicitly or explicitly invoke notions of efficiency without critical reflection on what they mean by efficiency.

In the refugee context, a notion of productive efficiency would involve using the most efficient combination of resources to produce a given output. This, of course, begs the question of what the "given output" would be and what notion of "cost" one would be trying to minimize. In the refugee regime, the desired output is effective refugee protection and "cost" would have a range of economic, social, and political dimensions. The challenge would therefore be to minimize the perceived cost of providing effective protection. Within states, this would be a question of social policy and selecting the right approach to asylum and refugee protection. Among states, this might be a matter of recognizing that some states are able to provide refugee protection at lower net cost and that there might therefore be a situation within which certain states have a comparative advantage in the provision of physical protection and others in the provision of financial compensation (Schuck 1997).

In the refugee context, a notion of allocative efficiency would involve the international community allocating resources in such a way that ensured that the greatest possible provision of "effective protection" was available given the constraint of state preferences and protection costs. In other words, given that states' willingness to contribute to asylum and refugee protection is finite, an allocatively efficient outcome would be one that ensured that the greatest quantity of effective protection was available globally, given this constraint. This might involve, for example, agreeing to a global division of responsibility for refugee protection among states that recognized that different states have different preferences and face different cost structures, and that is it more allocatively efficient for some states to play a cheque-book role (as Japan does) and for others to play a physical protection role (as many African states do). This argument is made, for example, by Hathaway and Neve (1997), who suggest that "common but differentiated responsibility-sharing" might offer a more sustainable basis for a global refugee regime than a regime based on the assumption that refugee protection is equally costly to provide in all states. While one might reasonably find other strong normative objections to such an argument – based on equity or legitimacy – Hathaway's suggestion would appear to find a degree of support based on efficiency criteria.

Equity

Equity refers to the distribution of costs and benefits within an international regime. It is a highly contested concept, which is rarely addressed in questions of institutional design. Discussing equity invokes notions of distributive justice, which can be seen in a variety of different ways. At its most simplistic equity might be regarded as synonymous with equality. For others, it is about equality of opportunity or about the legitimacy of the process through which resources, and costs and benefits, are allocated (Beitz 1989; Pogge 2002; Rawls 1971).

Equity is an important normative concept within forced migration. This is because the consequences of forced migration are often unequally distributed. Both the refugee and IDP regimes have significant North–South dimensions. In both cases, the countries of origin and destination are almost invariably found in the South. This places a disproportionate responsibility on many states that are least able to bear the costs of protection and durable solutions. Yet, in neither regime are there binding norms of burden-sharing compelling states outside of the region of origin to contribute to supporting protection in the South. Unsurprisingly, given that the overwhelming majority of the world's refugees come from and remain in the South, but that there is no binding norm of burden-sharing, the refugee regime has often been argued to be inequitable (Chimni 1998).

International organizations

A growing area in global governance has been the study of international organizations, which have increasingly been recognized to be important actors in their own right (Karns and Mingst 2004; Rittberger and Zangl 2006). International organizations (IOs) have a close relationship to the norms that exist in a given issue-area. IOs vary considerably but they generally comprise secretariats created to oversee the negotiation, implementation, monitoring, and enforcement of regimes. Some IOs – such as UNHCR, OHCHR, and ILO – have a normative function, existing to uphold and safeguard a particular state-given mandate. Others – such as IOM – have a service provision function, playing an implementing role but having little normative agenda. As well as having a secretariat, some IOs also provide a forum within which states meet to debate the regime and the governance of the IO. Within some IOs, such as the WTO or WHO, this forum function is highly developed; in others such as WFP or UNDP, it is considered less important. These differences notwithstanding, the global governance literature offers three broad basic approaches to understanding the role of IOs, which broadly build upon the realist, liberal institutionalist, and constructivist traditions.

From a realist perspective, IOs are viewed as having little independent significance in world politics. States are the most important actors in world politics. The existence and role of IOs merely reflects the prevailing interests of powerful states. From this perspective, IOs lack agency and automatively implement the will of the states that fund and sanction their existence. While IOs may serve an implementing function or provide forums within which inter-state negotiations take place, they cannot be considered to be autonomous actors of any significance. This view is exemplified by the work of Mearsheimer (1995) who has argued that liberal institutionalists over-state the independent influence that institutions, both as norms and as organizations, have in world politics. From this point of view, one would expect the work of an international organization such as UNHCR to be almost exclusively determined by the wishes of its main donors. The behavior of IOs is determined by their external structural environment.

Gradually, liberal institutionalism has increasingly addressed the question of the role of international organizations as political actors. For liberal institutionalism, states are still the most important actors in world politics, albeit that international institutions play a role in constraining or incentivizing certain forms of behavior. Nevertheless, recent authors have drawn upon the "principal-agent" problem in economics to conceptualize the conditions under which international organizations might constitute autonomous actors in world politics. The principal-agent problem describes a situation in which a principal hires an agent, and there is a contractual relationship between these actors. However, under conditions of asymmetric information, and, given that the agent has its own interests, the actions of the agent may not necessarily align perfectly with the preferences of the principal. A lot of economics literature has focused on the challenge of how to better align the interests of the agent with those of the principal. Analytically, though, this problem has also been identified as being useful in international relations for highlighting the conditions under which international organizations – as the agents of states – may have some degree of autonomy to make their own choices subject to the constraints of their state-given mandate (Hawkins et al. 2006).

Constructivist authors have drawn upon *organizational sociology* to suggest that IOs should not be analyzed as "black boxes" as they have so often been by rationalist authors. Rather, as organizations, they should be analyzed as organizations, with their own interests, cultures, and internal dynamics. Barnett and Finnemore (1999; 2004), for example, argue for the need to look at the internal workings of IOs to explain their role in world politics. They analyze a number of international organizations including UNHCR. They suggest that many organizations have had significant autonomy, expanding and adapting their work and mandate beyond the mandate given to them by states. They suggest that an important factor in explaining IO behavior is organizational sociology, resulting from bureaucratic politics and bureaucratic culture. These dynamics, they suggest, help to explain many of the "pathologies" of undesirable IO behavior – such as inefficiency, ineffectiveness, and unaccountability, which cannot be adequately explained by the type of "economistic" analysis offered by rationalist approaches to understanding the role of IOs.

These approaches are useful for analyzing the role of IOs in forced migration. Gil Loescher, in particular, has explored the extent to which UNHCR can be considered to be an autonomous actor in world politics. On the one hand, the Office is significantly constrained by its core donor states and has little material power of its own. On the other hand, it has, at times, been able to exert significant influence on the behavior of states and has been able to determine the direction of its own work and mandate. The conceptual work on the principal-agent problem and organizational sociology helps to place Loescher's largely historical analysis of the Organization within a theoretical framework. Throughout its history, UNHCR has had a relatively high degree of autonomy and independence (Loescher et al. 2008: McKittrick 2008). This can be attributed to a number of factors. Firstly, UNHCR is a normative organization. Its particular mandate of upholding the 1951 Convention has given it a normative basis for its work, which has given it a degree of authority to distance itself from states' short-term interests in a manner that is not always available to purely operational IOs such as IOM. Secondly, the position of the High Commissioner for Refugees has meant that individuals have played a key role as norm entrepreneurs in shaping the direction of the Office.

Power and institutions

Power is central to understanding the negotiation, implementation, monitoring, and enforcement of global governance. Yet much of regime theory traditionally takes an interest-based approach to world politics that sidelines the importance of power. However, an important component of analyzing power in global governance is to have a clear conceptual framework for understanding the concept. Barnett and Duvall (2005) set out an excellent and now widely accepted typology for analyzing power, based on four concepts that emerge from two analytical distinctions. Their starting point is the recognition that power is relational and describes a relationship between two actors, actor A and actor B. It involves actor A getting actor B to do something that actor B would not otherwise do.

The four concepts that Barnett and Duvall outline are 1) compulsory power; 2) institutional power; 3) structural power; and 4) productive power. These categories are based on two distinctions. Firstly, power can either be direct or diffuse. In other words, actor A can consciously and knowingly attempt to induce actor B to do something (direct) or actor A's influence over actor B can be less conscious and may be exercised through structures such as ideas or institutions (diffuse). Secondly, power can be either constraining or constitutive. In other words, actor A may influence actor B either by incentivizing the behavior of B (constraining) or by changing the identity and so the interests of B (constitutive).

Compulsory power is direct and constraining; institutional power is diffuse and constraining; structural power is direct and constitutive; and productive power is diffuse and constitutive. Compulsory power works through actor A coercing or inducing B to do something. Institutional power works through actor A influencing the institutional framework within which B makes its decisions. Structural power may work through actor A's instrumental use of ideas, culture or propaganda to persuade or change how B sees the world. Productive power works through the role of discourse in constituting how both A and B perceive the world and their interests in ways that are favourable to A. The four concepts are summarized in the table below.

Type of power	Direct v diffuse	Constraining v constitutive
Compulsory	Direct	Constraining
Institutional	Diffuse	Constraining
Structural	Direct	Constitutive
Productive	Diffuse	Constitutive

As with any issue-area of global governance, all four forms of power will exist simultaneously in the international politics of forced migration. One of the core power dynamics within the international politics of forced migration is along North–South lines. This is because the majority of displacement takes place in the South, while few people move on from South to North. However, Barnett and Duvall's typology is particularly useful because it highlights the multifaceted nature of power relations and the fact that North–South power relations are not reducible simply to an assessment of military or economic strength but are also influenced by factors such as institutions and ideas, which may present both an opportunity or a constraint for actors that are traditionally thought of as "weaker" actors in military or economic terms.

Regime complexity

There has been significant institutional proliferation in the late twentieth century. With the creation of new international institutions on a multilateral, regional, and bilateral level, the international institutional architecture has become increasingly dense. The literature on regime complexity attempts to explore the political consequences of this institutional proliferation (Alter and Meunier 2009; Raustiala and Victor 2004). Complexity refers to the way in which two or more institutions intersect in terms of their scope and purpose. Three main concepts describe different aspects of complexity. Firstly, institutions may be *nested*: regional or issue-specific institutions may be part of wider multilateral framework. Secondly, they may be *parallel*: obligations in similar areas may or may not contradict one another. Thirdly, they may be *overlapping*: multiple institutions may have authority over the same issue.

Complexity has been explored as an independent variable in world politics (Alter and Meunier 2009). Where more than one institution exists in a given issue-area, the institutions may have a complementary or a competitive relationship. The existence of nesting, parallel, and overlapping institutions has been identified as offering states an opportunity to engage in cross-institutional strategies, strategically choosing between multiple and competing institutions. Alter and Meunier (2009), identify three types of cross-institutional strategy that might be enabled by the existence of regime complexity. *Regime shifting* occurs when states move from addressing problems through one regime to addressing those problems through an alternative parallel regime, possibly relocating the most relevant politics for a given issue-area from one regime to another (Helfer 2004). *Forum-shopping* occurs where actors select the international venues based on where they are best able to promote specific policy preferences (Abbott and Snidal 1998; Busch 2007; Hafner-Burton 2005). *Strategic inconsistency* occurs where contradictory rules are created in a parallel regime with the intention of undermining a rule in another agreement (Raustiala and Victor 2004). The case study below applies these concepts to understand the changing politics of refugee protection in the context of institutional proliferation.

Case Study: Regime Complexity and the Politics of Refugee Protection

It is often assumed that the global refugee regime is relatively straightforward. The basis of the refugee regime is the 1951 Convention and its 1967 Protocol. The Office of the United Nations High Commissioner for Refugees (UNHCR) has responsibility for overseeing the regime, and its annual Executive Committee represents the regime's core arena for inter-state decision-making. However, over time the regime has become gradually more complicated, with the proliferation of a range of new international institutions. Although many of these institutions have ostensibly emerged to regulate other issue-areas, they have nevertheless had an important impact on the politics of refugee protection. Since the 1990s, two embryonic international regimes have begun to emerge in two issue-areas that were previously largely unregulated at the global level: migration and internal displacement. The creation of new institutions in these parallel areas has transformed the politics of refugee protection. This case study demonstrates the relevance of the literature on regime complexity for understanding change in the politics of refugee protection.

Institutional proliferation

At its creation, the refugee regime represented the main international institutional framework that existed to regulate any aspect of international human mobility. Over time, new parallel institutions have emerged that, to some extent overlap with the refugee regime. Some of these – such as the human rights regime – have been complementary, reinforcing the norms of the refugee regime; others, however, have some contradictory, threatening core tenets of the refugee regime. Since the 1990s, two new regimes have begun to emerge in parallel areas previously unregulated at the global level: international migration and internal displacement.

Based on the recognition that there were a significant number of people in "refugee-like situations" who had not crossed an international border, displaced by many of the civil conflicts of the post-Cold War era, the international community developed the Guiding Principles on Internal Displacement during the 1990s, which were complemented by a "collaborative" institutional framework through which different international organizations agreed a division of responsibility for IDPs. Although the Guiding Principles were based on "soft law," simply consolidating and applying existing norms from human rights and humanitarian law, the regime has gradually been translated into "hard law" through incorporation into national law and regional agreements.

Meanwhile, although there is no formal migration regime, a rapidly growing number of regional and inter-regional processes and agreements have emerged to aspects of both regular and irregular migration. Regional Consultative Processes (RCPs) – such as the Intergovernmental Consultations on Asylum, Refugees and Migration Policies (IGC), the Budapest Process, the Puebla Process, and the Colombo Process – have emerged to allow informal discussion and cooperation among states. Formal agreements have also emerged on a regional level in the EU and NAFTA contexts. There have also been steps at global level to develop global cooperation. The UN Secretary-General commissioned the Global Commission on International Migration (GCIM) between 2003 and 2005, which led to the creation of the Global Forum on Migration and Development (GFMD). Furthermore, since the 1990s, there has been a massive growth in the role of IOM as an operational migration agency.

Neither of these emerging parallel regimes focus directly on refugees. However, they nevertheless overlap significantly with the refugee regime. In particular, they allow states alternative mechanisms through which to cooperate to limit flow of spontaneous-arrival asylum seekers. The IDP regime, for example, has been used by states to justify an "internal flight alternative" for people fleeing persecution. The UK and Sweden, for example, have used this mechanism to return refugees to Afghanistan and Iraq. Meanwhile, the migration regime overlaps with the refugee regime insofar as it enables international cooperation to limit the mobility of spontaneous-arrival asylum seekers. The diagram below illustrates the way in which the human rights, migration and IDP regimes overlap with the refugee regime.

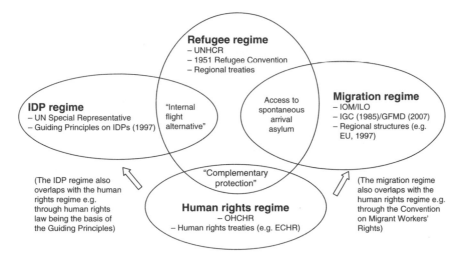

Figure 5.1   Diagram illustrating the main actors and institutions in the global refugee regime and how the regime exists in parallel to and partly overlaps with the migration, IDP, and human rights regimes. The intersections of the Venn diagram illustrate some of the ways in which the refugee regime overlaps with other regimes

Effect on politics of refugee protection

The proliferation of new institutions has had an effect on the politics of refugee protection. In particular, it has created opportunities for states to engage in regime shifting and forum-shopping. Northern states have increasingly been able to use the new alternative institutions to address their concerns with spontaneous-arrival asylum through regimes other than the refugee regime. By using institutions such as the EU, the IGC, and IOM, European states have been able to establish new forms of international cooperation in the area of asylum and migration. These new forms of cooperation on issues such as re-admission and border control have enabled Northern states to reduce the possibility for asylum seekers to move across international borders. Similarly, the IDP regime has created a mechanism through which states have been able to cooperate to ensure that people in need of protection receive it without having to necessarily cross an international border.

The new institutions have therefore enabled Northern states to bypass the refugee regime without explicitly violating their principal legal obligations. They have allowed Northern states to develop forms of cooperation to reduce the number of asylum seekers reaching their territory. Yet these new forms of cooperation have avoided overly violating the principle of *non-refoulement* (not refusing access to arriving refugees) that underpins the regime.

This has had the effect of implicitly reallocating burdens within the refugee regime. This is because the main form of responsibility-sharing within the regime is based upon states agreeing to reciprocally provide asylum to refugees who reach their territory. Given that the majority of the world's refugees originate from the South, Southern states already hosted the overwhelming majority of the world's displaced people. However, the new institutional proliferation and the resulting cross-institutional strategies have enabled Northern states to shift an even greater share of the costs of the refugee regime on to Southern states. Southern states have not been oblivious to this implicit renegotiation of the terms of the regime. They have noticed that Northern states have been using the new regimes to bypass the refugee regime and avoid contributing to the regime through upholding spontaneous-arrival asylum. In response, a number of Southern host states have reduced the quality and quantity of asylum that they offer (Betts and Milner 2006; Milner 2009). The outcome has been a net reduction in the overall level of international cooperation taking place within the regime.

IO response

UNHCR has not responded passively to this shift in strategy by states. Rather, it has demonstrated a significant degree of autonomy to define its own strategy response. Concerned with increasingly being bypassed, it has adopted a number of different strategies in an attempt to maintain its relevance. Firstly, it has shifted its own work and mandate into the areas into which states are shifting. Increasingly, UNHCR has taken on a role in relation to both IDPs and migration. In relation to IDPs, it has taken on a significant institutional role in relation to the protection of IDPs as part of an inter-agency response negotiated among different UN agencies (Loescher et al. 2008). In relation to migration, the Office has shown increasing interest in migration, not only to protect refugees within "mixed flows" but also in terms of possibly becoming involved in the protection of other groups of irregular migrants (Crisp 2008).

Secondly, UNHCR has begun to use issue-linkage in order to channel states' interest in migration into a commitment to refugee protection. For example, it has attempted to argue through a range of initiatives that Northern states might be able to best meet their interests in migration control through contributing to UNHCR's protection work in the South (Betts and Durieux 2007). It has identified states' interests in these wider issue-areas as an opportunity to encourage an interest in refugee protection, even if it is based on motives that do not derive from a concern with refugee protection per se.

Thirdly, UNHCR, has become an increasingly itinerant actor, engaging in other forums beyond the refugee regime. Rather than simply providing a forum within which states debate issues relating to asylum and refugee protection, UNHCR has been an autonomous political actor within other regimes. In particular, UNHCR has increasingly engaged in international forums such as the United Nations Development Group, the GFMD, and the Global Migration Group (GMG), for example.

In summary, rather than remaining exclusively within the confines of the refugee regime, UNHCR has pursued the states into the alternative regimes into which they are shifting. It has increasingly recognized that the politics of refugee protection no longer takes place purely within the refugee regime, but that it takes place in venues that focus on wider migration, humanitarianism, security, and development.

Regime complexity has therefore been an important factor in driving change in the politics and global governance of forced migration. The new institutional proliferation that has taken place in relation to IDPs and migration has enabled Northern states to engage in forum shopping and regime shifting, addressing their concerns with spontaneous-arrival asylum while bypassing their obligations under the refugee regime. This has contributed to a net reduction in international cooperation within the refugee regime. In response, UNHCR has adapted its own strategy, pursuing states into the alternative regimes into which they have shifted, and engaging in a wider political context.

Conclusion

Debate on global governance often lacks clarity. It is important when talking about the global governance of forced migration that the term is used precisely. This chapter has attempted to provide a working definition of global governance while highlighting a number of the ambiguous and problematic aspects of the concept. It has set out a range of conceptual tools that are available for understanding different aspects of the global governance of forced migration. The debates explored in this chapter are by no means exhaustive of potentially relevant issues within the burgeoning literature on global governance; but they highlight the enormous potential research agenda which exists for analyzing the global governance of forced migration. Issues such as compliance, power, complexity, and the role of IOs have immense scope to be explored in relation to different areas of forced migration.

Often global governance is seen in highly simplistic, technocratic ways. However, global governance in general, and the global governance of forced migration in particular, are becoming increasingly complex. The global governance of forced migration needs to be understood beyond simply the abstract, formal institutions that exist at the global level which are explicitly labeled "forced migration." A range of formal and informal institutions in a number of different issue-areas have an important influence on the politics of forced migration. With institutional proliferation, a range of actors including states and non-state actors are influenced in their behavior toward displaced people by the politics of a range of issue-areas: migration, IDPs, refugees, humanitarianism, development, and peace and security. In order to capture this complexity, and to fully appreciate the global governance of forced migration, there is therefore a need to challenge some of the existing categories and concepts of global governance. Although this chapter offers a starting point in that regard, there is still a great deal of thinking and analysis still to be done.

6

North–South Relations and the International Political Economy

The underlying causes of human displacement – conflict and authoritarian regimes, for example – are intimately connected to broader issues relating to the global economy. A range of issues that connect politics and economics, and relate to the global distribution of power and resources, contribute to the causes of forced migration. Underdevelopment, access to global markets, dependency on the export of primary products, developing-country debt, the legacy of colonialism, and structural adjustment, for example, all have an empirical relationship to the causes of conflict and whether an incumbent government is likely to respect or violate human rights (Collier 2007; Collinson 2003). It is precisely because many of these issues have dispropor-tionately significant consequences in the global South that the overwhelm-ing majority of the world's refugees and IDPs originate from and remain in the South. Forced migration and its underlying causes therefore need to be seen in the broader context of the international political economy and North–South relations (Castles 2003; Chimni 1998; Duffield 2001).

International Political Economy (IPE) is an area of International Relations which emerges from the recognition that world politics is intimately con-nected to global economy. It focuses both on how the structures of the global economy shape world politics, and vice-versa. In other words, it recognizes that in world politics inter-state relations and the behavior of states cannot be divorced from the role of markets, which shape interests and power rela-tions between states. IPE has focused on a range of topics, most notably globalization, trade, development, migration, and the role of non-state actors in world politics. A core element of IPE has historically been its focus on North–South relations. Economic relations affect inter-state politics, and reinforce inequalities and hierarchies between states. Within world politics, asymmetries in power have existed as long as the state system.

The North–South divide has been used as a means to crudely capture the most significant of these asymmetries in the post-colonial context.

North/South is often seen as synonymous with – although marginally less problematic than – other ways of highlighting asymmetric power relations between relatively weaker and stronger actors in the international system: developed/developing, First World/Third World, and core/periphery (Fawcett and Sayigh 2000). Duffield (2001: 4–7) defines "North" and "South" in socio-economic terms according to the degree and type of states' integration into the global economic system. Despite their diversity, Southern states have a number of identifying characteristics which strongly influence their relative position within the international system. Southern states can be considered to be post-colonial states, to have a high degree of dependency on the export of primary commodities, and to have relatively low GDP/capita. Meanwhile, Northern states are likely to be industrialized, high national income states with the capacity to externally project military and political power.

This division between North and South is not unproblematic. There is an increasing blurring and arbitrariness to the labels, which are formally defined by whether a country is a member of the OECD or not. There are immense differences within and between "Southern" states, which defy a simplistic dichotomy of North/South. At the margins, it seems problematic to identify relatively wealthy states such as South Korea and Uruguay, for example, as part of the "South." Meanwhile, the rise of China and India as major economic and political powers demonstrates the inadequacy of dividing the world between North and South. As Doty (1996) highlights, the North/South dichotomy is also problematic because it perpetuates a hierarchical view of the world which in turn shapes practice. Nevertheless, the North/South divide does capture important dynamics in world politics. During the 1970s and 1980s, it highlighted important differences in states' bargaining power as well as some of the main coalitions in world politics – such as the G77 – which continue to endure in many multilateral debates (Krasner 1985). Indeed, many debates in world politics – such as those on world trade and at the UN General Assembly – continue to divide along North–South lines. The label also arguably captures an important element of forced migration, highlighting fundamental differences in states' abilities to control borders, their proximity to conflict and human rights abuses, their influence in the international system, and whether they are (in the broader context of migration) predominantly sending or receiving countries.

This chapter therefore situates the study of forced migration in the broader context of IPE and North–South relations. It addresses two main areas. Firstly, it outlines the main debates in the IPE literature and highlights how they have been applied to develop a critical IPE approach to the study of forced migration. Secondly, it explores the question of North–South cooperation and the different ways in which this approach has been applied to understand international cooperation in relation to forced migration. The chapter then concludes with two case studies – one of which explores the "root causes" of forced migration from a critical perspective and the other of which explores North–South cooperation from a liberal perspective.

The IPE Approach

IPE's focus is on exploring the two-way relationship between the global economy and international politics. It emerged from a recognition that neither neo-classical economics nor political science offered the necessary analytical tools to capture a complex range of phenomena including trade, the international monetary system, migration, the international financial system, the role of multinational corporations, development, and regional integration. IPE incorporates theoretical tools borrowed from both disciples – international economics, regime theory, macroeconomics, and development theories, for example (Gilpin 2001). Nevertheless, it has also developed its own body of theory and offers three main theoretical approaches with diverging accounts of the relationship between economics and politics: mercantilism, liberalism, and Marxism.

Mercantilism is closely related to realism in IR theory. States are taken to be the main actors. Markets are used by states as a means to maximize military power. As such, states' economic relations are frequently conceived as zero-sum; states attempt to maximize their relative economic position vis-à-vis other states. Protectionism, private companies, and the international monetary regime, for example, are a means for states to extend, maximize, or project power. Mercantilism is the least commonly adopted of the three main IPE approaches. It contrasts with liberalism and Marxism in seeing markets as subordinated to states, where liberalism and Marxism are more focused on how markets shape politics.

Liberalism is generally the mainstream approach to IPE. It is closely related to liberal institutionalism in IR theory. Economic relations between states are seen as being positive sum. All states can mutually benefit from, for example, free trade and globalization. From a liberal perspective, the role of collective action should be to maximize these mutual benefits. International regimes and global governance can contribute to making cooperation in the economic realm efficient and mutually beneficial. As with Marxism, markets are seen as the drivers of inter-state politics. However, in contrast to Marxism, liberalism tends to take a positive view of the influence that markets play. For example, trade, globalization, and interdependence are seen as ways in which international cooperation and peace and security between states can be promoted (Keohane and Nye 1974).

Marxism underpins many of the alternative, critical approaches to IPE. Like liberalism, it sees the economy as underpinning politics. For Marxism, however, the relationship between prosperity and politics is not unambiguously positive. Rather, politics is driven by the capitalist pursuit of surplus value. The core of Marxism is the idea that capitalists (as the holders of capital) attempt to employ labor and, rather than paying labor at a wage rate equal to its marginal product, can pay a lesser wage and so in Marx's terms "extract surplus value." Within Marxist thought, politics is part of the "superstructure" through which the "base" of the capitalist mode of production maintains and extends its access to labor and raw material. In other words, markets are the drivers of international politics, and states' policies at the international level are merely a reflection of the interests of powerful economic elites.

Much of the critical IPE literature that relates to North–South relations has broadly Marxist underpinnings. *Leninism*, for example, suggests that imperialism represents the highest stage of capitalism. Lenin argued that once capitalists exhaust domestic sources of surplus value, they will resort to imperialism. In other words, states will serve as the vehicle through which capitalists engage in the extraction of surplus value. Building upon this logic, *dependency theory* (Cardoso and Faletto 1979; Frank 1969; Prebisch 1950) has argued that development and underdevelopment are "two sides of the same coin" and that development in the North is based upon underdevelopment in the South (Frank 1969). For dependency theorists states divide between "core" and "periphery" countries. The periphery represents primary product exporters, which are dependent upon exports to the core states, which are industrialized economies. Wallerstein's *world systems theory* extended the approach of dependency theory to relate it closely to international relations. He argued that the world divides between periphery, semi-periphery, and core states, defined by their position in the international division of labor (focusing on primary, secondary, and tertiary sectors of production, respectively). According to Wallerstein, inter-state relations and hierarchies are then determined by the global division of labor.

Critical IPE and "Root Causes"

The majority of the IPE literature that analyzes forced migration takes a critical perspective. The critical IPE approach explores forced migration in its broader context. Rather than just looking at the "symptoms" of human displacement, it attempts to identify the "root causes" of forced migration. The root causes approach traces the underlying causes of forced migration back to the inequalities and hierarchies of the international global economy. For example, it looks at the role of globalization, trade, capitalism, and structural adjustment programmes as underlying many of the reasons for forced migration (Castles 2003; Marfleet 2006). Furthermore, critical IPE also examines international responses to forced migration, often seeing humanitarianism as a fig-leaf response that at best ignores the underlying causes of forced migration and at worst legitimates the structures that perpetuate forced migration.

Causes

Stephen Castles (2003) argues for a political economy approach to forced migration. He takes a broadly Marxist perspective, arguing that forced migration needs to be understood in the broader context of the liberal capitalist global economy. For him, the structures of the global capitalist economy drive the underlying causes of human displacement. For Castles, the dominant liberal focus on humanitarianism and protection focuses mainly on the symptoms of forced migration rather than adequately questioning the "root causes" of forced migration. In doing so it sidelines and legitimates many of the causes of human displacement.

Castles (2003) argues that trans-boundary population movements have become increasingly significant in the context of globalization. He identifies that a so-called migration crisis was recognized during the 1990s and early 2000s in the context of the increased politicization of South–North migratory movements. Whether or not the people moving are recognized as refugees, a significant proportion of them are leaving extremely difficult economic, social, and political situations. Even non-refugee groups may be leaving as a "coping mechanism of last resort" or seeking "dirty, demanding and dangerous" jobs in the North in order to remit money to assist in family and community survival (Castles 2002). For Castles, the "migration crisis" therefore arises because of the vast inequalities between North and South with regard to economic conditions, social well-being, and human rights. From this perspective, addressing the "migration crisis" is a question of engaging with the sources of global inequality and overcoming the North–South divide that characterizes the international political economy.

The most obvious causal relationship that connects the structures of the global economy to forced migration is conflict. In the post-Cold War context, a number of academics identified the emergence of so-called "new wars," which, rather than being inter-state in nature were increasingly intra-state and characterized by significant human consequences. The most high profile of these conflicts of the 1990s took place in Somalia, Bosnia, Rwanda, East Timor, Burundi, and Kosovo, for example (Kaldor 1999). These types of intra-state conflict generated significant numbers of IDPs and refugees. Although identifying the causes of these conflicts is complex and challenging, many commentators saw these wars as stemming from "ancient tribal hatreds" based on, for example, ethnicity, nationalism, or religion (Huntington 1993; Kaplan 1993). This "primordialist" interpretation of the conflicts as being the result of inevitable differences in identity between groups is deeply problematic and has been widely criticised from a range of perspectives. For example, "constructivists" argue that the significance and meaning of identity categories is socially and historically constructed and should not be seen as fixed or inevitable (Fearon and Laitlin 2003; Mamdani 2001). Meanwhile, "instrumentalists" argue that the causes of so-called "ethnic wars" are generally economic or political interests rather than identity per se (Collier and Hoeffler 1998; Keen 2001; Stewart and Fitzgerald 2001).

The main critical IPE response to the "primordialist" (and other) accounts of the "new wars" is that they see the causes of the conflict as endogenous rather than exogenous. In other words, the accounts assume that the causes of violence and conflict stem from causes that are internal to a country rather than from international causes. In Duffield's (2001: 109–13) words, this leads to "internalizing the causes of conflict." For Duffield, regarding the causes of conflict as endogenous serves a political function. It legitimates a purely humanitarian response and it disguises the important role of exogenous factors such as trade, colonialism, and structural adjustment.

Economic factors and competition for resources have been identified as a significant factor in many of the "new wars." Economic inequalities contribute to ethnicity and religion becoming important identity categories because they lead to resentment relating to inequalities between groups. Most conflicts are not caused by unchanging, primordial differences such as Muslim–Christian or Hutu–Tutsi but because of underlying economic inequalities that lead to competition for resources, and, in this context, identity categories become important signifiers for horizontal inequalities between groups (Keen 2001; Stewart and Fitzgerald 2001).

In this context, a range of exogenous factors relating to the global economy have played an important role in exacerbating or triggering conflict. Violent conflicts in Sudan, Angola, Iraq, Nigeria, the Ivory Coast, Sierra Leone, Colombia, and Burundi, for example, have been significantly worsened by the connections between those conflicts and the international political economy.

As Turton (1997: 86) has put it, there is a relationship between "global connections and local violence." In particular, dependency on the export of primary products such as diamonds and oil, and processes of structural adjustment and externally imposed democratization have been correlated with increased likelihoods of violent conflict (Collier 2007; Mansfield and Snyder 2005; Reno 1999). A "root causes" approach to forced migration therefore implies the need to trace the causal relationships back from forced migration to the underlying structures of the global political economy.

Responses

Drawing upon extensive fieldwork in Sudan, Mark Duffield (2001) argues that humanitarian and development assistance are part of a Northern hegemonic strategy. Rather than being undertaken for altruistic reasons or to resolve the underlying causes of conflict, they are used by Northern states in order to engage in the transformation and subordination of the South. In particular, humanitarianism and development are used by the North as a means to contain – or to "securitize" – possible trans-boundary spill-overs that may result from conflict or underdevelopment in the South. In the context of increasing illicit transboundary flows from South to North, whether in terms of migration, arms, organized crime, or drugs, humanitarianism and development represent a means to contain such movements.

However, for Duffield, this approach fails to resolve the underlying causes of conflict, and trans-border movements. Rather, he suggests that humanitarian assistance in countries like Sudan has exacerbated rather than alleviated the conflict. For example, resources have been siphoned off to fund the war economy, while humanitarian action has served as a fig-leaf that has prevented meaningful political responses. Furthermore, it has disguised many of the underlying causes of the conflict – such as colonialism, structural adjustment, and global trade links. This approach has had the perverse consequence of actually exacerbating negative trans-boundary movements from South to North as the South has reconnected with the North through "parallel and shadow trans-border activity" (p. 5). Duffield's main suggestion is therefore that the North should disengage from the South entirely, and that the humanitarian project should cease.

Duffield's analysis is useful because it draws attention to the frequently non-altruistic motives underlying Northern engagement in the South. Indeed humanitarian responses have frequently had "mixed motives," of which the containment of refugees and other trans-boundary movements is just one (Chomsky 1999; Dubernet 2001). The analysis also highlights many of the uses and abuses of humanitarianism as a possible "fig leaf" to legitimate political inaction by the international community (Barnett and Weiss 2008; Rieff 2002). However, Duffield's suggestion that this should translate into a complete disengagement from the South by the North is overstated. There are circumstances under which humanitarian action may be motivated by self-interested motives but which nevertheless may be needed in order to save lives. Furthermore, while inequalities between North and South need to be addressed, the existing international system makes it unlikely that they will be overcome any time soon. In the short-term, humanitarianism and development assistance, albeit motivated by Northern states' own self-interest, may offer the best available means to alleviate the most serious forms of human suffering (Betts 2008).

Liberal IPE and North–South Cooperation

From a liberal IPE perspective, the analytical focus is not on the underlying structures that lead to hierarchy, inequality, and forced migration, but rather on the prospects for facilitating international cooperation in ways that are mutually beneficial for states. In a North–South context, a liberal IPE approach would focus upon developing cooperation and regulatory frameworks that could offer "win–win" outcomes for both North and South. As Duffield (2001) correctly identifies, a liberal form of global governance would include the type of institutionalized cooperation that facilitated humanitarian and development assistance. In Cox's (1981) terms a liberal perspective is self-consciously focused on a "problem-solving" approach rather than on a critical approach and, as such, takes the world as it finds it. The advantage of such an approach is that it can attempt to understand, explain, and find solutions to real and immediate problems. The disadvantage is that it is limited in its capacity to understand and engage with the underlying causes of those problems.

Suasion Games and Issue-Linkage

A central focus of liberal IPE is overcoming collective action problems. Liberal approaches generally regard international cooperation as an exercise in facilitating interest convergence. They attempt to identify cooperation problems and then to explain the conditions under which such cooperation problems can be overcome. As chapter 4 explained, the most commonly analyzed cooperation problem is the game theoretical analogy of Prisoner's Dilemma. Although Prisoner's Dilemma is the most common analogy used to describe sources of collective action failure, the problem with Prisoner's Dilemma is that it assumes that the two actors in the model

have symmetrical interests and power relations. Regime theory has identified the existence of other situation-structures, beyond Prisoner's Dilemma,
which may create different collaboration or coordination problems. One of
these is the idea of a Suasion Game, which has been used to understand the
power dynamics created by North–South relations (Martin 1993). This
situation will arise when, in a two-actor model, there is one player who is
privileged and must be persuaded to participate, while the other has little
choice but to cooperate (Hasenclever et al. 1997). In other words, it may
occur when the stronger actor has little to gain and the weaker actor little to
lose in the specific area, undermining the prospects for cooperation.

The Suasion Game therefore involves two actors – one stronger and one
weaker. Because of their different relative power, the two actors have different interests. Formally, the situation can be represented in game theory in
one of two ways. *Either* one (weaker) actor, A, has a dominant strategy to
cooperate, which the other (stronger) one, B, can exploit, *or* one actor, B,
has a dominant strategy to defect (stronger), while the other must cooperate
in order to avoid an even worse outcome (weaker).

In either case, the weaker actor's preferred strategy is to cooperate – either
because non-cooperation is not practically viable or because it would lead
to even greater costs. However, the stronger actor is in a position to choose
to defect and that is likely to be its preferred position. If the weaker actor A
refuses to cooperate it will simply be made worse off than if it cooperates on
the terms of the stronger actor B (box DD). An instance of unrequited
cooperation (CD) is therefore likely to be the outcome of the game satisfy-
ing only one actor and leaving the other aggrieved. The stronger actor B will
exploit the weaker actor A.

		Actor B	
		C	D
Actor A	C	4,3	3,4*
	D	2,2	1,1

Figure 6.1 Suasion Game. Number left (right) of comma refers to A's (B's) preference ordering (1 = worst outcome; 4 = best outcome). * = equilibrium

As Conybeare's (1984) analysis of the global trade regime illustrates, this
problem is particularly likely to occur in the context of North–South relations.
He uses the example of the prospects for a weak state using a retaliatory
tariff against a strong state. This, he suggests, would only make the small

state worse off, highlighting the extent to which a weaker actor or group of actors might be forced to accept only very small gains *or* scupper the prospects for cooperation entirely. Given that the majority of the world's refugees are in the South and that Northern states have few binding obligations to contribute to refugee protection in the South, one can immediately see how the Suasion Game analogy fits with the refugee regime. Actor A would be a first state of asylum and actor B would be a donor state outside of the region of origin. Southern host states of asylum are frequently faced with either accepting what is "on offer" or harming themselves by rejecting a relatively small contribution. In the context of the refugee regime, some states of first asylum might be able to consider opting for box DD by closing their borders in the short-run in order to induce the donors to shift to box CC in the long-run. This strategy worked for Macedonia, for example, when it closed its border in response to the mass influx of Kosovan refugees in 1999 (Barutciski and Suhrke 2001; Williams and Zeager 2004). However, in practice, Southern states rarely have the bargaining power and so are far more likely to opt for box CD than to risk a short-run shift to DD by closing the borders or expelling refugees.

From a liberal IPE perspective, the challenge then is to identify the conditions under which this Suasion Game can be overcome and Northern states will contribute to refugee and IDP protection and durable solutions in the South. As Martin (1993) suggests, one way of overcoming the Suasion Game is through issue-linkage. Issue-linkage can be defined as a situation where two different issues are combined and made conditional upon one another in a bargaining process (Aggarwal 1998; Haas 1980). Given that Northern states have very little interest in cooperation and Southern states have little power to influence Northern states, adding additional issues to the bargaining process offers a means to change the pay-offs in the Suasion Game by increasing Northern interest in cooperation and increase Southern leverage vis-à-vis Northern states. Historically, North–South cooperation has been most likely to occur in the global refugee regime when refugee protection has been linked to other issue-areas – such as security, migration, and development – in which Northern states have had an interest (Betts 2008). In other words, Northern states have rarely contributed to humanitarianism and protection in the South for its own sake, or for altruistic reasons, but have done so because they have perceived that they will derive benefits in relation to other issue-areas. Similarly, issue-linkage has been used by Northern states to induce Southern states to cooperate in areas relating to asylum and migration. For example, many of the EU's partnership agreements with states in Africa have been negotiated alongside issues such as trade and development. From a liberal perspective, issue-linkage therefore offers an opportunity to overcome collective action failure. Indeed, although North–South cooperation is an insufficient condition for ensuring that refugees and IDPs receive access to protection and durable solutions, it is undoubtedly a necessary condition for such access.

Alternative Approaches to North–South Cooperation

Aside from the dominant liberal conception of North–South cooperation, a range of more critical approaches can be applied in order to understand the deeper structures of knowledge and power that shape North–South relations. Doty (1996), for example, argues that even the framing of "North–South" shapes the relationship between states and reinforces a hierarchy between the two groups of states. For Doty, the notion of North–South is reproduced through a set of practices of representation which are disguised by the unproblematic way in which liberal and Marxist approaches deal with North–South relations. Drawing upon post-structuralist writers such as Foucault and Derrida, she argues that the binary relationship between North and South is part of what she calls an "imperial encounter." She explores, for example, how in the context of colonialism, independence, foreign assistance and human rights, and academic discourse, narratives of childhood, idleness, delinquency, progress, and inferiority have framed a hierarchical relationship between North and South which shapes the practice of how North and South relate to one another and the basis of their relations. From this perspective, North and South cannot be seen as unproblematic categories and North–South cooperation cannot simply be analyzed on the level of interest-based accounts of mutually beneficial collaboration. Instead, North–South cooperation is shaped by discourses and power relations that transcend the account offered by liberal IPE.

A number of more critical approaches to North–South cooperation have been developed in relation to forced migration in general, and the refugee regime in particular. The work of B. S. Chimni (1998) highlights the important role of knowledge in defining North–South relations in the refugee regime. He draws upon the concept of Gramscian hegemony, which is based on the notion that ideas and knowledge can reinforce the dominance of capitalist elites over the marginalized proletariat. He suggests that a North–South hierarchy in the refugee regime has historically been reinforced through the agenda-setting and knowledge dissemination role played by international institutions such as UNHCR. He demonstrates this empirically by analyzing the shift in the refugee regime which took place at the end of the Cold War. He argues that between 1950 and 1989 the dominant paradigm of the refugee regime entailed an "exilic bias," whereby those with a well-founded fear of persecution who were outside their country of origin were welcomed by host states. However, this shifted after 1989 to a "new approach" based on a "policy of containment." Where resettlement and asylum had been the norm, there was a shift toward privileging voluntary repatriation and the responsibility of the country of origin. For Chimni, the shift can be explained by the increase in South–North movement from the 1980s. "The new asylum seekers" increasingly came from the South and were seen as a different problem compared to the East–West movement of the early Cold War. For Chimni, the new non-entrée regime, with its focus on IDP protection and repatriation was based on "the myth of difference" between white asylum seekers fleeing Communism and non-white asylum seekers fleeing conflict and persecution in the South. Crucially, Chimni highlights how UNHCR served to legitimate this paradigm shift through its knowledge creation and dissemination roles, with the non-entrée regime and a range of containment policies becoming widely accepted.

Betts and Milner (2006) also develop a critical approach to North–South cooperation in the refugee regime. They explore attempts in the early 2000s by the European Union to develop an "external dimension" to its asylum policy through cooperative partnerships with African states. Although the initiatives have encompassed a broad spectrum of approaches, they were motivated by a common logic: all attempted to foster international cooperation with African states as a means to reduce the number of spontaneous-arrival asylum seekers reaching the EU. Betts and Milner argue that rather than this cooperation being a mutually beneficial form of cooperation between equal actors, African states have been "cooperated with." The proposals which implicate Sub-Saharan African states have been conceived in isolation from consideration of the political and structural realities of asylum in Africa, and with limited attempts to foster meaningful dialogue. By failing to take into account the constraints faced by African states, the European approaches made numerous false assumptions about the position of African states within the refugee regime. The overall European approach to the externalization of asylum policy saw cooperation as unproblematic and viewed refugee protection in Africa as perfectly substitutable for asylum in Europe. However, in practice, the assumptions made by European states about their African partners did not hold. Taking the example of Tanzania, as one of the proposed "partner" countries, Betts and Milner show how the assumption of a compliant and willing partner did not hold. Tanzania, as a longstanding refugee-hosting country, faced significant domestic political constraints on its ability to host additional refugees, which were not recognized by the European states that attempted to initiative cooperation. Rather than leading to cooperation, attempts by the UK government to develop cooperation on "protection in the region of origin" were rejected by the Tanzanian government and, instead, the "demonstration effect" of European states disengaging from their obligations toward asylum seekers contributed to legitimating an even stronger and less open stance toward the Burundian refugees already in Tanzania.

Case Study 1: Global Capitalism and Displacement in Africa

A range of empirical examples could be taken to illustrate the root causes approach. This case study analyzes two examples of internal conflicts in Sub-Saharan Africa: the civil war in Sierra Leone between 1991 and 1999, and the second civil war in Southern Sudan between 1983 and the present day. In both cases, it attempts to trace the causal relationship between global capitalism and forced migration. It argues that in both cases there was an important relationship between natural resources and global capitalism on the one hand, and conflict and displacement on the other.

Sierra Leone

From 1991, a rebel group known as the Revolutionary United Front (RUF) fought a war against the Sierra Leonean government in order to gain control over the country and its diamond mines. It recruited significant numbers of child soldiers and managed to fund the conflict mainly through the export of so-called "conflict diamonds." The conflict lasted until the signing of the Lome Accords in 1999. In addition to leading to the death of 75,000 people and the creation of many amputees, over 50 percent of population was displaced, the majority within the country and a significant minority as refugees in Guinea and other parts of West Africa.

The conflict has been attributed to a range of causes. However, it has proved challenging for academics to explain because of the absence of the obvious "ethnic" dimensions which are used to explain many of the conflicts in Sub-Saharan Africa. Among the competing explanations, some have emphasized economic explanations and others cultural explanations. In response to claims by Kaplan (1993) that the conflict was "irrational" and could be explained by "barbarism" and "anarchy," a number of academics argued that the conflict was not irrational but rather that the conflict served a range of economic functions from which its "rational" participants bene-fits. For example, Richards (1996) and Keen (2000) emphasize resource predation and individuals' desire to maximize their economic opportunities as reasons for the perpetuation of the conflict. In response to these economic explanations, a number of African scholars such as Abdullah (1998) have argued that the conflict cannot be seen as "rational" but is grounded in cultural explanations. For example, Abdullah emphasizes the role of youth culture – the glorification of violence, the depiction of violence in Hollywood films, and the sense of identity provided by RUF membership, as enabling the RUF to recruit disempowered young people with few economic prospects.

However, what Kaplan's "new barbarism" thesis and the alternative economic and cultural responses share is that they all identify the main causes of the conflict as primarily endogenous to the country. Yet, the international dimensions, which are neglected by the dominant explanations, are an important aspect of explaining the conflict and the resulting displacement. The conflict is particularly difficult to explain without seeing it in the context of Sierra Leone's wider relationship with the global economy.

Firstly, it is important to highlight the role of the IMF and its structural adjustment programmes (SAPs) of the late 1980s in contributing to the conflict. Following independence, Sierra Leone had been relatively conflict-free under the authoritarian rule of Shaka Stevens from 1968 until 1985 and under Joseph Momoh in the second half of the 1980s. The stability of the ruling APC government and of both Stevens and Momoh relied upon the government having access to the necessary foreign exchange to distribute resources to key supporters. The ongoing availability of social services, jobs, and patronage was necessary in order to maintain the government's support base. However, in the context of significant national debt, government corruption, and the mismanagement of its diamond resources, the IMF made economic restructuring a condition for rescheduling its debt. The resulting structural adjustment required the government to implement privatization, deregulation, and a reduction in its expenditure on social services. Implementation led to what Richards describes as a "crisis of patrimonialism." Alongside structural adjustment, a reduction in raw materials prices and a reduction in overseas development assistance exacerbated a declining state budget, undermining the state's capacity. President Momoh was therefore unable to maintain the patronage networks that kept the government in power or to finance the military to maintain his monopoly over the use of force within the territory. This collapse in state capacity created the context in which the RUF was able to recruit significant numbers of disaffected people and in which the government lacked sufficient military capability to win the war.

Secondly, private capital and international markets also played an important role in perpetuating the conflict. A crucial aspect of the conflict was the role of raw materials. Economic incentives for war came from illicit mining and exporting of diamonds and titanium oxide. Diamonds were exported, sold internationally both through established markets such as the Antwerp diamond markets and through the informal economy. The demand for conflict diamonds helped maintain the conflict by creating significant economic incentives for the RUF to maintain control of the country's mines and providing them with a source of revenues to maintain the war. Aside from providing a market for the conflict diamonds, private actors played a direct role in prolonging the conflict. For example, Sierra Ruptile, one of the main companies responsible for titanium oxide mining hired the private security firm, Executive Outcomes, to protect its mines. Meanwhile, a company called Sunshine, run by a former senior manager of de Beers, was recruited to clear the mines of RUF fighters. These actions contributed to the alienation of many of the illicit miners and the army, increasing the pool of disaffected Sierra Leoneans from which the RUF was able to recruit (Reno 1999).

Sudan

The second civil war in Sudan began in 1983 when President Numeiry divided the south of the country and attempted to impose Sharia Law in a predominantly Christian region. This led to a quarter of a century of violence between the Islamic government in Khartoum and the predominantly Christian and African Sudanese People's Liberation Movement/Army (SPLM/A). During that period hundred of thousand of IDPs have been created and refugees have fled the conflict into Northern Uganda and northwards toward Egypt.

The causes of the conflict are commonly seen as ethnic and religious because the war divides along African/Arab and Muslim/Christian lines. However, as Moro (2006) has argued, the causes of both the conflict and displacement can be attributed to competition for oil. Chevron discovered oil in the Upper Nile region of southern Sudan in 1978. Since then, a large number of MNCs have invested in drilling and exporting the country's oil on the basis of contract agreed with the Khartoum government. The government has securitized the oil fields and developed what Moro describes as a "scorched earth policy" toward the indigenous populations of the south. Since 1989 President El Bashir has used the oil revenues from the south to maintain his support base in Khartoum.

The conflict has important international dimensions insofar as the government's ability to export the oil and to provide contracts to foreign MNCs has been the underlying cause of the conflict. Although Western companies such as Chevron and Talisman have left because of public pressure and increased market risk, oil companies from a number of countries – notably from China, Malaysia, and India remain in the country and have been directly implicated in the violence around the oil fields. As in the case of Sierra Leone, the conflict illustrates the important role of natural resources and connections to the global economy as a source of conflict and hence also of forced migration. Without the possibility to exploit and export the oil reserves in the south, it is difficult to imagine that the civil conflict would have been so protracted or had such significant human consequences (Moro 2006).

Case Study 2: African Donor Cooperation in the 1980s

The two International Conferences on Assistance to Refugees in Africa (ICARA I and II) of 1981 and 1984 exemplify the challenges of facilitating North–South cooperation in the refugee regime. Both were one-off conferences that took place in Geneva and were convened by UNHCR in order to attract donor assistance to compensate African states for hosting significant numbers of refugees since the late 1960s. Yet both conferences led to few financial contributions by donors and were characterized by North–South polarization (Gorman 1986; 1993). They serve to illustrate how the Suasion Game logic described above applies to the problem of North–South cooperation in the refugee regime.

African states had hosted an increasing number of spontaneously settled rural refugees since the 1960s. Most had originally fled the anti-colonial liberation wars and there was a general assumption that they would eventually return to their countries of origin. However, by the late 1970s, it became increasingly clear that many of the refugees had actually left ongoing Cold War proxy conflicts and that the prospects for repatriation were remote. Consequently, the African states convened the Arusha Conference in 1979, at which they collectively committed to provide refugee protection but also called for greater international burden-sharing. This led to the African states and UNHCR jointly convening two conferences, which focused on the theme of the "Refugee Aid and Development" approach (RAD). The idea underpinning RAD was that development assistance could be provided by donors to support infrastructure projects that would simultaneously benefit refugees and the host communities.

In this context, UNHCR agreed to host the first ICARA conference in 1981. The conference was conceived as a pledging conference at which African states could submit a range of development projects and programs to the donor community for funding. Despite initial pledges, the limited donor contributions were highly earmarked and went largely to US strategic allies in African Cold Wars, notably in the Horn of Africa and Southern Africa. Furthermore, the money that was provided mainly went on food aid rather than on long-term solutions, as had been intended. The first conference left both African states and donors disappointed. African states were disappointed by the limited financial contributions made by Northern donors; donors were disappointed by African states' attempt to use the conference to attract assistance for projects that did little to provide durable solutions for refugees.

A second conference, ICARA II, was subsequently convened in 1984 in response to the failure of ICARA I. It was intended to be more conceptual and less of a pledging conference than ICARA I. Its greater focus on trying to facilitate durable solutions was reflected in the conference theme, "A Time for Solutions." Southern states wanted to attract additional development assistance for infrastructure projects as "compensation" for having hosted refugees. Northern states wanted durable solutions (especially local integration) to reduce the long-run need for humanitarian assistance. The United Nations Development Programme (UNDP) was given a mandate to focus on infrastructural development, and UNHCR had responsibility for ensuring refugees' access to durable solutions. As with ICARA I, however, the second conference led to few new pledges. There was a polarization in expectations. The African states were interested in development assistance, the Northern donors in removing long-run humanitarian obligations. Once Ethiopian famine began in 1984, donor attention was diverted from ICARA and there was little lasting legacy from the conference other than ongoing mistrust between donors and African states.

The ICARA conferences illustrate the Suasion Game logic of North–South cooperation. As with the Suasion Game, the Northern states had little interest in contributing voluntarily to support refugee protection in the South. Meanwhile, the Southern states had little capacity to influence the Northern states. They were therefore left with the same choice as the "weaker" actor in the Suasion Game: to take the little that was offered by the Northern donors or to scupper cooperation entirely. As Martin's (1993) analysis of the Suasion Game highlights, issue-linkage may have offered the opportunity to overcome the Suasion Game by creating a stronger interest in cooperation on behalf of the Northern donors or increasing the bargaining power of African host states. However, the institutional design of the conferences created few opportunities for issue-linkage. This was because refugee protection was largely addressed in isolation and UNHCR made the assumption that donor states would altruistically support projects and programs in the South even in the absence of having any wider interest in doing so. Had ICARA been differently conceived to include wider discussions and a wider set of interests, it may have been possible to facilitate the type of issue-linkage needed for cooperation to take place (Betts 2008).

Conclusion

Clearly the world does not divide between "North" and "South" and the categorization is by no means unproblematic. Nevertheless, North–South relations are central to the politics of forced migration. Most human displacement takes place in the South because most of the world's conflicts and human rights abuses take place in the South. Southern states also host the majority of the world's refugees and IDPs. Meanwhile, the economic and political means to address both the underlying causes and consequences of forced migration often lie with Northern states. Understanding, explaining, and addressing forced migration therefore depends upon analyzing displacement in the broader context of North–South relations.

IPE offers two radically different approaches for analyzing North–South relations in the context of forced migration. Firstly, it offers a *liberal approach*, which focuses on trying to identify the conditions under which mutually beneficial North–South cooperation can occur to address the most serious consequences of forced migration. Indeed, North–South cooperation represents a necessary but insufficient condition for ensuring that refugees and IDPs receive access to protection and durable solutions. The liberal approach provides insights into the conditions under which collective action can take place across North–South lines, and Northern states will be motivated to address the problems of the South. Secondly, IPE offers a *critical approach*, which focuses on examining the root causes of forced migration and their relationship to the global political economy. It situates forced migration in the broader context of trade, conflict, and underdevelopment, for example.

The main critique of the liberal approach by critical theorists is that it sidelines consideration of the underlying causes of forced migration and thereby legitimates the structures that underlie the causes of forced migration. The main liberal critique of the critical approach is that offers few practical suggestions for how to address the most serious human consequences of forced migration. Although the approaches have a generally antagonistic relationship, they need not be seen as mutually exclusive. Rather, they have different – but potentially complementary – analytical and prescriptive purposes. The liberal approach is "problem-solving," highlighting the conditions that enable liberal global governance to provide humanitarian and development assistance. Meanwhile, the critical approach offers a broader contextual framework, which reminds us that there are deeper structures of power, hierarchy, and inequality that underlie both the root causes of forced migration and the solutions advocated within liberal global governance.

7

Globalization

Globalization has become one of the most prominent issues in IPE. Discussion of "globalization" in academia and the media emerged during the 1990s from the empirical observation that state borders were becoming less important in relation to economic, political, social, and cultural life. The concept was used to describe the notion that there are a range of social phenomena which are not confined by or reducible to the territorial state or inter-state relations. Globalization is often used to describe a broad range of empirical phenomena, conjuring images of trans-national corporations, the internet, the dominance and spread of western culture, and global financial markets, for example. Yet, much of the commentary on globalization lacks a precise definition of globalization or an adequate conceptual framework for analyzing it.

Generally "globalization" is defined as the increase in trans-boundary flows and interconnections (Held and McGrew 2002). Yet even this definition is limited and begs the question of what, if anything, is qualitatively "new" about globalization? Many would argue that there has been international trade and economic interdependence for a long time (Hirst and Thompson 1996). Indeed, Jan-Aart Scholte (2005) is extremely skeptical about the way in which the term has been used, suggesting that it has far too often been used in a manner that is synonymous with terms such as "internationalization," "liberalization," "universalization," or "westernization," which already exist and for which an additional concept would be redundant.

Scholte is therefore one of the very few authors to provide a clear and analytical definition of globalization and a conceptual framework that can contribute to understanding and explaining globalization. He defines it as having two elements: trans-planetary interconnectivity and supra-territoriality; the former representing flows and connections across borders (e.g. international trade), and the latter representing social relations that transcend territorial geography (e.g. the internet). On the one hand trans-planetary interconnectivity is not qualitatively new but has quantitatively increased since the 1970s. On the other hand, supra-territoriality is the qualitatively new aspect of globalization.

Aside from attempting to define "globalization," academic debates on the topic have focused on a range of questions. Is it new? What are its causes and consequences? Is it normatively desirable? How these questions have been answered has generally depended upon the perspective of the author. Ideas about globalization have been divided into three sets of thinkers: Hyper-globalizers, Skeptics, and Transformationists (Held and McGrew 2002). The first group generally believe that globalization is new, is leading to radical change, and is making the nation-state less relevant (Beck 1999; Ohmae 2005). The second group generally believe that globalization is not new and is not bringing profound or qualitatively new change (Hirst and Thompson 1996). The third group attempts to transcend the extreme positions of the other two and to argue that the nation-state is still relevant but globalization is nevertheless bringing significant change to many areas of social life (Held and McGrew 2002; Scholte 2005). Its approach is therefore to try to identify what changes are occurring as a result of globalization and why. This third position has become the academic mainstream in analyzing globalization.

One area which has been particularly affected by globalization is human mobility. The movement of people, within and across borders, and the character of that movement, has been both cause and consequence of globalization. Jet-age travel, communications, the creation of a trans-national labor force, the emergence of trans-national criminal networks and human smugglers, for example, have all contributed to an increase in international migration. Meanwhile, increased human mobility has also led in turn to increased remittance flows and the formation of trans-national identities, for example. Within this broader context, globalization has had a complex relationship with forced migration. Globalization has had an impact on many of the underlying causes of human displacement, the type of movements that have resulted, and the response by states and other actors.

This chapter therefore attempts to provide a starting point for exploring the relationship between forced migration and globalization. It divides into three main parts. Firstly, it begins by setting out a conceptual framework for analyzing globalization. Drawing upon Scholte's work, it sets out a number of analytical tools for defining and examining the causes, consequences, and normative implications of globalization. Secondly, it applies aspects of this framework to explore the relationship between globalization and forced migration. Thirdly, it examines the relationship between globalization and forced migration through a case study of the so-called "asylum-migration nexus."

The Concept

Defining and developing an analytical framework for understanding globalization is conceptually challenging. The term has been used in a range of ways and often hijacked in the service of particular ideological or normative perspectives. However, the work of a number of so-called transformationists, most notably that of David Held and Jan-Aart Scholte, has added significant clarity to the concept. This section draws heavily on their work to set out a conceptual framework for analyzing globalization that can then be applied to explore the relationship between globalization and forced migration.

Definition

Despite the proliferation of literature on globalization, it has rarely been clearly defined in a coherent and generally accepted way. Scholte (2005: 14) suggests that the study of globalization has been characterized by "analytical disarray." He puts forward four different ways in which the word globalization has been used: to mean "internationalization" – as the increase in cross-border relations and interdependence; "liberalization" – as the removal of state-imposed restrictions on movement between countries; "universalization" – as standardization, homogenization, and the creation of a global culture; and "westernization" – as the emerging of dominance of Western values such as democracy. However, for Scholte, globalization is none of these things. If a term already exists to describe each of these phenomena, the term "globalization" would not be needed. It would be a redundant concept. For Scholte and other transformationists, globalization represents "a reconfiguration of social geography." It has two key elements, which Scholte calls "trans-planetary interconnectivity" and "supra-territoriality."

Globalization = Trans-planetary interconnectivity + Supra-territoriality

The concept of *trans-planetary interconnectivity* relates to the increase in flows across international borders, whether economic, political, social, cultural, or environmental. Obvious examples include telecommunications, aeroplane travel, finance, the mass media, and human rights campaigns.

The notion of trans-planetary interconnectivity in closely related to some of the most commonly used definitions of globalization as, for example, "the widening, deepening and speeding up of worldwide interconnections" (Held and McGrew 2002), and "a proliferation of cross-border flows and transnational networks" (Castles 2002). For Scholte, while trans-planetary interconnectivity is one aspect of globalization, it does not represent something qualitatively new. International travel and trade have been historically significant even prior to the twentieth century. What has, however, happened since the 1970s is that there has been a significant quantitative increase in trans-planetary interconnectivity.

The concept of *supra-territoriality* relates to a reconfiguration of social geography beyond territorial space. In Scholte's words (2005: 61) it represents "social connections that substantially transcend territorial geography" and are both simultaneous and instantaneous. The most obvious example of this is the internet, which creates a social space outside of territorial geography. Other examples might include telecommunications, finance, mass media, and climate change. The concept is closely related to other ideas within the literature on globalization. In particular, Castells (1996) has talked about the emergence of a "network society" in which there has been a shift from a global social geography based on "a space of places" to one based on "a space of flows." For Castells, the world is made up of interconnected nodes that are linked in ways that transcend territory. Sassen (2001) underlines this analysis in her discussion of the network of global cities, in which New York, London, and Tokyo are simultaneously connected by the internet and financial markets, for example. For Scholte, it is this notion of supra-territoriality that is the qualitatively new aspect of globalization.

Causes and consequences

Scholte also sets out a typology for explaining the causes and consequences of globalization. He identifies the four main areas of social organization: production, governance, identity, and knowledge. He argues that change in these areas is both the cause and the consequence of globalization. In other words, each area can be seen as both the *explanans* (something that explains) and the *explanadum* (something to be explained) of globalization. This relationship can be illustrated below. For example, in the area of "knowledge," technological change in relation to the internet has led to both supra-territoriality and trans-planetary interconnectivity. This, in turn, has had a major impact upon the organization of, for example, "governance" (for example, facilitating e-governance) and "production" (for example, expanding the scope for the commodification of information).

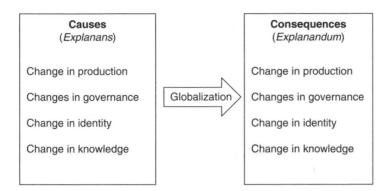

Production

Production processes are no longer confined within the boundaries of a single state but extend across states. Trans-national commodity chains, intra-firm trade, outsourcing, offshore centers, global companies, and increased market concentration have meant that production takes place on an increasingly trans-national scale. Meanwhile, with the emergence of new technologies resulting from the possibilities for new forms of supra-territorial geography, a range of new products are now bought and sold for money which were previously unavailable. Securities, derivatives, currency trading, IT, telecommunications, mass media, genetic modification, biofuels, and pharmaceuticals have also emerged as new areas of economic activity. There have also been significant organizational changes in production that have driven and been driven by globalization. Increasingly, large firms now operate on a global scale. On the one hand, these new forms of production are a consequence of globalization. For example, they have resulted from globalization making transactions and movements across borders increasingly efficient. On the other hand, these changes have also contributed to globalization. For example, they have led to the creation of new forms of governance in order to regulate new areas such as biotechnology and finance, and they have created new identities in the forms of a trans-national labor force and trans-national consumers.

Governance

A range of new levels of governance, beyond the nation-state, have emerged. Where once the nation-state was the main level of law-making and standard-setting, now multi-level governance exists. There has been a decline in territorialism, and national, regional, international, and trans-national forms of governance co-exist. New actors beyond the state have also played an increasingly prominent role in governance. The firm and civil society, in particular, have become increasingly involved in formulating, implementing, enforcing, and reviewing rules. These changes have in part been driven by globalization. As the issues and problems have emerged that transcend the scope of the nation-state, so it has been necessary to develop governance mechanisms that similarly go beyond national borders. The internet, climate change, and financial flows, for example, cannot be regulated by a single state acting in isolation. Consequently, new forms of regional and global governance have emerged. Meanwhile, as authority has diffused beyond the nation-state, so non-state actors have had opportunities to become involved in governance. These new forms of governance have, in turn, contributed to globalization in other areas. For example, the development of European governance has contributed to the creation of a European trans-national identity. Similarly, the emergence of common regulatory standards across borders has facilitated new forms of production across trans-national commodity chains.

Identity

There has been a proliferation of identities. Beyond the notion of nationality, the relationship between identity and territory has changed. Micro-nationalist politics has emerged at the sub-state level as indigenous groups, regions, and ethnic groups have found the means to assert their autonomy. As people and information have moved across borders, processes of hybridization and fragmentation have led to the creation of new cultures and forms of self-identification. For example, in the context of migration, global diasporas have become a significant source of new trans-national identities. As with the other areas of social organization, change in identity can be understood as both a consequence and a cause of globalization. New forms of technology have enabled identities to transcend territorial space. For example, the internet has allowed the reassertion of trans-national identities and the formation of a range of diaspora networks. Similarly, changes in production and the emergence of a trans-national labor force have contributed to the creation of global diasporas. On the other hand, the new identities have also driven globalization, leading to change in other areas of social organization. For example, the emergence of diaspora groups has led to the creation of new forms of governance in which states have tried to develop policies with extra-territorial scope to control their diasporas abroad (Gamlen 2008). It has also contributed to the development and use of new technologies to facilitate trans-national social interaction such as methods for moving capital or communicating across borders.

Knowledge

Although many technologies – such as trans-national shipping and trans-national communications – predate debates on globalization, a range of new technologies have emerged which have transformed social organization. The most obvious example is the internet, which has facilitated the creation of a genuinely supra-territorial space for social interaction. It has been a significant catalyst for a range of other significant social changes such as global financial markets, the organization of trans-national advocacy groups, and the global distribution of goods and services. In that sense, the internet has been a major cause of globalization and change in areas ranging from production to identity. However, beyond the internet, other technologies such as telecommunications, biotechnology, and nanotechnology are also deeply implicated in the causes and consequences of globalization. They will lead to significant future changes in production and governance.

Analytical Perspectives

Approaches to globalization can be divided into three broad schools of thought: hyper-globalizers, skeptics, and transformationists (Held and McGrew 2002). They diverge in their conclusions about the extent of globalization's implications for social organization, and whether or not it represents a new or old phenomenon. In many ways the division of academic approaches to globalization into these three groups is artificial; however, it highlights key differences.

Firstly, *hyper-globalizers* argue that globalization is radically new and is changing economic, political, and social structures around the world. For hyper-globalizers, globalization represents a qualitatively new phenomenon, in which the nation-state is declining in importance. The market is eroding state authority, in which the state's regulatory autonomy is constrained by the mobility of goods, services, and capital. Meanwhile, the spread of liberal values such as democracy is creating a cosmopolitan cultural and political framework within which old communitarian loyalties based on territory are no longer relevant. The broad characterization has both positive and negative variants. For Ohmae (2005), for example, the triumph of the market and liberalization are to be celebrated. For Beck (1999), on the other hand, market power is eroding democracy and the welfare state and the decline of the state is to be lamented.

Secondly, *skeptics* respond critically to hyper-globalizers. For skeptics, there is nothing that empirically supports the extreme claims that globalization is fundamentally changing economic, political, or social organization. The state remains the most important actor in world politics with the authority to govern within its territory. Although there are indeed a range of trans-border flows, these, according to skeptics, are nothing qualitatively new. Trans-national cultures, the international movement of goods, services, people, and capital have existed in previous historical eras. Indeed, even on a quantitative level Hirst and Thompson (1999) have argued that there was more global trade in the early twentieth century than there is at the start of the twenty-first century.

Thirdly, *transformationists* attempt to transcend the debate between hyper-globalizers and skeptics, arguing that the two extreme positions represent a false dichotomy. For them, globalization does not necessarily mean the end of the state and the triumph of the free market. However, neither is it just a continuation of past trends. Globalization is transforming social organization. The question for transformationists is to identify how, and in what areas, globalization is changing social relations. In many ways, the transformationist agenda has become the mainstream of globalization research, attempting to analytically explore and unpack what globalization is and how, causally, it is changing different aspects of society (Held and McGrew 2002; Scholte 2005).

Normative Perspectives

The debate between hyper-globalizers, skeptics, and transformationists is largely an analytical debate, in the sense that it focuses on debates of interpretation about the empirical nature and consequences of globalization. A different, but equally common, debate relates to the normative question of whether globalization is "good" or "bad" and from whose perspective. Just as Held and McGrew (2002) have developed a typology to identify different positions within the analytical debate, so too Scholte (2005) provides a typology for positions within the normative debate based on four perspectives: neo-liberalism, rejectionism, reformism, and transformism.

Firstly, at one extreme, *neo-liberalism* would see globalization as normatively desirable. It would argue that the free movement of capital, goods, services, and people across borders is desirable and should be left to market forces. From this perspective, liberalization, deregulation, privatization, and fiscal austerity should be promoted in order to ensure the maximum benefits are derived from trans-boundary economic movements. Reducing the role of the state and facilitating trans-boundary movements will increase the efficiency of markets, extending prosperity to a wide range of people. Globalization will also contribute to spreading liberal values such as democracy and freedom. This position is exemplified by the dominant "Washington Consensus" view of the US government and the Bretton Woods institutions from the 1990s.

Secondly, *rejectionism* takes the opposite view to neo-liberalism. It sees globalization as negative. It rejects the opening up of state borders and instead promotes a return to self-sufficient country units. From this point of view, liberalization and global markets represent a threat to domestic industry, the welfare state, and national culture. Rejectionists would therefore advocate protectionism and a return to greater state control. This position is exemplified by the position of the French government in many international debates relating to globalization and to a number of the so-called anti-globalization protestors.

Thirdly, *reformism* takes a more nuanced view. It opposes neo-liberalism; however, it does not completely reject the benefits that come from globalization. Rather, it argues that what impact globalization has and who benefits and who loses from globalization is a consequence of the type of policy interventions that are applied in response to globalization. The challenge from this perspective is to use policy interventions to enhance the positive aspects of globalization by working toward social democratic principles of governance at the national, regional, and global levels.

Fourthly, *transformism* also takes a more nuanced view than the first two categories but is more radical than reformism. It argues that, at the moment, globalization, as it is currently conceived, has many potentially negative aspects to it. These negative consequences are not inevitable and globalization could have very positive social outcomes. However, in order for it to do so changes that are more fundamental than policy interventions would be required. Rather, it would be necessary to fundamentally reconstruct the structures of production and knowledge. In particular, it would be necessary to challenge the basis of the global capitalist mode of production and the neo-liberal ideological framework that underpins globalization.

In setting out his own normative position, Scholte (2005) rejects the two extremes of neo-liberalism and rejectionism. Instead, he argues that the most appropriate response combines reformism with some elements of transformism. In other words, whether or not globalization is "good" or "bad" depends upon the policy responses and the type of governance structures that are created to regulate it and channel both trans-planetary interconnectivity and supra-territoriality into positive outcomes. However, it may also be necessary to re-think some of the structural and ideological underpinnings of the global liberal order in order for globalization to have its most positive outcomes, especially for many people who are marginalized in the international political economy.

Implications for Forced Migration

Globalization has significant implications for forced migration. In particular, the changes in production, governance, identity, and knowledge identified above have had profound consequences for forced migration. The relationship between forced migration and globalization can be analyzed on three different levels: the underlying causes of displacement, movement and mobility, and international responses to forced migration. This section explores these relationships by drawing upon the conceptual framework outlined above.

Underlying causes of displacement

Most sources of internal or cross-border displacement can be attributed to persecution, conflict, environmental change, serious economic distress, or change in land use. In turn, many of the underlying causes of these types of displacement are closely connected to the consequences of globalization. As trans-world interconnectivity and supra-territoriality transform production, governance, knowledge, and identity, many of the underlying sources of forced migration may be exacerbated or mitigated.

Identifying exactly how globalization (as an independent variable) affects the underlying causes of forced migration (as a dependent variable) is an empirical question that relies upon carefully tracing the causal mechanisms that relate the two concepts. The flow diagram below provides a basis for identifying and exploring different aspects of that relationship. Globalization (as interplanetary interconnectivity and supra-territoriality) may affect production, governance, knowledge, or identity. A change in any one of these areas may then have an impact on conflict, persecution, environmental change, economic distress or land use, changing patterns of forced migration.

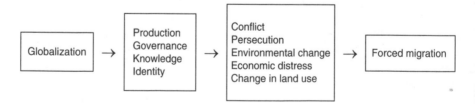

In some cases a change in social organization resulting from globalization may reduce forced migration by mitigating the underlying causes of forced migration. In other cases it may increase forced migration by exacerbating the underlying causes of displacement. In most cases, the relationship between a source of change and forced migration will be contingent upon the precise nature of the change that takes place. There are too many possible causal relationships to explain all of them. However, the relationships can be illustrated by taking some examples.

For example, a range of hypotheses emerge from the literature about the possible relationship between globalization and conflict. In relation to the globalization of governance, it has been suggested that the structural adjustment policies of the World Bank and IMF may have contributed to conflicts in Sub-Saharan Africa by eroding state capacity, and so led to displacement (Milner 2009). The creation of global governance over and above the level of the nation-state has created a layer of governance that has forced many developing countries to comply with policies of liberalization, privatization, and deregulation conceived in the developed world. In turn, many of these policies have reduced governments' tax base and so their capacity to provide public services or maintain a strong military.

In relation to the globalization of production, it has been suggested that, under certain conditions, international trade in primary products such as diamonds and oil may contribute to conflict by financing and incentivizing violence (Collier 2007). Indeed the global economy has created many opportunities for developing countries to export their primary products. However, in many cases, being dependent upon primary commodity exports has been a mixed blessing. Aside from being susceptible to volatile, internationally determined prices, dependency on extractive industries in particular has often led to conflict as different factions in states such as Sudan, Nigeria, Indonesia, Angola, and the DRC have competed to control access to natural resources.

In relation to the globalization of identity, processes of fragmentation and pluralization of ethnicity, religion, and nationality at the end of the Cold War have been identified as sources of internal conflict either as a factor in their own right (Huntington 1993) or as a signifier for inequalities between groups (Stewart 2008). Globalization has challenged the relationship between territory, citizenship, and identity leading the growing emphasis on forms of identity that are not co-terminous with the boundaries of the state. Trans-national identities, micro-nationalist politics, and diaspora groups, for example, have all contributed to the pluralization of identities within states and the privileging of religion and ethnicity in politics.

In relation to the globalization of knowledge, the increasingly dominant ideology of liberal democracy and democratic peace theory has led to attempts to facilitate democratization in many areas of the world. In many situations this has led to conflict rather than democratic consolidation

(Mansfield and Snyder 2005). It has frequently been claimed that there is a strong empirical relationship between liberal democracies on the one hand, and peace and prosperity on the other (Reuveny and Li 2003; Russett 1993). Yet, in many situations, attempts to engage in promoting democratization have led to conflict, with voting dividing upon ethnic or religious lines (Mann 2005).

It is also possible to explore a range of hypotheses about the relationship between globalization and other sources of forced migration. For example, sources of persecution may be linked to globalization in a number of ways. The globalization of knowledge through increasing access to the internet and the global media may have helped to subvert authoritarian dictatorships and to make human rights abuses more transparent, increasing the opportunity costs of persecution to a given regime. Indeed, the globalization of human rights norms by trans-national advocacy groups may have contributed to reducing sources of persecution (Keck and Sikkink 1998). On the other hand, in some instances the globalization of production and governance in the economic realm may have contributed to increasing sources of persecution in some cases by, for example, enabling dictatorships to comply with international agreements in the economic realm as a means of bypassing the enforcement of international standards in relation to human rights (Hafner-Burton 2009).

Similarly, sources of environmental displacement are affected by globalization. For example, climate change and the emission of greenhouses gases are closely related to globalization insofar as they exemplify how emissions in one state generate externalities on a global scale. Environmental change is also closely connected to changes in production patterns and the use of new technologies that have contributed to the growing use of fossil fuels (Myers 1997; Piguet 2008). Meanwhile, trans-national corporations and international financial institutions have been profoundly implicated in many of the large dam projects that have led to change in land use and development-induced displacement (Khagram 2004).

Potential hypotheses about the causal relationships between globalization and the underlying causes of forced migration are almost unlimited, and further empirical research is needed to substantiate the relationship. Nevertheless, it is clear that different aspects of globalization have far-reaching and diverse affects on forced migration. Some of these are positive in the sense of mitigating the underlying causes of displacement; others are negative in terms of exacerbating root causes. In the majority of cases, though, there is no inevitability to whether the relationship is positive or negative. Rather, globalization's impact on forced migration will be contingent on a range of other factors such as the motives of different actors and the types of policies that are adopted to mediate the relationship between globalization and forced migration. The key challenge for research is to unpack the conditions under which globalization mitigates or exacerbates the causes of forced migration.

Movement and mobility

Globalization has also changed the dynamics of forced migration by having a profound impact upon people's mobility. Until the 1980s most refugee movements were either East–West involving people fleeing Communism or were regionally confined within the developing world. Since the 1980s, this has changed. An increasing proportion of people displaced in the developing world have spontaneously moved onward to developed countries, often as part of broader migratory flows (Chimni 1998). This South–North movement has emerged as the ability and aspiration of people to move transcontinentally has been transformed by globalization.

Improved transportation and communications have enabled people to move on a global scale. The era of "jet-age migration" has therefore contributed to the phenomenon of trans-world asylum seekers. New private actors such as human smugglers have played an important role in enabling people to move irregularly across international borders. Aside from the means to travel, the desire to move onward from regions of origin to Europe or North America, for example, has been fueled by new aspirations. The internet, the global media, and communications across borders have contributed to significant "pull factors" in addition to the "push factors" that are commonly assumed to drive forced migration. Images of life in the developing world have attracted a significant proportion of refugees and displaced people to move onward from their region of origin. In the context of "mixed flows," both refugees and non-refugees increasingly used asylum channels as a means to access developed-country labor markets, in many cases doing so-called "3-D jobs" (dirty, demanding, and dangerous) (Castles 2002), and using remittances to support families and communities in the country of origin or in host countries in the region of origin (Lindley 2007).

In the context of this form of trans-continental movement, transnationalism has become an increasingly important phenomenon. Faist (2004) defines trans-nationalism as "sustained ties across borders." As people have moved they have developed and maintained social, cultural, and economic ties – most notably through remittance sending, diasporas, and the development of social networks. Trans-nationalism is not the same as globalization but evolves within the linkages created by globalization. For example, it has been facilitated by increased communication and travel. Trans-nationalism has contributed to the development of identities not based primarily on attachment to a specific territory. Instead, communities with multiple identities have emerged through both the development of cosmopolitan identities and the strengthening of ethnic identity in exile (Castles 2002).

While the implications of trans-nationalism go far beyond forced migration, they have particular relevance in the context of forced migration. Van Hear (2006) examines trans-national relations amongst Sri Lankan Tamil, Palestinian, and Afghan refugees. He highlights the complex relationships between homeland, country of first asylum, and the wider diaspora in third countries. The dynamics across these three groups of states represent important dynamics but are also crucial for livelihoods, with remittance-sending connecting all three of these groups in economically and socially significant ways. Remittances have become an important part of the survival strategy of many refugee communities in first countries of asylum as well as a means of maintaining social ties.

Responses by states

The new dynamics of trans-continental mobility have contributed to changing state responses to forced migration. Before the 1980s most Western states were positively predisposed to receiving refugees fleeing Communism. Since the 1980s there has been growing concern in industrialized countries to manage migration. Immigration and integration have become increasingly politicized and states have attempted to introduce policies to demonstrate that they are able to control migration. Many developed countries have been in the contradictory position of trying to create a trans-national workforce to address labor shortages while simultaneously excluding "irregular" immigrants spontaneously arriving from the South.

In this context, Bauman (1998) has highlighted how the world now divides between "tourists," who have access to mobility, and "vagabonds," who are locally confined and lack the ability to travel. This stratified global hierarchy is underpinned by the selective immigration policies of states. Duffield (2001) and Chimni (1998) similarly argue that migration control is part of the broader context of North–South relations, in which much of liberal global governance exists to ensure the containment and exclusion from the North of people in the global South.

These broader attempts to limit and control the South–North flow of irregular migrants have led to particular policy innovations in relation to forced migration. Since the early 2000s, a range of policy initiatives have emerged, underpinned by the common logic of attempting to shift the space in which protection is available to forced migrants back toward refugees' regions and countries of origin.

From 2003, for example, there was an emerging international debate about the concept of "protection in the region," whereby a number of European states and UNHCR argued that enhancing refugee protection in the South could represent a means for Northern states to avert onward movement. The argument that was made was that a primary reason for so-called "irregular secondary movement," in which refugees left camps and settlements in first countries of asylum and moved spontaneously to the developed world, was the absence of adequate protection in the South. If the quality and quantity of protection and access to durable solutions for refugees in the South could be strengthened, this might lead to a reduction in onward movement (Betts and Milner 2006).

Alongside this, a number of European states also proposed using extra-territorial asylum processing: This involved the idea of transferring the site at which asylum claims were assessed from European territory to the territory of a third transit country nearer to an asylum seeker's country of origin. For example, the European Union discussed plans to establish "transit processing centers" in North Africa and former Soviet countries along Europe's eastern border. The proposals followed the use of extra-territorial processing measures by the United States in the 1990s (for Haitian asylum seekers whose claims were assessed at Guantanamo Bay), and by Australia in the early 2000s (on Nauru and Christmas Island) (Noll 2003).

In addition to this, there have been claims that some of the new reforms relating to IDP protection may also have been influenced by a common logic. The new emphasis of "in-country" protection has allowed the use of "internal flight alternative" as a means to legitimate the return of asylum seekers and refugees to their country of origin on the grounds that they could have found effective protection somewhere within their country of origin (Prosser 2008). One interpretation of the emergence and development of a normative and institutional framework for IDP protection is that it represents a genuine response to a significant protection gap; an alternative interpretation is that it is part of a broader shift toward containing protection within the region of origin (Dubernet 2001).

A further variant on this broad strategy by Northern states of trying to reduce the need for transcontinental South–North movement has been the broader "migration and development" debates that have taken place in, for example, the UN framework and the Global Forum for Migration and Development (GFMD). Some commentators have argued that many of these debates have been underlined by a sedentarist logic, whereby there has been a false assumption that development in the region of origin may reduce the likelihood of people resorting to irregular migration, whether through asylum channels or not (Castles and Wise 2008).

All of these strategies demonstrate how states are attempting to address an important aspect of globalization – increased human mobility – within the territorialized framework of the state system. While globalization is changing the dynamics of forced migration, entwining displacement with growing human mobility, states' policy responses are underpinned by an assumption that the nation-state can reassert its authority. Questions relating to asylum and irregular migration therefore represent one of the areas in which the nation-state system is being fundamentally challenged by globalization.

Case Study: The "Asylum-Migration Nexus"

The politics and practice of refugee protection have become increasingly complicated in the context of globalization. This has led to a range of policy labels and academic debates highlighting the existence of "nexuses" that connect asylum and refugee protection on the one hand, to a number of other issue-areas on the other hand. These nexuses have been used to describe asylum's relationship to migration, development, and security, for example. The most high profile of these nexuses has been the so-called asylum–migration nexus.

Discussion of the asylum–migration nexus emerges from the growing difficulty to clearly distinguish between asylum and other forms of trans-border movement. Although the dominant international legal and normative framework is premised upon a clear delineation between refugees and voluntary economic migration, globalization and the impact it has had on the ability and motive to move across borders has created a blurring of the boundaries between these two areas.

The asylum–migration nexus is closely connected to globalization insofar as aspects of interconnectivity and supra-territoriality have led to the emergence of the "trans-world asylum seeker" since the 1980s. Given the opportunity to travel trans-continentally created by new forms of transportation and trans-national social networks, and the aspiration to travel trans-continentally created by the internet, the global media, and the creation of a global workforce, the nature of asylum has changed. Asylum has become more closely intertwined with other forms of human mobility. In particular, the growth in spontaneous-arrival South–North asylum seeking has taken on many of the same features as other forms of irregular migration.

Castles and Van Hear (2005) highlight three different levels on which the nexus operates: routes, causes, and policies. The *routes* taken by asylum seekers and other irregular migrants are frequently similar. The restrictive policies of many Northern states have made spontaneously reaching the territory of Europe, Australia, or North America extremely challenging, even for refugees. Asylum seekers, like irregular migrants, have therefore frequently resorted to entering countries through irregular channels such as by using human smuggling networks. The same transit migration routes across the Mediterranean, the Gulf of Aden, or the Caribbean, for example, have been used by both asylum seekers and irregular migrants.

The *causes* of asylum and migration are increasingly blurred. International refugee law is premised upon the notion of a clear distinction between people who face political persecution and those who do not. In reality, a range of people flee desperate situations such as environmental degradation or severe economic and social distress but do not meet the definition of a "refugee." Similarly, many refugees, who face a well-founded fear of persecution, may also have "mixed motives" for traveling trans-continentally, including aspirations to work and remit money to their families. Furthermore, as people's circumstances change during transit, they may even engage in "category jumping" – shifting between different categories of migrant.

The *policies* adopted to address asylum and migration have become increasingly undifferentiated. Non-entrée measures and tighter border controls have been adopted in a blanket manner, which in practice makes it almost equally difficult for asylum seekers and other irregular migrants. Northern states' migration control policies have rarely incorporated refugee- and asylum-sensitive components. Innovations such as Frontex, the EU's border control agency, and the security fences in Ceuta and Melilla, or along the US–Mexican border, for example, have few measures to ensure that asylum seekers are not excluded alongside other categories of migrant.

The asylum–migration nexus has a range of implications for protection. In particular it has implications for *how* to protect, *where* to protect, and *who* to protect. In relation to "how to protect" the nexus has led to a policy focus on ensuring refugee protection "in the context of mixed flows." UNHCR has been keen to ensure that transit and destination states are able to screen and identify refugees and separate them from broader migratory movements. For example, in 2007 it developed a "10-point" plan of how to ensure refugees would receive protection and not be forcibly returned to countries of origin as part of the blanket removal orders that transit and destination countries commonly apply to irregular migrants (UNHCR 2007).

In relation to "where to protect," the nexus has led to debate on whether it would be possible to consider a "new asylum paradigm" (Schuster 2005), which might territorially separate the place in which an asylum seeker is identified, the place where the asylum claim is assessed, and the place where protection is provided. Indeed, concern with spontaneous-arrival asylum led a number of states to consider whether the territory on which protection is provided could be de-coupled from the territory on which an asylum seeker first arrives (Noll 2003). For example, in 2003 the UK Government proposed that it might be possible for an asylum seeker identified in Europe to have his or her claim assessed at a transit processing center in North Africa, and then either sent to a third country to receive protection or returned to the country of origin (depending on whether the claim is successful or not). These types of proposal have a long history but their revival highlights the extent to which states have attempted to find new ways to provide refugee protection in the context of the asylum–migration nexus (Hathaway and Neve 1997; Schuck 1997; Shacknove 1993).

In relation to "who to protect," there has also been growing debate on whether, in the context of globalization, it any longer makes sense to uphold the sharp, dichotomous distinction between "refugee" and other types of "irregular migrant." In practice, a range of people who cross borders, who do not fall within the framework of international refugee law, are nevertheless in need of (and entitled to) international protection. People fleeing serious economic and social distress or environmental degradation, stranded migrants, trafficked migrants, and people who have developed needs as a result of suffering trauma or violence during transit all have protection needs. In theory, these people have entitlements under international human rights law. In practice, however, these rights are rarely respected and most "other irregular migrants" are returned to their country of origin. However, in the context of the asylum–migration nexus, UNHCR and a range of other international actors have begun a debate on how to ensure that categories of vulnerable people who cross borders but are not refugees may also receive access to their human rights (Crisp 2008; Dowd 2008).

Conclusion

Globalization is challenging to define and analyze. It is questionable whether it represents a single coherent phenomenon or a series of emerging trends in society, politics, and the economy. Nevertheless, the work of Scholte (2005), in particular, provides an instructive definition and analytical framework for analyzing the concept. This chapter has tried to apply elements of that framework to elucidate the relationship between globalization and forced migration.

It is possible to examine the relationship between globalization and forced migration on different levels: underlying causes, mobility and movement, and states' responses. The precise causal relationship in each of these areas needs to be unpacked through empirical research. Nevertheless, broad trends can be identified. Globalization appears to be exacerbating some causes of displacement and mitigating others. Exactly how it is affecting conflict, persecution, and environmental change, for example, is contingent upon a range of mediating factors but it is nevertheless possible to see broad trends that are reshaping the causes and dynamics of forced migration.

Meanwhile, globalization is leading to greater opportunity and aspiration to move trans-continentally as part of broader irregular migratory movements. Yet states are continuing to address the dynamics of increased human mobility through a Westphalian state-centric framework, trying to control and manage asylum and irregular migration. This has led to attempts to shift protection space ever closer to the country of origin through policies such as "protection in the region of origin," "extra-territorial protection," and "internal flight alternative." How sustainable and effective these strategies of containment will be in a globalized world is open to question.

Given the increasingly complex dynamics of forced migration and their relationship to broader aspects of human mobility, old labels and categories are being challenged and recreated. Phenomena such as the "asylum–migration nexus," "mixed flows," and "irregular migration" are illustrative of the inadequacy of existing labels. In the context of globalization, policy-makers and academics may need to re-think old conceptual tools and policy distinctions.

8

Regionalism

The "region" is an increasingly important unit of political organization. Regionalism broadly relates to patterns of interdependence and international cooperation within geographically contiguous areas of territory. Different regions vary greatly in terms of the degree of formalized cooperation that exists. The most prominent example of regionalism is the EU, which has developed significant levels of institutionalized cooperation and policy integration. However, there are also many other examples of formal regional groups – NAFTA, ASEAN, MERCOSUR, COMESA, ECOWAS, and SADC, for example. These organizations vary in purpose and in the scope of their activities. Some, such as NAFTA and MERCOSUR, have a primarily economic focus, existing to facilitate free trade and the movement of goods, services, and people. Some, such as ASEAN, have a primarily security focus, existing to ensure mutual respect for sovereignty. The EU is exceptional in having developed significant levels of collective action across a wide range of issue-areas.

Regionalism is challenging to define, and has a number of different dimensions. Hurrell (1995) highlights five different aspects of regionalism, which need to be distinguished from one another: regionalization (the emergence of non-state led economic interdependence); regional awareness and identity (the creation of an imagined community across borders); regional inter-state cooperation (collective action to address common problems); state-promoted regional integration (the harmonization and standardization of policies, especially to remove barriers to the movement of goods, services, and people); and regional cohesion (the creation over time of a coherent, consolidated regional unit). These are analytically distinct aspects of regionalism but, in practice, they frequently overlap. It is important when one speaks about regionalism to be clear on which of these phenomena one is referring to.

Regionalism is not new. It emerged in practice and as an important source of academic debate in the 1960s (Fawcett 1995). However, regionalism has been revived and has developed new dimensions since the end of the Cold War. In the Cold War context, regional associations were subordinated to East–West relations. NATO, the Warsaw Pact, SEATO, CENTO, ANZUS, OAS, and OAU were generally the handmaidens of the superpowers, and even the European Community was viewed by the US as a bulwark against Soviet expansion into Western Europe. The end of the Cold War led to a revival of multilateralism and the decentralization of power within the international system. In this context, the EU rapidly expanded and developed new forms of cooperation, and other regions attempted to emulate the example of the EU.

Academic work on regionalism has generally focused on trying to explain regional inter-state cooperation (including regional integration) – especially in the European Union. It has tried to explain when it exists and why; and the conditions under which attempts to develop collaboration and coordination are a "success" or a "failure" (Caporaso 1998; Mattli 1999). This work has relevance for forced migration. Indeed, a range of forms of regional cooperation have developed in relation to asylum and immigration, refugee protection standards, and even IDP protection. In the European Union a common asylum and immigration policy has emerged (Byrne 2003; Lavenex 1999; Thielemann 2003). In the African Union debate has begun on the creation of the world's first "hard law" framework on IDP protection (Beyani 2006). There have also been longstanding regional mechanisms relating to refugee protection – such as the OAU Refugee Convention of 1969 and the Cartagena Declaration of 1984 for Latin America. The broader literature on regionalism may help to explain variation in the emergence of regional approaches to forced migration.

Many aspects of forced migration are inherently regional in nature. Firstly, cross-border movements by refugees are regionally concentrated. In practice when people flee conflict or persecution they generally remain within their region of origin and the majority of the world's refugees are hosted by states that neighbor the country of origin. Secondly, the conflicts that give rise to refugee or IDP movements are often part of regional complexes. For example, the conflict in Sierra Leone in the 1990s cannot be understood without seeing it in the broader context of the West African region and dynamics with Liberia and Guinea. Thirdly, the provision of protection to refugees and IDPs is often a regional public good. In other words, the benefits of one state providing protection accrue to the other states in the given region irrespective of whether they contribute to protection. This is because they too benefit from the resulting stability. Fourthly, asylum policies are an integral element of regional integration. This is because once a region, such as the EU, attempts to facilitate the free movement of people within that region or to develop a common external border, it will also need to consider how to develop a common immigration and asylum policy. Because of these dynamics, many of the responses to forced migration and forms of international cooperation to address asylum, refugee protection, and IDPs emerge at a regional level.

This chapter therefore explores the relationship between regionalism and forced migration. It divides into three parts. The first part sets out the main theories of regionalism derived from International Relations. It explains the varieties of regionalism and theories that have been developed to explain regional inter-state cooperation. The second part explains the relevance of regionalism for forced migration. In particular, it sets out a typology of the different types of regional cooperation that exist in relation to forced migration based on five elements: common legal frameworks, ad hoc cooperation, policy harmonization, informal dialogue, and coalitional bargaining. Finally, the chapter relates the theories of regionalism to the empirical context of forced migration in two case studies: the development of a common EU asylum and immigration policy and the development of informal "regional consultative processes" (RCPs) in the area of asylum and migration.

Theories of Regionalism

Regionalism is challenging to define. It is often poorly defined in academic work. This is partly because it is an inherently ambiguous term and there is little consensus on its meaning. Beyond hinting at geographical proximity and contiguity, and patterns of interdependence, there is nothing "natural" or "scientific" about a given region. The definition of a given "region" is socially constructed and politically contested (Hurrell 1995: 38). Hurrell (1995) therefore explores the question: what do we mean by regionalism? He identifies five analytical varieties of regionalism that need to be distinguished from one another.

Firstly, *regionalization* relates to social and economic integration. In particular, it occurs with increasing interdependence on an economic level. As flows of goods, services, and people within a given region increase, so states become dependent upon one another in order to maximize their own welfare, and one states' actions have externalities for another state. For Hurrell, this is a market- rather than state-led process. Regionalization contrasts, for example, with state-promoted regional integration insofar as it is explicitly not state- or policy-led but is an informal and undirected process.

Secondly, *regional awareness and identity* relates to the creation of a sense of belonging and a common culture amongst the population of a given region. Just as the notion of an "imagined community" has been used to understand nationality and nationalism as forms of identity within a state (Anderson 1983), so too one can think of imagined communities existing across borders. In the European context for example, a great deal of consideration has been given to the notion of a common European identity and the elements of culture that underpin it. Language, rhetoric, common perceptions of an external threat, historical narratives, and common values, for example, may all underpin a sense of identity and belonging that transcends the state but is nevertheless geographically limited to some extent.

Thirdly, *regional inter-state cooperation* refers to collective action to address common problems. Just as intergovernmental agreements are often created at the multilateral level, so too ad hoc agreements or institutionalized cooperation frequently arise at the regional level. Cooperative arrangements may emerge to manage common external or internal challenges. In some cases regional cooperation may be preferred by states to global cooperation because the nature of the problem may be regional or because it may be easier to achieve agreement with a more limited number of states.

Fourthly, *state-promoted regional integration* is a distinct sub-category of regional cooperation. It relates to state policy-making decisions that reduce barriers to the movement of goods, services, capital, and people. It relates in particular to the attempt to engage in the harmonization and standardization of policies. A significant proportion of the literature on regionalism focuses on regional integration, particularly in relation to the EU, which has been explored as the "model" for regional integration.

Fifthly, *regional cohesion* relates to the notion that the combination of the other four varieties of regionalism may lead to a coherent and consolidated regional unit, which might be considered to constitute a political actor in its own right. Such a unit might take on a variety of forms, being based on, for example, supra-nationalism, a set of overlapping intergovernmental agreements, a mixture of supra-nationalism and inter-governmentalism (as in the EU), consociationalism, a regional hegemon, or a neo-medieval structure of overlapping structures of authority.

These aspects of regionalism are analytically distinct from one another but commonly overlap in practice. In reality, there may be feedbacks between them and progress in one area may support that in another. All of them have relevance for aspects of the causes, consequences, and responses to forced migration. However, the most important aspect from an IR perspective is explaining regional inter-state cooperation – both at the level of intergovernmental agreements (collaboration) and the level of regional integration (coordination).

Explaining Regional Cooperation

Explanations of regional cooperation draw upon broader explanations of international cooperation within international relations. A range of IR theories can contribute to explaining different sources of regional cooperation. Hurrell (1995), for example, sets out an analytical framework for explaining regionalism. His approach is based on the so-called "levels of analysis" approach to international relations, which identifies the sources of state behavior at a range of levels such as the system level (inter-state politics) and the unit level (domestic politics) (Putnam 1988; Singer 1961; Waltz 1979; Woods 1996). In attempting to explain the development of regionalism (mainly as regional inter-state cooperation), Hurrell (1995: 45–73) can be analyzed on three levels: systemic, regional, and domestic.

At the *system level*, neo-realism sees regionalism as a part of broader configurations of power in the international system. From a neo-realist perspective, regionalism is not dissimilar to the role that alliance formation plays in the balance of power. Regional alliances serve as the means by which groups of states join together to ensure that they have sufficient and equal power to deter attack by rival states or alliances. Alternatively, the region may simply be an expression of a regional hegemon, such as South Africa, Brazil, or India, attempting to dominate the region internally and project its power externally.

Within the context of Cold War bipolarity, hegemony can also be seen as playing an important role in the emergence of regionalism. For example, the US played an important role in the emergence of the EU through providing funding and political support because it saw the EU as an important means through which to preserve the balance of power in Europe. The EU represented a means to deter the expansion of the Warsaw pact from the East. From this perspective, the development and trajectory of regionalism would be strongly influenced by the systemic context of bipolarity or multi-polarity, and the diffusion of power that has come with multi-polarity might contribute to explaining the expansion in size and scope of the EU since the end of the Cold War.

From this neo-realist perspective, even regional economic cooperation would be seen as part of the power maximizing strategy of states in the international system. Economic success underlies military power. By using regional integration as a means to maximize their economic power, they may enhance their relative military power vis-à-vis external actors. Attempts to develop trade, free movement of goods, services, capital, and people might therefore be considered part of the state strategy of maximizing relative power in order to ensure survival within the state system.

From a system-level perspective, attempts to address an issue-area such as forced migration in a regional context are difficult to explain. They would have to be seen as part of the much broader context described above. In particular, cooperation in specific areas would emerge from the wider context of the balance of power and be led, not by a concern with human displacement but by the wider context of states trying to maximize their security and economic interests, and so developing quasi-permanent economic and security alliances. Insofar as new issues emerged that needed to be addressed for the alliance to fulfil its basic security and economic functions, cooperation might develop.

At the *regional level*, liberal institutionalism in particular sheds light on the drivers of cooperation. Economic interdependence creates a "demand" for regimes at the regional level. If states realize that externalities exist such that one states' policies affect another state and that states can be collectively better off with cooperation than competition they may develop institutionalized cooperation. In particular, regional institutions, like international institutions in general, can play an important role in reducing transaction costs and reducing uncertainty in ways that enable states to derive mutual benefit from institutionalized cooperation (Keohane 1982). From this perspective, regional cooperation may be preferred to global cooperation insofar as the scale of externalities or public goods is confined to a given region, or insofar as the supply of institutions is easier to achieve with a smaller number of states in a given region.

Beyond liberal institutionalism, other theories also have relevance for explaining factors that influence the emergence of regional cooperation. In particular, neo-functionalism suggests that regionalism can take on its own path-dependent and self-sustaining logic. Once a regional layer of bureaucracy is created, the centralized, technocratic structures that it brings into being may take on their own dynamic. In particular, neo-functionalism suggests that regional cooperation emerges as a result of functional spill-over from cooperation in one area to that in another. In other words, regionalism may be partly explained as the consequence of previous decisions. Constructivism also highlights a number of important factors that may explain cooperation at the regional level. A common identity, the historical emergence of norms, processing of learning, and the development of knowledge all play important roles in the emergence of regional cooperation (Checkel 1999).

From a regional-level perspective, regional cooperation in an issue-area such as forced migration would emerge either because of the perception of a mutual benefit from cooperation in that area (liberal institutionalism), because the prior development of cooperation in other issue-areas such as the creation of a free-trade area created a logic for further cooperation (neo-functionalism), or because a set of values and ideas created a common preference for cooperation in that area (constructivism). In the area of forced migration, for example, states might realize that regional institutions offer a more efficient means than unilateralism to address issues of asylum, refugee protection, and IDPs. Alternatively, cooperation in this area might arise from the functional spill-over of cooperation in other areas such as the free movement of goods, services, capital, and labor. Once cooperation exists in these areas of economic cooperation it may be difficult to avoid the need for new cooperative agreements in relation to issues of border control, immigration, and integration. Finally, from a constructivist perspective, common values of human rights, justice, and security might underpin a common vision of a region such as the EU's role with respect to forced migration.

At the *domestic level*, a range of factors also influence the development of regional cooperation. Interest groups may play an important role in promoting or obstructing cooperation and integration. Cooperation in a given area may involve winners and losers. The ability of different groups to assert their interests in national politics will contribute to shaping the state's position in inter-state negotiations. As liberalism predicts, regime type may also matter. For example, whether states are democracies may shape their interest in engaging in regional cooperation. As democratic peace-theory suggests, democracies are less likely to go to war with one another. This may or may not create a stronger impetus toward regional integration (Doyle 1997; Kant 1795; Russett 1993). Domestic politics may also influence the trajectory of regional cooperation because, over time, regional-level agreements may be implemented and become embedded within domestic legal frameworks. This process of embedding international norms within domestic politics and law may in turn contribute to a form of path dependency which leads to further regional cooperation.

These examples of domestic factors may also have relevance for explaining regional cooperation in relation to forced migration. Different groups may have different interests at stake in the areas of immigration, asylum, and refugee protection, for example. So groups may be economically threatened by the presence of non-citizens on their territory. They may fear competition for jobs, social services, or natural resources. Other groups – such as human rights NGOs – may push strongly for a rights-based framework. The variety of domestic interest groups will therefore shape the nature and scope of regional cooperation. Similarly, forced migration is an area in which the incorporation of regional legal standards into domestic law has played an important role in constraining domestic politics and influencing states' positions in subsequent international debates. The ECHR, for example, has been incorporated in European states' domestic legislation in ways that limit European states' autonomy with respect to the development of asylum and immigration policies. This in turn constrains the positions that they can adopt in discussions on further regional cooperation.

Explaining Regional Integration

An important sub-theory of regional cooperation is the area of regional integration. Indeed the process of integration has arguably had the greatest attention in the literature because of the literature's Eurocentric focus on the EU. Although integration is part of regional cooperation it refers more specifically to the coordination and standardization of policies across states in order to pass authority to a supranational level. For Mattli (1999: 44) it is "the process of providing common rules, regulations and policies for a region." In order to operationalize the concept, he defines it more narrowly as "the voluntary linking in the economic domain of two or more formerly independent states to the extent that authority over key areas of domestic regulation is shifted to the supranational level" (p. 41).

Different regions vary in the scope of their integration. Regional organizations are often categorized in different ways according to their degree of integration. A free-trade area is defined as an area in which barriers to the mobility of goods, services, and people have been removed. A customs union is a free-trade area with a common external border. A monetary union is a customs union with a single currency and a common monetary policy. A political union includes the coordination of a range of other policy areas including fiscal policy, welfare provision, justice and home affairs, and foreign policy.

The region with the greatest degree of integration is the EU. It has gradually moved from the category of free-trade area to being a monetary and political union. Indeed, the Treaty of Rome created the European Community (EC) in 1957, giving rise to a customs union. In 1992, the Maastricht Treaty led to the first steps to develop a political union with three pillars of integration: European Community law (EC), a common security and foreign policy (CSFP), and justice and home affairs (JHA). By 1999, a monetary union was brought into existence through the creation of the Eurozone and the European Central Bank (ECB). In the 2000s, the EU has gone even further in developing the attributes of a sovereign state, even proposing the creation of a constitutional treaty in the Treaty of Lisbon in 2007.

There are a range of political science theories that attempt to explain regional integration (Mattli 1999). Each one sheds light on a different factor that underlies regional integration, and they have generally been developed in relation to trying to explain the emergence of the EU. Functionalism, neo-functionalism, intergovernmentalism, and supranationalism represent the four main theories of regional integration.

Functionalism: suggests that regional integration emerges because it is necessary to meet the emerging challenges that result from interdependence. Mitrany (1966) argued that integration will occur as part of a gradual and teleological process toward peace and prosperity. For Mitrany, the piece by piece transfer of sovereignty will lead to "a working peace." From this point of view, regionalism begins from technocratic cooperation. It is not political or politicized but a web of technocratic elites engage in transferring sovereignty. Although analytically functionalism is interesting because it highlights the role of technocratic elites in the process of integration, it is highly normative and teleological it its approach.

Neo-functionalism builds upon functionalism. However, it is more analytical and less normative. It identifies the principal driver of integration as being "functional spill-over" (Haas 1958; 1961). Bureaucracies exist on three different levels: supranational, state, and sub-state. At each level actors have utilitarian self-interests. Once integration is achieved in one area, so this leads to a logic of integration being needed in another area. In this sense, integration takes on a path-dependent form with previous integration being what defines subsequent integration. For example, the creation of a free-trade area leads to debate about a common currency which in turn leads to debate about the need for a common fiscal policy, which leads to debate about a common welfare policy. Neo-functionalism highlights the key role of bureaucrats and path dependency in the integration process. However, one area in which it struggles is that it cannot explain what initially led to the start of the integration process.

Intergovernmentalism explains integration at the level of inter-state bargaining. It results from a series of bargains between states. States negotiate pooling sovereignty on the basis of convergences in their preferences. Intergovernmentalism draws heavily upon liberal institutionalism and sees integration as being similar to the process through which states create regimes, with regional institutions facilitating cooperation by reducing transactions costs, providing information, and facilitating issue-linkage. One of the core weaknesses of intergovernmentalism in the context of regional integration is its assumption of fixed preferences and its exclusion of domestic actors. Liberal intergovernmentalism attempts to address this weakness by including domestic actors in the analysis (Moravcsik 1993). For liberal intergovernmentalism, integration is a two-stage approach. Firstly, it involves national preferences being determined by the opportunities and constraints of economic interdependence for different domestic actors. Secondly, it involves international bargains which are determined by relative power and interest convergence at the inter-state level.

Supranationalism sheds light on the role of supra-state authority in driving integration. Here, integration is a top-down process in which a supra-national authority exerts an influence on integration. Once a supranational entity is created, it becomes an autonomous, interested, and influential actor. For example, the European Commission has been extremely influential in driving the European integration process. Supranationalism can therefore be contrasted with intergovernmentalism insofar as state bargaining is not the only driving process underlying integration (Weiler and Wind 2003).

The four approaches simply place emphasis on different sources of integration. In summary, functionalism points to the normative desirability of peace driving the process; neo-functionalism highlights a path-dependent and bureaucratically led process; intergovernmentalism sees it as driven by inter-state bargaining and preference formation; supranationalism highlights the autonomous role of a supranational authority to which sovereignty is transferred. Although these approaches therefore shed light on different factors in the integration process, they do not really constitute an overarching explanatory theory that can explain variation in regional integration.

In response to the inadequacy of the existing approaches to explain variation in integration, Mattli (1999) attempts to develop a theory to explain relative "success" and "failure" of regional integration. For example, why is it that the EU has so successfully integrated while there has been so little integration in the Andean Pact or ECOWAS? In order to answer this question, Mattli highlights two principal conditions that have been necessary for integration to take place. On the demand side there have needed to be significant gains from cooperation. In particular, integration would need to offer significant possibilities for reducing transaction costs or providing economies of scale in addressing externalities. On the supply side political leaders have needed to be willing and able to accommodate this demand at each step of the integration process. In particular, there has needed to be undisputed leadership in order for politicians to be able to retain power and carry their domestic constituency in the transfer of sovereignty.

For Mattli, the core cooperation problem in relation to integration is different from other areas of international cooperation. Integration is a coordination problem rather than the collaboration problem of Prisoner's Dilemma described in chapter 3. This is because regional integration involves not only collaboration to remove border barriers but also the adoption of standardized common regulations and policies. Where PD involves the challenge of how to get away from a single stable inefficient equilibrium (at which free-riding takes place), the Coordination Dilemma (CD) involves a choice between multiple stable and efficient equilibria.

	Actor B	
	C	D
C	4,3	2,2
D	1,1	3,4

Actor A (rows)

Figure 8.1   Coordination Problem: Number left (right) of comma refers to A's (B's) preference ordering (1 = worst outcome; 4 = best outcome)

In the diagram above, CC represents the repeated outcome of the iterated game. State A gets its optimum outcome; however, state B receives its second best outcome. Since the Coordination Dilemma involves agreement on which equilibrium to move to, it has *distributional consequences*. One actor may have to sacrifice its optimum scenario for coordination in deference to the preference of another. Coordination will thus occur under two conditions. Firstly, strong leadership at the regional level by, for example, actor A will be needed. In other words, an authoritative regional hegemon is needed whose standards might be accepted and adopted. Secondly, strong domestic leadership will be needed – especially by actor B – to sell the second-best outcome to electorates.

Relevance to Forced Migration

In many ways, the nature of forced migration is inherently regional. The causes, consequences, and responses to forced migration all have important regional aspects. Many of the conflicts that lead to refugee and IDP movements are the result of regional dynamics. The conflict in the Balkans, the Great Lakes, and West Africa, for example, are not reducible to a single state. The consequences of displacement are usually regional, with refugee movements generally being confined to countries that neighbor the country of origin. Furthermore, many of the most successful historical attempts to respond to forced migration have been led by regional actors. Historically, ASEAN, the OAU, and the EU, for example, have played an important role in providing solutions to refugee crises.

The provision of protection and durable solutions to refugees and IDPs has sometimes been suggested to constitute a global public good for which the benefits of one state's provision accrue to all other states, irrespective of whether or not they contribute to providing protection (Suhrke 1998). In practice, however, protection is not a global public good. The security and humanitarian benefits that result from a given state's contribution to protection are usually specific to a given region.

Indeed, protection may be more appropriately considered to be a regional public good. Once provided, the benefits of stability and security from refugees and IDPs receiving care and maintenance and access to human rights accrue to other states in the region who might be affected by receiving those refugees or the spill-over of conflict if another state in the region did not provide that protection. Given that the non-excludable nature of these benefits will create an incentive for states to free-ride on the contributions of their neighbors, this regional public goods logic represents a strong argument for regional cooperation in the areas of forced migration.

Where regional cooperation has taken place in relation to forced migration, it has generally emerged as a result of pre-existing structures of regional cooperation in other issue-areas. Regional cooperation in the area of forced migration has taken on a variety of forms. Indeed, this section sets out a typology of the five main varieties of regional cooperation in the area of forced migration: common legal frameworks, ad hoc cooperation, policy harmonization, informal dialogue, and coalitional bargaining.

Common legal frameworks

The refugee regime has not simply been defined by international treaties with global coverage. Rather, many of the legal mechanisms which protect the rights of refugees and other displaced people are regional treaties. Even the 1951 Convention was originally conceived as a regional treaty, with its geographical coverage confined to the Europe region until 1967. In recognition that forced migration patterns vary in different regions, additional regional instruments have been created to supplement the 1951 Convention and its 1967 Protocol. The 1969 OAU Convention created a refugee treaty for Africa, which differs from the 1951 Convention insofar as it accords refugee status to those fleeing not only individual persecution but also generalized violence. The 1984 Cartagena Declaration provides a refugee treaty for Latin America which incorporates all of the aspects of the 1951 Convention but again goes further in some areas. Meanwhile, in 2004, the European Council passed a directive on asylum, which went beyond the 1951 Convention by, for example, ensuring access to protection for people persecuted by non-state actors and people fleeing gender-based persecution (Goodwin-Gill and McAdam 2007).

Beyond refugees, the African Union's has developed an African Union Convention on Internally Displaced Persons. This is significant because it represents the first form of multilateral "hard law" framework to emerge on the IDP issue, and draws heavily on the Guiding Principles on Internal Displacement (Beyani 2006). Furthermore, regional human rights instruments such as the ECHR provide standards that require European states to ensure the protection of a range of people who may not necessarily be refugees. For example, it has been repeatedly recognized under ECtHR cases that there may be groups of people who are "excludable" from the 1951 refugee convention but who nevertheless cannot be "removed" from the country in which they claim asylum because of a reasonable concern about how they would be treated if they were returned to their country of origin (McAdam 2007). In most cases therefore, the existence of regional legal frameworks appears to complement and reinforce the more inclusive multilateral frameworks of refugee and IDP protection.

Ad hoc cooperation

Historically, many solutions to long-standing refugee crises have emerged from ad hoc regional cooperation. In the absence of strong, formal legal mechanisms relating to international burden-sharing, international responses to mass influx situations, humanitarian crises, or protracted refugee situations have often required ad hoc cooperation. Given the regionally-confined nature of many of these situations, it has been incumbent upon the countries of the affected region to attempt to develop cooperation amongst themselves and then, where possible, to appeal to extra-regional actors for support.

For example, in attempts to develop burden-sharing arrangements to overcome long-standing refugee situations – such as ICARA, CIREFCA, and the Indo-Chinese CPA – there has been an important regional dynamic. In the ICARA conferences of the 1980s, the OAU was an important actor;

in CIREFCA, the so-called Contadora Group of Central American states was an important actor; and in the CPA, ASEAN was an important actor (Betts 2008). These regional groups ensured cooperation within the region that enable those states to agree on how to agree to share responsibility within the region and a basis on which to approach the wider international community in search of additional support.

Policy harmonization

Formal regional integration has begun to occur in the area of asylum and immigration within the EU. In the context of attempts to develop a monetary and political union, states have tried to negotiate a common asylum policy, burden-sharing mechanisms, and a so-called external dimension to their asylum policies. The logic behind standardizing and harmonizing asylum policies has been driven by the recognition that, given the absence of internal borders within the Union and a common external border, one state's asylum policy decisions will affect other European states. Furthermore, if one state's asylum policies are more generous than that of another, it will risk attracting a disproportionately high proportion of asylum seekers. Having common standards reduces the risk that individual European states will competitively reduce their asylum standards and engage in a "race to the bottom" as they try to deter asylum applications.

At the moment, this type of policy harmonization is exclusive to the EU and there have not been attempts to develop common standards to the same extent anywhere else in the world. Attempts to negotiate common standards have been slow and arduous and there have been significant disagreements amongst European states about which standards should be adopted. Attempts to develop burden-sharing mechanisms within the EU have been particularly problematic and so burden-sharing mechanisms have remained limited (Thielemann 2003).

Informal dialogue

Beyond the formal level, a growing array of informal dialogues known as "Regional Consultative Processes" (RCPs) have emerged in the broad area of migration, many of which have implications for forced migration. Most RCPs are not transparent or politicized dialogues but take place behind closed doors among networks of civil servants. They represent what might be referred to as trans-governmental policy networks (Koehler 2008; Slaughter 2000). The first such RCP was the co-called Intergovernmental Consultations on Asylum, Refugee and Migration Policies in Europe, North America and

Australia (IGC), which came into existence in 1985. The IGC's aim was to facilitative behind-closed-doors dialogue among like-minded countries, which might or might not lead to more formal cooperation.

Since the IGC's inception, it has served as a model for the development of a range of similar processes throughout the world, some based on geographical regions and others, like the IGC, based on the participation of "like-minded" states. Of those that address forced migration, the so-called Bali Process emerged in 2000 in order to develop cooperation between Australia, New Zealand, and a number of states in Asia to combat human trafficking and smuggling. Meanwhile, many other such as the Mediterranean "five-plus-five" dialogue and the Budapest Process have focused on irregular migration and thereby had significant implications for access to spontaneous-arrival asylum (Nielsen 2007).

Coalitional bargaining

In multilateral debates on forced migration, states rarely engage in bargaining in isolation. Rather, they tend to form coalitions to strengthen their bargaining power. Sometimes these coalitions are issue-specific; in other cases the coalitions endure across debates on a range of issues. For example, in the 1970s and 1980s, the developing-country coalitions of the Non-Aligned Movement (NAM) and the G77 played an important and visible role in the UN General Assembly.

In the context of humanitarian debates in the UN, a number of core coalitions are particularly important for understanding the collective positions of states. In UNHCR's annual Executive Committee discussions, for example, voting and arguing often divide into regional groups. The African Group, the Arab League, the Group of Latin American Countries (GRULAC), and the EU, for example, frequently speak with a united voice.

Having identified these five forms of regional cooperation in the area of forced migration, the challenge is to explain why regional cooperation has taken place, and to explain variation in terms of where we do and do not see regional cooperation in this area. While the theories described above focus on explaining overall regional cooperation, the challenge in explaining regional cooperation on forced migration is a slightly different one. It focuses on trying to explain regional cooperation in one specific issue-area, which is, of course, linked to and influenced by broader cooperation in other issue-areas. Nevertheless, the theories of regional cooperation and integration offer a useful starting point for exploring the reasons for regional cooperation on forced migration. The two case studies therefore attempt to explore the relevance of the theories of regionalism for explaining regional cooperation on forced migration.

Case Study 1: The Harmonization of EU Asylum and Immigration Policy

The EU is the only region in the world that has attempted to develop a common asylum and immigration policy, which includes common minimum standards on asylum, limited burden-sharing mechanisms, and an "external dimension" to asylum policy. There is a common underlying logic behind this integration: the internal market (Guild 2006). The creation of a free-trade area led to acknowledgment that the free movement of labor within the EU was necessary for an efficient market. The creation of free movement within the EU and a common external border in turn led to acknowledgment of the need for common asylum and immigration standards, given the significant extent of externalities that resulted from one state's decisions in relation to asylum and immigration policy. Without standardization in this area, one state's decision to admit an individual would be a decision to admit to the entire EU. Furthermore, no state would have any incentive to maintain high asylum standards for fear of attracting a disproportionately high number of asylum applications.

This logic of moving from internal market to common asylum and immigration policy can be traced historically to examine how the two are related. The EU integration process has evolved through a series of intergovernmental treaties and the evolution of concern with asylum and immigration can be seen within the main treaties and summits that have taken place since the late 1980s.

The Single European Act (SEA) of 1986 focused on completing the Union as a free-trade area. It set out the short-term goal of abolishing intra-EU state borders by 1992, allowing the free movement of goods, persons, and capital. Building on the SEA, the Schengen Implementing Agreement and Dublin Agreements of the early 1990s created free movement within the so-called Schengen zone of Schengen Agreement signatory states. Consequently, by the early 1990s, the EU had significant amounts of internal free movement and a common external border.

Given the shift toward freedom of movement within the EU, a new focus on justice and home affairs emerged in the 1990s. The Maastricht Treaty of 1992 bought into existence three "pillars" of the EU's work, the third of which was Justice and Home Affairs (JHA). This new focus stemmed from the acknowledgment that, once intra-EU freedom of movement existed, there was a need for common responses to many of the challenges and consequences of free movement and a common border – including on policing, border security, and asylum and immigration.

The Amsterdam Treaty of 1997 was the first to focus on developing common standards for asylum and immigration. It led, in particular, to the entry into force of the Dublin Convention, which established the notion of the "safe third country principle" as a basis for assigning responsibility for assessing asylum claims within Europe. Dublin's focus was on the idea that asylum seekers should claim asylum in the first safe country that they reach and should not be entitled to engage in "asylum shopping" on their own terms. Hence Dublin empowered asylum-receiving states to send asylum seekers back to another Dublin signatory state in the event that they had already passed through that country en route.

Building upon the Amsterdam Treaty, a number of successive treaties began to develop the details of a common asylum and immigration policy. The Tampere Summit of 1999 focused specifically on asylum, calling for the development of common minimum standards of asylum and for "mutual recognition" of other states' asylum decisions. The Seville Summit of 2002 set out the basis of developing an external dimension to the EU's asylum and immigration policy. It recognized the need to engage in partnerships with third countries, especially in Europe's border regions, in order to effectively "manage" asylum and immigration. The EU's subsequent focus on asylum has therefore been in trying to establish minimum common asylum standards within the EU and the basis for partnerships with third countries outside the EU. The European Council directive on asylum procedures in 2004 went a long way toward establishing common standards, while in 2005, Europe created its own border agency, Frontex, to manage its common external border.

While the EU has managed to develop common minimum standards in relation to asylum legislation, it has struggled to agree on the basis for a burden-sharing framework. Indeed, some European states, notably those that border the Mediterranean, have received a disproportionately high proportion of Europe's refugees and asylum seekers. In this context, they have appealed to northern European states to share responsibility, whether through financial transfers or resettlement. Yet, despite establishing a nominal "European Refugee Fund," there has been very little agreement on what form an EU burden-sharing initiative would take (Thielemann 2003).

The question then is: how can theories of regional integration shed light on the process of European integration in the area of asylum and immigration? The different theories shed light on different elements of the integration process. *Neo-functionalism* would explain the process in terms of technocratic spill-over from one issue-area to another. It would see the process as being led by the logic of creating an internal market and spilling over into a justification of ever-deeper integration in other areas. *Intergovernmentalism* sheds light on the inter-state bargaining and the dynamic of negotiations at the specific summits such as Maastricht, Amsterdam, Tampere, and Seville. At each of these conferences, it might highlight the role of issue-linkages and side payments across issue-areas as facilitating interest-convergence on the area of asylum and immigration. *Supranationalism* highlights the role of supra-state authority. Indeed, the European Commission has played an important role. Its Directorate-General for Justice and Home Affairs has produced a range of White Papers that have shaped the European debate on asylum and immigration and the framework within which cooperation has taken place.

All of the theories have something to offer in identifying different factors that have contributed to integration. However, in terms of explaining how the overall internal market agenda led to a common asylum policy, neo-functionalism arguably provides the best explanation. Indeed, it demonstrates how integration on asylum has been driven by economic integration. Once a common logic of free movement of goods, services, and capital was accepted, this led to the logic of freedom of movement for people within the EU. This in turn led to the need to manage a common external border, which in turn necessitated common asylum standards within Europe and a common external dimension to asylum policy.

On the other hand, explaining why there has been limited progress in some areas of the integration process requires different explanations. The development of common standards has been time-consuming and remains incomplete. Mattli's (1999) notion of the Coordination Dilemma is useful for explaining some of the core challenges to developing common standards. Indeed, in the absence of a clear hegemon able to provide leadership and persuade other member states to adopt its standards, and given the controversy of the issue in domestic politics, it has been challenging to agree on which standards to adopt for the common framework. In terms of the lack of progress on burden-sharing, the problem has again been a different one, being the classic Prisoner's Dilemma problem, in which some states have simply had little incentive to engage in burden-sharing given the option of free-riding on other European states' provision of asylum.

Case Study 2: Regional Consultative Processes

RCPs are an increasingly important aspect of regionalism within the area of human mobility. They have a very different rationale in comparison to cooperation within the EU. They are informal, entirely state-led, and issue-area specific. Although they are sometimes linked to broader regional groups, they are generally stand-alone processes that focus on migration and sometimes address aspects of forced migration in the broader migration context (Koehler 2008; Nielsen 2007; Thouez and Channac 2005).

RCPs are diverse. The IGC emerged in 1985 with an initial focus mainly of addressing spontaneous-arrival asylum from developing to developed countries. The Regional Consultative Mechanism (RCM), which is often referred to as the "Puebla Process," was created in 1996 by 11 governments in North and Central America to explore avenues for cooperation in relation to migration management. The Bali Process was created in 2000 with a particular focus on human trafficking and smuggling from Asia to Australia. In Africa, the Migration Dialogue for Southern Africa (MIDSA) and the Migration Dialogue for West Africa (MIDWA) were both created in 2000, the former being based on SADC and COMESA countries and the latter on ECOWAS countries. Others include the Budapest Process, the Abu Dhabi Process, and the Colombo Process (Nielsen 2007). Some RCPs are not necessarily based on geographical "regions" but on inter-regional dialogue or on groups of "likeminded states."

The main focus of the RCPs has generally been on irregular migration but many have touched on forced migration either directly – in the case of the IGC or the Bali Process – or indirectly through the implications controlling irregular migration has for access to spontaneous arrival asylum. Indirectly, the RCPs have created a venue for dialogue and cooperation that has offered many states a means of bypassing formal multilateral processes and instead choosing to work through these less transparent and more exclusive forums.

The RCPs are not captured by theories of regionalism and regional integration. They represent a very different process compared to formal regional cooperation. They are informal, issue-area specific, not always geographical. Perhaps most importantly, they can be seen not so much as "regional cooperation" in themselves but as trans-national policy networks that may sometimes lead to new forms of bilateral, regional, or inter-regional cooperation. The notion of a trans-governmental policy network describes a linked cluster of civil servants who relate to one another in a technical and de-politicized environment. Rather than being public, politicized and involving elected representatives, RCPs generally involve technocrats speaking behind closed doors (Keohane and Nye 1974; Slaughter 2000).

This growing mechanism for international cooperation is not captured by theories of regionalism and regional integration. The informal, depoliticized, and state-led characteristics of RCPs make them analytically distinct. RCPs therefore require an understanding not of formal regional cooperation but of trans-governmental policy networks, for which there is so far an absence of theory.

Conclusion

The region is an important level of analysis in world politics. Regional cooperation in relation to forced migration has taken place in five areas, highlighted by the typology in this chapter: common legal frameworks, ad hoc cooperation, policy harmonization, informal dialogue, and coalitional bargaining. The theories of regional cooperation help to explain why regional cooperation takes place and why there is variation in success and failure across regions. This chapter has applied those theories to a slightly different context: regional cooperation in a particular issue-area. Nevertheless, the theories offer a useful starting point for explaining why cooperation in relation to forced migration has taken place on a regional level and what has driven that regional cooperation.

The most developed regional cooperation is in the EU, which has begun to develop a common asylum and immigration policy with both internal and external dimensions. Theories of regional integration usefully highlight the factors that have driven this process and also its limitations. Each of the main theories of integration shed light on different factors underlying the process. Neo-functionalism highlights the role that cooperation in other areas has played in creating a technocratic logic for cooperation on asylum. Intergovernmentalism highlights the processes of negotiation that have taken place at inter-state meetings such as the Tampere and Seville Summits. Supranationalism highlights the important role of the European Commission in driving the process.

Overall, the harmonization of asylum and immigration policy in the EU has been led by other issue-areas. In particular, it has been driven by the logic of the internal market. Neo-functionalism's account to functional spillover highlights how cooperation in one area has created an impetus toward cooperation in relation to other areas such as asylum policy. However, in practice, cooperation has remained weak. The weaknesses can be partly explained by the Coordination Dilemma described by Mattli, whereby it has been difficult to agree on which common asylum standards to adopt. In the absence of decisive leadership at regional and national levels, decisions on coordination have stalled.

New forms of regional cooperation are rapidly emerging in the broad area of migration, which have implications for issues such as access to asylum, human trafficking and smuggling, and the re-admission and return of asylum seekers. The so-called RCPs have a different logic from formal regional governance. They represent issue-area specific and informal transgovernmental policy networks. These types of cooperation are not adequately explained by existing theories of regionalism and regional integration, which focus mainly on formal regional organizations and geographical regionalism. The characteristics of RCPs require an alternative conceptual framework in contrast to formal regional organization. Nevertheless, they highlight the centrality of regional cooperation to forced migration. In future, regions are likely to become increasingly important in world politics in general and forced migration in particular. In forced migration, as in many other issue-areas, states are increasingly bypassing the global, multilateral level in favor of not only formal regional cooperation but also informal mechanisms of regional dialogue.

Bibliography

Abbott, K. W., R. O. Keohane, A. Moravcsik, A.-M. Slaughter, and D. Snidal (2001). The Concept of Legalization. In J. Goldstein, M. Kahler, R. O. Keohane, and A.-M. Slaughter (eds.), *Legalization and World Politics*, pp. 17–36. Cambridge, MA: MIT Press.

Abbot, K. W., and D. Snidal (1998). Why States Act Through Formal International Organizations. *Journal of Conflict Resolution* 42 (1): 3–32.

Abdullah, I. (1998). Bush Path to Destruction: The Origin and Character of the Revolutionary United Front/Sierra Leone. *The Journal of Modern African Studies*, 36: 203–35.

Adorno, T., and T. W. Horkheimer (1972). *Dialectic of Enlightenment*. New York: Herder and Herder.

Aggarwal, V. (1998). Reconciling Multiple Institutions: Bargaining, Linkages, and Nesting. In V. Aggarwal (ed.), *Institutional Designs for a Complex World*. Ithaca, NY: Cornell University Press.

Alderson, K., and A. Hurrell (eds.) (2000). *Hedley Bull on International Society*. London: Palgrave Macmillan.

Alter, K., and S. Meunier (2009). The Politics of International Regime Complexity. *Perspectives on Politics*, 7(1): 13–24.

Anderson, B. (1983). *Imagined -Communities: Reflections on the Origin and Spread of Nationalism*. London: Verso.

Angell, N. (1910). *The Great Illusion: A Study of the Relation of Military Power to National Advantage*. London: Heinemann.

Axelrod, R. (1984). *The Evolution of Cooperation*. New York: Basic Books.

Ayoob, M. (1995). *The Third World Security Predicament: State Making, Regional Conflict and the International System*. London: Lynne Rienner Publishers.

Bache, I., and M. Flinders (eds.) (2005). *Multi-Level Governance*. Oxford: Oxford University Press.

Bagshaw, S. (2005). *Developing a Normative Framework for the Protection of Internally Displaced Persons*. New York: Transnational Publishers.

Barnett, M. N., and R. Duvall (eds.) (2005). *Power in Global Governance*. Cambridge: Cambridge University Press.

Barnett, M. N., and M. Finnemore (1999). The Politics, Power, and Pathologies of International Organizations. *International Organization*, 699–732.

Barnett, M., and M. Finnemore (2004). *Rules for the World: International Organizations in Global Politics*. New York: Cornell University Press.

Barnett, M., and T. Weiss (eds.) (2008). *Humanitarianism in Question: Politics, Power, Ethics*. Ithaca, NY: Cornell University Press.

Barrett, S. (2007). *Why Cooperate? The Incentive to Supply Global Public Goods*. Oxford: Oxford University Press.

Barutciski, M. (2002). A Critical View on UNHCR's Mandate Dilemmas. *International Journal of Refugee Law* 14 (2/3): 365–81.

Barutciski, M. (2006). International Law and Development-Induced Displacement/ Resettlement, in Chris de Wet (ed.), *Development-Induced Displacement and Resettlement*, pp. 71–104. Oxford: Berghahn.

Barutciski, M., and A. Suhrke (2001). Lessons from the Kosovo Refugee Crisis: Innovations in Protection and Burden-sharing. *Journal of Refugee Studies* 14 (2): 95–134.

Bauman, Z. (1998). *Globalization: The Human Consequences*. Cambridge: Polity Press.

Beck, U. (1999). *What is Globalization?* Cambridge: Polity Press.

Beitz, C. R. (1989). *Political Equality: An Essay in Democratic Theory*. Princeton, NJ: Princeton University Press.

Bellamy, A. J. (2008). Conflict Prevention and the Responsibility to Protect. *Global Governance* 14 (2): 135–56.

Bellamy, A. J. (2009). *Responsibility to Protect*. Cambridge: Polity Press.

Betts, A. (2003). Public Goods Theory and the Provision of Refugee Protection: The Role of the Joint-Product Model in Burden-Sharing Theory. *Journal of Refugee Studies* 16 (3): 274–96.

Betts, A. (2005). *International Cooperation Between North and South to Enhance Refugee Protection in Regions of Origin*. Refugee Studies Centre Working Paper 25. Oxford: RSC.

Betts, A. (2006). What Does "Efficiency" Mean in the Context of the Global Refugee Regime? *British Journal of Politics and International Relations* 8 (2): 148–73.

Betts, A. (2008). North–South Relations in the Global Refugee Regime: The Role of Linkages. *Global Governance* 14 (2): 157–78.

Betts, A., and J.-F. Durieux (2007). Convention Plus as a Norm-Setting Exercise. *Journal of Refugee Studies* 20 (3): 509–35.

Betts, A., and J. Milner (2006). *The Externalisation of EU Asylum Policy: The Position of African States*. Oxford: COMPAS Working Paper WP-06-35.

Betts, A., and A. Schmidt (2009). Regimes as Practice: International Institutions and Refugee Protection. Unpublished Paper.

Beyani, C. (2006). Recent Developments. The Elaboration of a Legal Framework for the Protection of Internally Displaced Persons in Africa. *Journal of African Law* 50 (2): 187–97.

Biersteker, T. J., and C. Weber (eds.) (1996). *State Sovereignty as Social Construct*. Cambridge: Cambridge University Press.

Booth, K. (1991). Security and Emancipation. *Review of International Studies* 17 (4): 123–36.

Booth, K. (1997). Security and Self: Reflections of a Fallen Realist. In K. Krause, and M. C. Williams (eds.), *Critical Security Studies: Concepts and Cases*, pp. 83–120. London: Routledge.

Booth, K. (ed.) (2004). *Critical Security Studies and World Politics*. Boulder, CO: Lynne Rienner Publishers.

Bradley, M. (2008). *Principle and Pragmatism in Protection: ICRC, UNHCR and R2P in Darfur*. Oxford University, Refugee Studies Centre. Unpublished dissertation.

Buchanan, A., and R. O. Keohane (2006). The Legitimacy of Global Governance Institutions. *Ethics and International Affairs* 20 (4): 405–37.

Bull, H. (1977). *The Anarchical Society: A Study of Order in World Politics*. London: Palgrave Macmillan.

Bull, H., and A. Watson (1984). *The Expansion of International Society*. Oxford: Clarendon Press.

Busch, M. L. (2007). Overlapping Institutions, Forum Shopping, and Dispute Settlement in International Trade. *International Organization* 61: 735–61.

Buzan, B. (1991). *People, States and Fear: An Agenda for International Security Studies in the Post-Cold War Era* (2nd edn.). Boulder, CO: Lynne Rienner Publishers.

Buzan, B., O. Waever, and J. de Wilde (eds.) (1998). *Security: A New Framework for Analysis*. Boulder, CO: Lynne Rienner Publishers.

Byrne, R. (2003). Harmonization and Burden Redistribution in the Two Europes. *Journal of Refugee Studies* 16 (3): 336–58.

Calleo, D. P. (1987). *Beyond American Hegemony: The Future of the Western Alliance*. New York: Basic Books.

Caporaso, J. (1998). Regional Integration Theory: Understanding Our Past and Anticipating Our Future. *Journal of European Public Policy* 5 (1): 1–16.

Cardoso, F. H., and E. Faletto (1979). *Dependency and Development in Latin America*. Berkeley: University of California Press.

Carr, E. H. (1946). *The Twenty Years' Crisis, 1919–1939: An Introduction to the Study of International Relations*. (2nd edn.). London: Macmillan.

Castells, M. (1996). *The Rise of the Network Society, The Information Age: Economy, Society and Culture Vol. I*. Oxford: Blackwell.

Castles, S. (2002). Migration und Community Formation under Conditions of Globalization. *International Migration Review* 36 (4): 1143–68.

Castles, S. (2003). The International Politics of Forced Migration. *Development* 46: 11–20.

Castles, S., and N. Van Hear (2005). *Developing DFID's Policy Approach to Refugees and Internally Displaced Persons: A Research Consultancy by the Refugee Studies Centre for the Conflict and Humanitarian Affairs Department, Department For International Development – UK*. Oxford: Refugee Studies Centre.

Castles, S., and R. D. Wise (eds.) (2008). *Migration and Development: Perspectives from the South*. Geneva: International Organization for Migration.

Cernea, M. (2000). Risks, Safeguards, and Reconstruction: A Model for Population Displacement and Resettlement. In M. Cernea and C. McDowell (eds.), *Risks and Reconstruction: Experiences of Resettlers and Refugees*, pp. 11–55. Washington DC: World Bank.

Cernea, M. (1997). The Risks and Reconstruction Model for Resettling Displaced Populations. *World Development* 25 (10): 1569–87.

Chayes, A., and A. Chayes (1996). *The New Sovereignty: Compliance with International Regulatory Agreements*. London: Harvard University Press.

Checkel, J. T. (1999). Norms, Institutions and National Identity in Contemporary Europe. *International Studies Quarterly* 43 (1).

Chimni, B. (1998). The Geopolitics of Refugee Studies: A View from the South. *Journal of Refugee Studies* 11 (4): 350–74.

Chomsky, N. (1999). *The New Military Humanism: Lessons from Kosovo*. London: Pluto Press.

Clapham, C. (1996). *Africa and the International System: The Politics of State Survival*. Cambridge: Cambridge University Press.

Collier, P. (2007). *The Bottom Billion: Why the Poorest Countries Are Failing and What Can Be Done About it*. Oxford: Oxford University Press.

Collier, P., and A. Hoeffler (1998). On the Economic Causes of Civil Wars. *Oxford Economic Papers* 50 (4): 563–73.

Collinson, S. (2003). *Power, Livelihoods and Conflict: Case Studies in Political Economy Analysis for Humanitarian Action*. London: Overseas Development Institute.

Commission on Global Governance (1995). *Our Global Neighbourhood*. Oxford: Oxford University Press.

Conybeare, J. (1984). Public Goods, Prisoner's Dilemma and the International Political Economy. *International Studies Quarterly* 28: 5–22.

Cox, R. W. (1981). Social Forces, States and World Orders: Beyond International Relations Theory. *Millennium: Journal of International Studies* 10 (2): 126–55.

Crawford, N. C. (2002). *Argument and Change in World Politics: Ethics, Decolonization, and Humanitarian Intervention*. Cambridge: Cambridge University Press.

Crisp, J. (2003). A New Asylum Paradigm? Globalization, Migration and the Uncertain Future of the International Refugee Regime. *New Issues in Refugee Research*, Working Paper No. 100. Geneva: UNHCR.

Crisp, J. (2008). *Beyond the Nexus: UNHCR's Evolving Perspective on Refugee Protection and International Migration*. Geneva: UNHCR Policy Development and Evaluation Service.

Cronin, B. (2003). *Institutions for the Common Good: International Protection Regimes in International Society*. Cambridge: Cambridge University Press.

Deere, C. (2008). *The Implementation Game: The TRIPS Agreement and the Global Politics of Intellectual Property Reform in Developing Countries*. Oxford: Oxford University Press.

Donnelly, J. (2000). *Realism and International Relations*. Cambridge: Cambridge University Press.

Doty, R. L. (1996). *Imperial Encounters: The Politics of Representation in North–South Relations*. Minneapolis: University of Minnesota Press.

Dowd, R. (2008). *Trapped in Transit: The Plight and Human Rights of Stranded Migrants*. New Issues in Refugee Research Paper No. 156, UNHCR.

Downs, G. W., D. M. Rocke, and P. N. Barsoom (1996). Is the Good News About Compliance Good News About Cooperation? *International Organization* 50 (3): 379–406.

Doyle, M. W. (1997). *Ways of War and Peace*. New York: W. W. Norton and Company.

Drezner, D. W. (2007). *All Politics Is Global: Explaining International Regulatory Regimes*. Princeton, NJ: Princeton University Press.

Dubernet, C. (2001). *The International Containment of Displaced Persons: Humanitarian Spaces Without Exit*. Aldershot: Ashgate Publishing.

Duffield, M. (2001). *Global Governance and the New Wars*. London: Zed Books.

Dumper, M. (2008). Palestinian Refugees. In G. Loescher et al. (eds.), *Protracted Refugee Situations: Political, Human Rights and Security Implications*, pp. 189–213. Tokyo: UNU Press.

Dunne, T., and N. J. Wheeler (eds.) (1999). *Human Rights in Global Politics*. Cambridge: Cambridge University Press.

Eagleton-Pierce, M. (2008). Unravelling the Received Idea of "Governance." Paper for Oxford/Sciences-Po Joint Doctoral Seminar "Regional and Global Institutions in the 21st Century," April 30–May 1, 2008. Oxford.

Faist, T. (2004). Towards a Political Sociology of Transnationalism. *European Journal of Sociology* 45 (3): 19–54.

Falkner, R. (2007). *Business Power and Conflict in International Environmental Politics*. Basingstoke: Palgrave Macmillan.

Fawcett, L. (1995). Regionalism in Historical Perspective. In L. Fawcett, and A. Hurrell (eds.), *Regionalism in World Politics: Regional Organization and International Order*, pp. 9–36. Oxford: Oxford University Press.

Fawcett, L., and A. Hurrell (eds.) (1995). *Regionalism in World Politics: Regional Organization and International Order*. Oxford: Oxford University Press.

Fawcett, L., and Y. Sayigh (2000). *The Third World beyond the Cold War: Continuity and Change*. Oxford: Oxford University Press.

Fearon, J., and D. Laitin (2003). Ethnicity, Insurgency, and Civil War. *American Political Science Review* 97 (1): 75–90.

Franck, T. M. (1990). *The Power of Legitimacy Among Nations*. Oxford: Oxford University Press.

Frank, A. G. (1969). *Capitalism and Underdevelopment in Latin America: Historical Studies of Chile and Brazil*. New York: Monthly Review Press.

Gamlen, A. (2008). *Why Engage Diasporas?* COMPAS Working Paper No.5, Oxford University, COMPAS.

Gibney, M. (2004). *The Politics and Ethics of Asylum: Liberal Democracy and the Response to Refugees*. Cambridge: Cambridge University Press.

Gibney, M. (2008). Asylum and the Expansion of Deportation in the United Kingdom. *Government and Opposition* 43 (2): 146–67.

Gilpin, R. (1975). *US Power and the Multinational Corporation: The Political Economy of Foreign Direct Investment*. New York: Basic Books.

Gilpin, R. (2001). *Global Political Economy: Understanding the International Economic Order*. Princeton, NJ: Princeton University Press.

Goldstein, J., M. Kahler, R. O. Keohane, and A.-M. Slaughter (eds.) (2001). *Legalization and World Politics*. Cambridge, MA: MIT Press.

Gong, G. W. (1984). *The Standard of "Civilization" in International Society*. Oxford: Oxford University Press.

Goodwin-Gill, G., and J. McAdam (2007). *The Refugee in International Law*. Oxford: Oxford University Press.

Gorman, R. F. (1986). Beyond ICARA II: Implementing Refugee-Related Development Assistance. *International Migration Review* 20 (2): 283–98.

Gorman, R. (1993). Linking Refugee Aid and Development in Africa, in Gorman, R. (ed), *Refugee Aid and Development: Theory and Practice*. London: Greenwood.

Gramsci, A. (1971). *Selections from the Prison Notebooks (1929–1935)*, trans. Q. Hoare and G. Nowell-Smith. New York: International Publishers.

Grieco, J. (1988). Anarchy and the Limits of Cooperation: A Realist Critique of the Newest Liberal Institutionalism. *International Organization* 42 (3): 485–507.

Guild, E. (2006). The Europeanisation of Europe's Asylum Policy. *International Journal of Refugee Law* 18 (3–4): 630–51.

Haas, E. B. (1958). *The Uniting of Europe: Political, Social, and Economic Forces, 1950–1957*. Stanford: Stanford University Press.

Haas, E. B. (1961). International Integration: The European and the Universal Process. *International Organization* 15 (3): 366–92.

Haas, E. B. (1980). Why Collaborate? Issue-Linkages and International Regimes. *World Politics* 32 (3): 357–405.

Haas, P. M. (1989). Do Regimes Matter? Epistemic Communities and Mediterranean Pollution Control. *International Organization* 43 (3): 377–403.

Habermas, J. (1993). *Justification and Application: Remarks on Discourse Ethics*. Cambridge, MA: MIT Press.

Haddad, E. (2008). *The Refugee: The Individual between Sovereigns*. Cambridge: Cambridge University Press.

Hafner-Burton, E. M. (2005). Forum Shopping for Human Rights: The Politics of Preferential Trade. Paper presented at APSA Annual Meeting, September 2005.

Hafner-Burton, E. M. (2009). *Forced to be Good: Why Trade Agreements Boost Human Rights*. Ithaca, NY: Cornell University Press.

Hall, R. B. (1997). Moral Authority as a Power Resource. *International Organization* 51(4): 591–622.

Hall, R. B., and T. J. Biersteker (2002). *The Emergence of Private Authority in Global Governance*. Cambridge: Cambridge University Press.

Hampshire, J. (2008). Disembedding Liberalism? Immigration Politics and Security in Britain since 9/11. In T. Givens, G. P. Freeman, and D. L. Leal, *Immigration Policy and Security: U.S., European, and Commonwealth Perspectives*. New York: Routledge.

Hasenclever, A., P. Mayer, and V. Rittberger (1997). *Theories of International Regimes*. Cambridge: Cambridge University Press.

Hathaway, J. C., and R. A. Neve (1997). Making International Refugee Law Relevant Again: A Proposal for Collectivized and Solution-Oriented Protection. *Harvard Human Rights Journal* 10.

Haufler, V. (2006). Global Governance and the Private Sector. In C. May (ed.), *Global Corporate Power*, pp. 95–105. Boulder, CO: Lynne Rienner Publishers.

Hawkins, D. G., D. A. Lake, and D. L. Nielson (eds.) (2006). *Delegation and Agency in International Organizations*. Cambridge: Cambridge University Press.

Held, D., and A. McGrew (eds.) (2002). *Governing Globalization: Power, Authority and Global Governance*. Cambridge: Polity Press.

Helfer, L. R. (2004). Regime Shifting: The TRIPs Agreement and New Dynamics of International Intellectual Property Lawmaking. *Yale Journal of International Law* 29.

Helton, A. C. (2002). *The Price of Indifference: Refugees and Humanitarian Action in the New Century*. Oxford: Oxford University Press.

Hinsley, F. H. (1966). *Sovereignty*. New York: Basic Books.

Hirst, P. Q., and G. F. Thompson (1999) *Globalization in Question: The International Economy and the Possibilities of Governance*. Cambridge: Polity Press.

Hobsbawm, E. J. (1990). *Nations and Nationalism since 1780: Programme, Myth, Reality*. Cambridge: Cambridge University Press.

Huntington, S. (1993). The Clash of Civilizations? *Foreign Affairs* 72 (Summer 1993): 22–49.

Hurrell, A. (1995). Regionalism in Theoretical Perspective. In L. Fawcett, and A. Hurrell (eds.), *Regionalism in World Politics: Regional Organization and International Order*, pp. 37–73. Oxford: Oxford University Press.

Hurrell, A. (2007). *On Global Order: Power, Values and the Constitution of International Society*. Oxford: Oxford University Press.

Hyndman, J. (2000). *Managing Displacement: Refugees and the Politics of Humanitarianism*. Minneapolis: Minnesota University Press.

Inayatullah, N. (1996). Beyond the Sovereignty Dilemma: Quasi-States as Social Construct. In C. Weber, and T. J. Biersteker, *State Sovereignty as Social Construct*, pp. 50–80. Cambridge: Cambridge University Press.

Jackson, R. J. (1990). *Quasi-States: Sovereignty, International Relations and the Third World*. Cambridge: Cambridge University Press.

Juma, M. K., and P. M. Kagwanja (2008). Somali Refugees: Protracted Exile and Shifting Security Frontiers. In G. Loescher, and J. Milner (eds.), *The Politics, Human Rights and Security Dimensions of Protracted Refugee Situations*. Tokyo: United Nations University Press and Brookings Institute Press.

Jupille, J., M. Mattli, and D. Snidal (2008). Explaining Institutional Choice in Trade. Paper presented at the Global Economic Governance Programme, University of Oxford, 25 April.

Kaldor, M. (1999). *New and Old Wars: Organized Violence in a Global Era*. Cambridge: Polity Press.

Kant, I. (1795). Perpetual Peace: A Philosophical Sketch.

Kaplan, R. D. (1993). *Balkan Ghosts: A Journey Through History*. New York: St Martin's Press.

Karns, M. P., and K. A. Mingst (2004). *International Organizations: The Politics and Processes of Global Governance*. London: Lynne Rienner Publishers.

Kaul, I., I. Grunberg, and M. Stern (eds.) (1999). *Global Public Goods: International Cooperation in the 21st Century*. Oxford: Oxford University Press.

Keck, M. E., and K. Sikkink (1998). *Activists Beyond Borders: Advocacy Networks in International Politics*. Ithaca: Cornell University Press.

Keen, D. (2000). Incentives and Disincentives for Violence. In M. Berdal, and M. Malone (eds.), *Greed and Grievance: Economic Agendas in Civil Wars*. London: Lynne Rienner Publishers.

Keen, D. (2001). The Political Economy of War. In V. F. F. Stewart, and Associates (eds.), *War and Underdevelopment: Volume 1*. Oxford: Oxford University Press.

Keene, E. (2002). *Beyond the Anarchical Society: Grotius, Colonialism and Order in World Politics*. Cambridge: Cambridge University Press.

Keohane, R. O. (1982). The Demand for International Regimes. *International Organization* 36 (2): 325–55.

Keohane, R. (1984). *After Hegemony: Cooperation and Discord in the World Political Economy*. New Jersey: Princeton University Press.

Keohane, R. O. (1989). *International Institutions And State Power: Essays In International Relations Theory*. Boulder: Westview Press.

Keohane, R. O., and J. S. Nye (1974). Transgovernmental Relations and the International Organisations. *World Politics* 26 (1): 39–62.

Khagram, S. (2004). *Dams and Development: Transnational Struggles for Water and Power*. Ithaca: Cornell University Press.

Kindleberger, C. P. (1973). *The World in Depression 1929–1939*. London: Penguin Press.

Kingsbury, B. (2007). International Public Law: What is the Public and What Does Law Seek to Govern? Governing the Globe Lecture Series, Oxford.

Koehler, J. (2008). What States Do and How They Organize Themselves in Regional Consultative Processes (RCPS). Paper presented at workshop on "Migration and International Cooperation," 7–8 August 2008, IOM Headquarters, Geneva.

Koh, H. H. (1997). Why Do Nations Obey International Law? *Yale Law Journal* 106 (8): 2599–659.

Koremenos, B., C. Lipson, and D. Snidal (eds.) (2003). *The Rational Design of International Institutions*. Cambridge: Cambridge University Press.

Krasner, S. D. (1983). Structural Causes and Regime Consequences: Regimes as Intervening Variables. In S. D. Krasner, *International Regimes*, pp. 1–21. New York: Cornell University Press.

Krasner, S. D. (1985). *Structural Conflict: The Third World Against Global Liberalism*. Berkeley: University of California Press.

Krasner, S. D. (1999). *Sovereignty: Organized Hypocrisy*. Princeton, NJ: Princeton University Press.

Krause, K., and M. C. Williams (eds.) (1997). *Critical Security Studies: Concepts and Cases*. London: Routledge.

Lavenex, S. (1999). *Safe Third Countries: Extending the EU Asylum and Immigration Policies to Central and Eastern Europe*. New York: Central European University Press.

Lindley, A. (2007). *The Early Morning Phonecall: Remittances from a Refugee Diaspora*. COMPAS Working Paper No. 47, Oxford University, COMPAS.

Linklater, A. (1982). *Men and Citizens in the Theory of International Relations*. London: Macmillan.

Linklater, A. (1998). *The Transformation of Political Community: Ethical Foundations of the Post-Westphalian Era*. Cambridge: Polity Press.

Linklater, A., and H. Suganami (2002). *The English School of International Relations: A Contemporary Reassessment*. Cambridge: Cambridge University Press.

Lischer, S. K. (2005). *Dangerous Sanctuaries: Refugee Camps, Civil War, and the Dilemmas of Humanitarian Aid*. Ithaca: Cornell University Press.

Loescher, G. (1993). *Beyond Charity: International Cooperation and the Global Refugee Crisis*. Oxford: Oxford University Press.

Loescher, G. (2001). *The UNHCR and World Politics: A Perilous Path*. Oxford: Oxford University Press.

Loescher, G. (2003). Refugees as Grounds for International Action. In E. Newman, and J. van Selm (eds.), *Refugees and Forced Displacement: International Security, Human Vulnerability, and the State*, pp. 31–49. Tokyo: United Nations University Press.

Loescher, G., A. Betts, and J. Milner (2008). *UNHCR: The Politics and Practice of Refugee Protection into the Twenty-First Century*. Abingdon: Routledge.

Loescher, G., and J. Milner (2005). *Protracted Refugee Situations: Domestic and International Security Implications*. Abingdon: Routledge (Adelphi Paper).

MacFarlane, S. N., and Y. F. Khong (2006). *Human Security and the UN: A Critical History*. Bloomington: Indiana University Press.

Malkki, L. H. (1995). Refugees and Exile: From "Refugee Studies" to the National Order of Things. *Annual Review of Anthropology* 24: 495–523.

Mamdani, M. (2001). *When Victims Become Killers: Colonialism, Nativism and the Genocide in Rwanda*. Princeton: Princeton University Press.

Mann, M. (2005). *The Dark Side of Democracy: Explaining Ethnic Cleansing*. Cambridge: Cambridge University Press.

Mansfield, E. D., and J. L. Snyder (2005). *Electing to Fight: Why Emerging Democracies Go to War*. Cambridge, MA: MIT Press.

Mares, P. (2003). Distance Makes the Heart Grow Fonder: Media Images of Refugees and Asylum Seekers. In E. Newman, and J. van Selm, *Refugees and Forced Displacement: International Security, Human Vulnerability, and the State*, pp. 330–49. Tokyo: United Nations University Press.

Marfleet, P. (2006). *Refugees in a Global Era*. London: Palgrave Macmillan.

Martin, L. (1993). The Rational State Choice of Multilateralism. In J. Ruggie (ed.), *Multilateralism Matters: The Theory and Praxis of an Institutional Form*, pp. 91–121. New York: Columbia University Press.

Mattli, W. (1999). *The Logic of Regional Integration: Europe and Beyond*. Cambridge: Cambridge University Press.

Mattli, W. (2003). Public and Private Governance in Setting International Standards. In M. Kahler, and D. A. Lake (eds.), *Governance in a Global Economy: Political Authority in Transition*, pp. 199–225. Princeton, NJ: Princeton University Press.

Mattli, W., and T. Buthe (2003). Setting International Standards: Technological Rationality or Primacy of Power? *World Politics* 56 (1): 1–42.

McAdam, J. (2007). *Complementary Protection in International Refugee Law*. Oxford: Oxford University Press.

McKittrick, A. (2008). *UNHCR as an Autonomous Organization: Complex Operations and the Case of Kosovo*. RSC Working Paper, Oxford University, Refugee Studies Centre.

Mearsheimer, J. J. (1995). The False Promise of International Institutions. *International Security* 19 (3): 5–49.

Mearsheimer, J. J. (2001). *The Tragedy of Great Power Politics*. New York: W. W. Norton and Company.

Milner, H. V. (1992). International Theories of Cooperation Among Nations: Strengths and Weaknesses. *World Politics* 44 (3).

Milner, J. (2000). *Sharing the Security Burden: Towards the Convergence of Refugee Protection and State Security*. RSC Working Paper No. 4, Oxford University, Refugee Studies Centre.

Milner, J. (2009). *Refugees, the State and the Politics of Asylum in Africa*. Basingstoke: Palgrave Macmillan.

Mitrany, D. (1966). *A Working Peace System*. Chicago: Quadrangle Books.

Moravcsik, A. (1993). Preferences and Power in the European Community: A Liberal Intergovernmentalist Approach. *Journal of Common Market Studies* 31 (4): 473–523.

Moravcsik, A. (1997). Taking Preferences Seriously: A Liberal Theory of International Politics. *International Organization* 51 (4): 513–53.

Morgenthau, H. (1948). *Politics Among Nations: The Struggle for Power and Peace*. New York: Alfred A Knopf.

Moro, L. N. (2006). Oil, War and Forced Migration in Sudan. *St Antony's International Review* 2 (1): 75–90.

Morris, E., and S. J. Stedman (2008). Protracted Refugee Situations, Conflict and Security: The Need for Better Diagnosis and Prescription. In G. Loescher, and J. Milner (eds.), *The Politics, Human Rights and Security Dimensions of Protracted Refugee Situations*. Tokyo: United Nations University Press and Brookings Institute Press.

Myers, N. (1997). Environmental Refugees. *Population and Environment* 19 (2): 167–82.

Newman, E. (2003). Refugees, International Security, and Human Vulnerability: Introduction and Survey. In E. Newman, and J. van Selm, *Refugees and Forced Displacement: International Security, Human Vulnerability, and the State*, pp. 3–30. Tokyo: United Nations University Press.

Newman, E., and J. van Selm (eds.) (2003). *Refugees and Forced Displacement: International Security, Human Vulnerability, and the State*. Tokyo: United Nations University Press.

Nielsen, A.-G. (2007). Cooperation Mechanisms. In R. Cholewinski, R. Perruchoud, and E. Macdonald (eds.), *International Migration Law: Developing Paradigms and Key Challenges*, pp. 405–26. Cambridge: Cambridge University Press.

Noll, G. (2003). Visions of the Exceptional: Legal and Theoretical Issues Raised by Transit Processing Centres and Protection Zones. *European Journal of Migration and Law* 5: 303–41.

Nye, J. S. (2008). *The Powers to Lead*. New York: Oxford University Press.

Nyers, P. (2006). *Rethinking Refugees: Beyond States of Emergency*. Abingdon: Routledge.

Ohmae, K. (2005). *The Next Global Stage: The Challenges and Opportunities in Our Borderless World*. New Jersey: Wharton School Publishing.

Olson, M. (1965). *The Logic of Collective Action: Public Goods and the Theory of Groups*. London: Harvard University Press.

Olson, M., and R. Zeckhauser (1967). Collective Goods, Comparative Advantage and Alliance Efficiency. In R. McLean, *Issues of Defence Economics*. New York: NBER.

Österud, Ö. (1997). The Narrow Gate: Entry to the Club of Sovereign States. *Review of International Studies* 23: 167–84.

Paris, R. (2001). Human Security: Paradigm Shift or Hot Air? *International Security* 26 (2): 87–102.

Phuong, C. (2004). *The International Protection of Internally Displaced Persons*. Cambridge: Cambridge University Press.

Piguet, E. (2008). *Climate Change and Forced Migration*. New Issues in Refugee Research – Research Paper No. 153, UNHCR, Policy Development and Evaluation Service.

Pogge, T. (2002). *World Poverty and Human Rights: Cosmopolitan Responsibilities and Reforms*. Cambridge: Polity Press.

Poku, N. K., and D. Graham (eds.) (2000). *Migration, Globalisation and Human Security*. London: Routledge.

Power, S. (2008). *Chasing the Flame: Sergio Vieira de Mello and the Fight to Save the World*. London: Penguin.

Prebisch, R. (1950). *The Economic Development of Latin America and Its Principal Problems*. New York: United Nations.

Prosser, B. (2008). Exploring the Solution of Internal Relocation Through an Examination of the Recent UK Case, AH and Others. Presentation at 5th Students Forced Migration Conference, Oxford University.

Putnam, R. D. (1988). Diplomacy and Domestic Politics: The Logic of Two-Level Games. *International Organization* 42: 427–60.

Raustiala, K., and A.-M. Slaughter (2002). International Law, International Relations and Compliance. In W. Carlsnaes, T. Risse, and B. A. Simmons (eds.), *The Handbook of International Relations*, pp. 538–58. London: Sage Publications.

Raustiala, K., and D. G. Victor (2004). The Regime Complex for Plant Genetic Resources. *International Organization* 58: 277–309.

Rawls, J. (1971). *A Theory of Justice.* Cambridge, MA: Harvard University Press.

Reno, W. (1999). *Warlord Politics and African States.* Boulder, CO: Lynne Rienner Publishers.

Reus-Smit, C. (2001). Human Rights and the Social Construction of Sovereignty. *Review of International Studies* 27: 519–38.

Reuveny, R., and Q. Li (2003). Economic Openness, Democracy, and Income Inequality: An Empirical Analysis. *Comparative Political Studies* 36 (5): 575–601.

Richards, P. (1996). *Fighting for the Rain Forest: War, Youth and Resources in Sierra Leone.* Oxford: James Currey Ltd.

Rieff, D. (2002). *A Bed for the Night: Humanitarianism in Crisis.* London: Vintage.

Risse, T. (2004). Global Governance and Communicative Action. *Government and Opposition* 39 (2): 288–313.

Risse, T., S. C. Ropp, and K. Sikkink (eds.) (1999). *The Power of Human Rights: International Norms and Domestic Change.* Cambridge: Cambridge University Press.

Rittberger, V., and B. Zangl (2006). *International Organization, Polity, Politics and Policies.* New York: Palgrave Macmillan.

Roberts, A. (1998). More Refugees, Less Asylum: A Regime in Transformation. *Journal of Refugee Studies* 11 (4): 375–95.

Robinson, W. C. (1998). *Terms of Refuge: The Indochinese Exodus and the International Response.* London: Zed Books.

Robinson, W. C. (2004). The Comprehensive Plan of Action for Indo-Chinese Refugees, 1989–1997. *Journal of Refugee Studies* 17 (3): 319–33.

Rosenau, J. (1992). Government, Order and Change in World Politics. In E. Czempiel and J. Rosenau (eds.), *Governance Without Government*, pp. 1–29. Cambridge: Cambridge University Press.

Roy, A. (1999). *The Greater Common Good.* Bombay: India Book Distributor (Bombay) Ltd.

Ruggie, J. G. (ed.) (1993). *Multilateralism Matters: The Theory and Praxis of an Institutional Form.* New York: Columbia University Press.

Ruggie, J. G. (2004). Reconstituting the Global Public Domain: Issues, Actors, and Practices. *European Journal of International Relations* 10 (4).

Russett, B. (1993). *Grasping the Democratic Peace: Principles for a Post-Cold War World.* New Jersey: Princeton University Press.

Salehyan, I., and K. S. Gleditsch (2006). Refugees and the Spread of Civil War. *International Organization* 60 (2): 335–66.

Sassen, S. (2001). *The Global City: New York, London, Tokyo.* Princeton, NJ: Princeton University Press.

Schmidt, A. (2008). From Global Prescription to Local Treatment – the International Refugee Regime in Africa. Paper presented at the ISA Conference in San Francisco, March 2008.

Scholte, J. A. (2004). *Globalization and Governance: From Statism to Polycentrism.* Warwick University/ESRC Centre for the Study of Globalisation and Regionalisation Working Papers, No. 130/04.

Scholte, J. A. (2005). *Globalization: A Critical Introduction.* London: Palgrave Macmillan.

Schuck, P. (1997). Refugee Burden-Sharing: A Modest Proposal. *Yale Journal of International Law* 22 (2): 243–97.

Schuster, L. (2005). *The Realities of a New Asylum Paradigm.* COMPAS Working Paper No. 20, Oxford University, COMPAS.

Scott, J. C. (1998). *Seeing Like a State: How Certain Schemes to Improve the Human Condition Have Failed.* London: Yale University Press.

Sell, S. K. (2003). *Private Power, Public Law: The Globalization of Intellectual Property Rights.* Cambridge: Cambridge University Press.

Shacknove, A. (1993). From Asylum to Containmen. *International Journal of Refugee Law* 5 (4): 516–33.

Singer, J. (1961). The Level-of-Analysis Problem in International Relations. *World Politics* 14 (1): 77–92.

Skran, C. (1995). *Refugees in Inter-War Europe: The Emergence of a Regime.* Oxford: Clarendon Press.

Slaughter, A.-M. (2000). Governing the Global Economy through Government Networks. In M. Byers (ed.), *The Role of Law in International Politics: Essays in International Relations and International Law.* Oxford: Oxford University Press.

Stedman, S. J., and F. Tanner (eds.) (2003). *Refugee Manipulation: War, Politics, and the Abuse of Human Suffering.* Washington DC: Brookings Institution Press.

Steiner, N. (2003). Arguing about Asylum: The Complexity of Refugee Debates in Europe. In N. Steiner, M. Gibney, and G. Loescher, *Problems of Protection: The UNHCR, Refugees, and Human Rights*, pp. 179–95. London: Routledge.

Stewart, F. (2008). *Horizontal Inequalities and Conflict: Understanding Group Violence in Multiethnic Societies.* London: Palgrave Macmillan.

Stewart, F., V. FitzGerald, and associates (eds.) (2001). *War and Underdevelopment: Volume 1.* Oxford: Oxford University Press.

Strang, D. (1996). Contested Sovereignty: The Social Construction of Colonial Imperialism. In C. Weber, and T. J. Biersteker, *State Sovereignty as Social ConstructI*, pp. 22–49. Cambridge: Cambridge University Press.

Suhrke, A. (1998). Burden-Sharing During Refugee Emergencies: The Logic of Collective Action Versus National Action. *Journal of Refugee Studies* 11 (4): 396–415.

Suhrke, A. (2003). Human Security and the Protection of Refugees. In E. Newman and J. van Selm, *Refugees and Forced Displacement: International Security,*

Human Vulnerability, and the State, pp. 93–108. Tokyo: United Nations University Press.

Thielemann, E. (2003). Between Interests and Norms: Burden-Sharing in the European Union. *Journal of Refugee Studies* 16 (3): 253–73.

Thouez, C., and F. Channac (2005). *Regional Consultative Processes for Migration: An Evaluation Based on IMP's Work*. New York: United Nations Population Fund.

Towle, R. (2006). Processes and Critiques of the Indo-Chinese Comprehensive Plan of Action: An Instrument of International Burden-Sharing? *International Journal of Refugee Law* 18 (3–4): 537–70.

Turton, D. (ed.) (1997). *War and Ethnicity: Global Connections and Local Violence*. New York: University of Rochester Press.

UNHCR (2008). *2007 Global Trends: Refugees, Asylum-seekers, Returnees, Internally Displaced and Stateless Persons*. Geneva: UNHCR.

van Hear, N. (2006). Refugees in Diaspora: From Durable Solutions to Transnational Relations. *Refuge* 23 (1): 9–14.

van Selm, J. (2003). Refugee Protection Policies and Security Issues. In E. Newman and J. van Selm, *Refugees and Forced Displacement: International Security, Human Vulnerability, and the State*, pp. 66–92. Tokyo: United Nations University Press.

Vincent, J. (1974). *Nonintervention and the International Order*. Princeton, NJ: Princeton University Press.

Waever, O. (1993). Societal Security: The Concept. In O. Waever, B. Buzan, M. Kelstrup, and P. Lemaitre, *Identity, Migration and the New Security Agenda in Europe*, pp. 17–40. New York: St. Martin's Press.

Wallerstein, I. M. (2004). *World Systems Analysis: An Introduction*. Durham, NC: Duke University Press.

Walt, S. M. (1985). Alliance Formation and the Balance of World Power. *International Security* 9 (4): 3–43.

Waltz, K. (1979). *Theory of International Politics*. New York: McGraw-Hill.

Weiler, J. H., and M. Wind (eds.) (2003). *European Constitutionalism Beyond the State*. Cambridge: Cambridge University Press.

Weiner, M. (1995). *The Global Migration Crisis: Challenges to States and to Human Rights*. New York: Harper Collins Publishers.

Weiss, T. G., and D. A. Korn (2006). *Internal Displacement: Conceptualization and its Consequences*. Abingdon: Routledge.

Wendt, A. (1992). Anarchy Is What States Make of it: The Social Construction of Power Politics. *International Organization* 46 (2): 391–425.

Wendt, A. (1999). *Social Theory of International Politics*. Cambridge: Cambridge University Press.

Wheeler, N. J. (2000). *Saving Strangers: Humanitarian Intervention in International Society*. Oxford: Oxford University Press.

Whitaker, B. E. (2008). Funding the International Refugee Regime: Implications for Protection. *Global Governance* 14 (2): 241–58.

Wight, M. (1977). *Systems of States*. Leicester: Leicester University Press.

Wilkinson, R. (ed.) (2005). *The Global Governance Reader*. London: Routledge.

Wilkinson, R., and S. Hughes (2002). *Global Governance: Critical Perspectives*. London: Routledge.

Williams, J. H. P., and L. A. Zeager (2004). Macedonian Border Closings in the Kosovo Refugee Crisis: A Game-theoretic Perspective. *Conflict Management and Peace Science* 21 (4): 233–54.

Woods, N. (ed.) (1996). *Explaining International Relations since 1945*. Oxford: Oxford University Press.

Woods, N. (2002). Global Governance and the Role of Institutions. In D. Held, and A. McGrew (eds.), *Governing Globalization: Power, Authority and Global Governance*, pp. 25–45. Cambridge: Polity Press.

World Bank (1994). *Resettlement and Development: The Bankwide Review of Projects Involving Involuntary Resettlement 1986–1993*. Washington DC: World Bank.

Wyn Jones, R. (1999). *Security, Strategy, and Critical Theory*. London: Lynne Rienner Publishers.

Zetter, R. (1991). Labelling Refugees: Forming and Transforming a Bureaucratic Identity. *Journal of Refugee Studies* 4 (1): 39–62.

Zolberg, A. R., A. Suhrke, and S. Aguayo (1989). *Escape from Violence: Conflict and the Refugee Crisis in the Developing World*. Oxford: Oxford University Press.

Index

Abdullah, I. 140
Abu Dhabi Process 182
Adorno, T. 35
Afghanistan
  asylum seekers 76, 77
  refugees 64, 123, 158
African Group 178
African National Congress 12
African states
  anti-colonial liberation
    wars 142
  asylum/security 73
  displacement/global
    capitalism 139–42
  ECOWAS 164, 173, 182
  sovereignty/legitimacy 73
  structural adjustment 30
  Sub-Saharan 138
African Union 8, 105, 165
  Convention on Internally Displaced
    Persons 176
Algerian refugees 38
Alter, K. 121
Amsterdam Treaty 180, 181
anarchy 21, 22, 32, 99
Andean Pact 173
Anderson, B. 46, 53, 167
Angola 12, 132, 155
anti-colonial liberation wars 142
anti-immigration sentiment 37
ANZUS (Australia, New Zealand,
    United States Security Treaty) 165

APEC (Asia-Pacific Economic
    Cooperation) 105
Arab League 178
Arab–Israeli conflict 69
Arendt, H. 74
Arusha Conference 142
ASEAN states (Association of South
    East Asian Nations) 91–2, 94,
    95–6, 105, 164, 175, 177
asylum
  EU policy 165, 179–81
  European Council 176
  extra-territorial 159
  policies 165–6
  securitization 75–6
asylum seekers
  European Union 76, 138
  funds spent on 115
  irregular routes 161
  terrorists 64, 76
  white/non-white 138
asylum-migration nexus 160–2, 163
Augsburg, Peace of 45
Australia 76, 88, 159
authoritarian regimes 11, 127
Axelrod, R. 85
Ayoob, M. 72, 73

balance of power 24, 61
Bali Process 178, 182
Bangladesh 10, 77
Barnett, M. N. 87, 118, 119, 120

Barre, S. 77
Bauman, Z. 158
Beck, U. 146, 151
Bellamy, A. J. 68
benevolent leadership model 83, 88
Betts, A. 81, 89, 107, 124, 125, 136, 138, 143, 159
Biersteker, T. J. 48, 52, 53
biopower 61, 74–5
bipolarity 61–2, 66, 67, 112
Booth, K. 70
Bosnia 50, 57, 66, 132
Bradley, M. 107
Bretton Woods Institution 100, 153
Buchanan, A. 114
Budapest Process 122, 178, 182
Bull, H. 30, 46, 51
burden-sharing 87–90, 97, 124, 176–7, 180
bureaucracy 45, 46, 111, 172
Burmese 77
Burundi 77, 132
Buzan, B. 60, 69, 71

Cambodia 63
Canada 29
capitalism 34, 130, 139–42
capital/labor 34–5
Carr, E. H. 48
Cartagena Declaration 6, 101, 165, 176
Castells, M. 148
Castles, S. 131, 148, 157, 158, 160–1
CENTO 165
Ceuta security fence 161
Chayes, A. H. 111
cheating 84, 85, 111
Chechnya 8, 50
Chevron 141
child protection 8
Chimni, B. 36, 117, 137–8, 158
China 9, 12, 38, 128
Chomsky, N. 50
Christmas Island 159

CIREFCA (International Conference of Refugees in Central America) 82, 89, 90, 92–3, 95, 176, 177
citizenship
  displacement 65
  Linklater 35
  obligations 53–4
  refugees 59
  rights 14, 73
  sovereignty 58
  states 31, 45
civil society 150
civilian casualties 67
Clapham, C. 73
climate change 10, 26, 66, 100
coalitional bargaining 178
coercion 43, 88
coercive leadership model 83
Cold War
  aftermath 165
  compliance 112
  displacements 11–12
  domestic policies 41
  forced migration 12–13
  proxy conflicts 39
  self-interest 25
  sovereignty 47
  strategic studies 61–2
  USSR 38
collaboration 80, 96
  see also cooperation
collective action
  failure 84, 88–9, 100
  regionalism 164, 167
collective bargaining position 95–6
Colombia 132
Colombo Process 122, 182
colonialism 12–13, 46–7, 127
  see also post-colonialism
COMESA (Common Market for Eastern and Southern Africa) 105, 164, 182
commodities 11, 149, 150
common monetary policies 171

common security and foreign policy
(CSFP) 171
common welfare policy 172
communication networks 157, 158
Communism 25, 62–3, 157, 158
communitarianism 51–2, 54
complex governance perspective 51
compliance 110–13
Comprehensive Plans of Action
(CPAs) 82, 90–3, 95–7
see also Indo-Chinese CPA
conflict
cultural causes 139–40
democratization 156
displacement 127, 139
endogenous/exogenous 66, 124, 132
globalization 155
multinational corporations 141
new barbarism 139–40
primordialist perspective 132
private actors 141
proxy 39
refugees 63
security 60
states 62, 66, 132
conflict diamonds 141
Congo, Democratic Republic of 13, 155
constraining influences 103
constructivism
compliance 111, 112
cooperation 85–7, 98
Copenhagen School 70
identity formation 41, 132
institutions 86
nation-state 44
ontology of 32–4
organizational sociology 118
regionalism 169, 170
sovereignty 48, 52–3
Contadora Group of Central
American 177
containment 57, 133, 138
Contras 12–13, 63
Convention on the Status of Refugees
(1951)

access to rights 78–9
adherence to 32
asylum 112
global refugee regime 100–1
League of Nations 40
liberal institutionalism 27
Protocol (1967) 38, 121–5, 176
refugees defined 5–6, 38
as regional treaty 175–6
Conybeare, J. 135–6
cooperation
ad hoc 176–7
constructivism 85–7, 98
hegemony 25
humanitarian aid 27
international 20, 25–6, 80–1, 93–4,
123, 164
inter-state 87, 167
liberal institutionalism 84–5, 89
multilateral 88
mutual 84–5
neo-functionalism 183
neo-realism 82–3
North–South 128–9, 134–9
regimes 170
regional 168–71, 175, 183
reluctance 22
transaction costs 85, 108
unrequited 84–5, 135
Coordination Dilemma 174, 181, 183
Copenhagen School 70, 71–2
corruption 140
cosmopolitanism 41, 51–2, 54
cost/benefit analysis 86
Côte d'Ivoire 12, 132
counter-veiling tendency 47
countries of temporary refuge 95
country of origin involvement 95
Cox, R. W. 34, 70, 134
CPA: *see* Comprehensive Plans of
Action
crime, organized 13, 74, 146
Crisp, J. 63
critical security studies 61, 69–72,
77–9

critical theories 20, 34–7, 44, 70
CSFP (common security and foreign policy) 171
culture, trans-national 152
customs union 171

Dadaab camps 77, 78
dam-building projects 9–10, 12, 71
Darfur 107
debt 127, 140
decision-making 50
decolonization 46
defection, mutual 84–5
defensive realism 23
delegation 109
Democratic Peace Theory 28
democratization 133, 151, 156
dependency theory 34, 130
deportation 75
Derrida, J. 137
destination countries: *see* host community
developing countries
  coalitional bargaining 178
  quasi-sovereignty 72–3
  structural adjustment 29–30, 73, 127, 140, 155
development projects 9–10, 11, 12, 69
development-induced displacement and resettlement (DIDR)
  causes 8–10
  normative changes 34
  rights/values 79
  soft law 101
  studies on 17
  Welsh School 71
deviance 74
diamonds 11, 12, 133, 139, 155
diaspora groups 29, 41, 150, 155
DIDR: *see* development-induced displacement and resettlement
discourse ethics 35–6, 74–5
disease, communicable 66, 67
displacement
  amputees 139

authoritarian regimes 127
causes 127, 131–3, 154–7
citizenship 65
Cold War 11–12
conflict 127, 139
environmental 156
global capitalism 139–42
security 60
terrorism 64
see also development-induced displacement and resettlement; internally displaced persons
domestic policies 29, 41, 115
Doty, R. L. 128, 137
Downs, G. W. 111
Dubernet, C. 70–1, 159
Dublin Agreement 179, 180
Duffield, M. 132, 133–4, 158
Durieux, J.-F. 89, 125
Duvall, R. 119, 120

East–West relations 165
ECHR (European Court of Human Rights) 171, 176
Ecomomic Community of West African States (ECOWAS) 164, 173, 182
effectiveness 110–13, 114–16
e-governance 148
EITI (Extractive Industries Transparency Initiative) 100, 105
El Bashir, Omar 141
El Salvador 63
enforcement theory of compliance 111
English School of International Relations 30–2
  nation-state 44
  order/justice tension 58
  refugees 54–5
  solidarist international society 41
  sovereignty 48, 50–2
  WWII aftermath 54
environmental factors 10, 11, 12, 15, 67, 69
epistemic communities 86

Esquipulas II peace deal 92, 94
Ethiopia 63, 143
ethnic wars 132
Eurocentrism 72–3
European Central Bank 171
European Commission 102, 173, 181,
    183
  Directive (2004) 101
European Community law 171
European Council 176
European Court of Human Rights
    (ECHR) 171, 176
European Refugee Fund 180
European Union
  asylum seekers 76, 138
  asylum/immigration policy 165,
    179–81
  burden-sharing 180
  integration process 123, 172, 179
  internal market 183
  Justice and Home Affairs 72, 171,
    179, 181
  refugees 175
  regionalism 100, 122, 164, 172
  state autonomy 171
  and US 168
Eurozone 171
exclusion, logic of 133
Executive Outcomes 141
externally displaced persons 96
Extractive Industries Transparency
    Initiative (EITI) 100, 105

Faist, T. 157
feminism 20
feudalism 45
Finnemore, M. 87, 118
five-plus-five dialogue 178
forced migration
  categories 1, 4–10, 36
  causes 11–12, 157
  Cold War 12–13
  global governance 101, 126
  global politics 1–2, 11–14, 60

globalization 154–60
human rights 4–5
international cooperation 80–1
International Relations 14–17
liberalism 28–9
nation-state 158–60
normative taboos 32
North–South relations 144
rationalist approaches 48–9
regional cooperation 183
regionalism 166, 169–70, 174–8
responses 13–14, 133–4
security 24, 62
sovereignty 44–5, 58–9
states 128
Forced Migration Studies 2, 3, 5
foreign exchange factors 140
foreign policy 28, 29
forum-shopping 121
Foucault, M. 35–6, 74–5, 137
fragmentation process 150
Franck, T. M. 111
Franco, Leonardo 94, 98
Frank, M. 130
Frankfurt School 35
freedom of movement 181
free-riding 26, 81, 84, 85, 100, 111, 175
free-trade area 171, 179
Friends of River Narmada 10
Frontex 161, 180
functionalism 172, 173

G77 128, 178
GCIM (Global Commission on
    International Migration) 122
Geneva conference 95
GFMD: *see* Global Forum on
    Migration and Development
Gilpin, R. 129
global capitalism 139–42
Global Commission on Global
    Governance 103
Global Commission on International
    Migration (GCIM) 122

Global Compact 100, 105
global economy 127, 131
Global Forum on Migration and
    Development (GFMD) 122, 125, 159
global governance
    ambiguities 104–7
    creation/persistence 103–4, 108–10
    definitions 99–103, 102–3
    efficiency 114–16
    enforcement 100
    forced migration 101, 126
    institutions 102–3
    international organizations 117–19
    International Relations 99, 104
    legitimacy 114
    normative debates 104, 113–17
    overview 102–7
    regime theory 104
    stages in 99–102
Global Migration Group (GMG) 125
global politics 1–2, 11–14, 60
    see also world politics
global refugee regime
    case study 37–42
    compliance 112
    LNHCR 100–1
    North–South cooperation 136–7
    Schmidt on 107
    states 16
    UNHCR 121
globalization
    causes 146, 148–9
    as concept 147–51
    conflict 155
    defined 145, 147–8
    emerging trends 162–3
    forced migration 154–60
    International Political
        Economy 145–7
    knowledge 155–6
    migration and security 39
    nation-states 146, 163
    normative perspectives 152–3
    persecution 156

production processes 148, 149, 155
    state authority 49
    transboundary threats 67
GMG (Global Migration Group) 125
Goldstein, J. 108–9
Gong, G. W. 46
Goodwin-Gill, G. 176
governance
    complex 51
    and government 99, 102
    levels of 105, 149–50
    multiple actors 99–100
    norms 106–7
    structural adjustment 155
    see also global governance
Graham, D. 68
Gramsci, A. 34–5, 137
Greek city-states 45
greenhouse gas emissions 100
Group of Latin American Countries
    (GRULAC) 178
Guantanamo Bay 159
Guatemala 95
guerrillas in exile 63
*Guiding Principles on Internal
    Displacement* (UNHCR) 7, 8, 56,
    57, 68, 122, 176
Guinea 73, 165

Haas, E. B. 86
Habermas, J. 35
Haddad, E. 31, 49, 51–2, 54, 59
Haitian asylum seekers 159
Hamas 63
Hampshire, J. 75
Hasenclever, A. 81, 83, 103
Hathaway, J. C. 116
hegemonic stability theory 23, 40, 83
hegemony
    coercion 88
    cooperation 25
    Gramsci 34–5, 137
    humanitarian aid 133–4
    knowledge 35

hegemony (*cont'd*)
  neo-realism 108
  regionalism 168
  self-interest 88
  US 112, 168
Held, D. 145, 146, 147, 148, 151, 152
Hirst, P. Q. 145, 146, 152
Hobbes, T. 21
Hobsbawm, E. 46
Holy Roman Empire 45
Homeland Security 72
Honduras 13, 63, 97
Hong Kong 38, 91
Horkheimer, M. 35
host community 63, 65, 69, 79, 138
Huguenots 55
human mobility 68–9, 146
human rights
  cosmopolitan values 41
  forced migration 4–5
  international law 47, 162
  international norms 32–3, 101
  International Relations 15
  NGOs 170–1
  refugees 54
  religion 69
  respect for/violation of 127
  sovereignty 31, 44, 48, 52
human security 61, 66–9
human trafficking 13, 146, 157, 161, 178
humanitarian aid
  cooperation 27
  domestic politics 29
  as hegemonic strategy 133–4
  refugee crisis 64
  United Nations 7–8
  violence 74
humanitarian corridors 70–1
humanitarian emergencies 66
Humanitarian Evacuation Programme
    (UNHCR) 42, 89
Hungarian Revolution 38
Huntington, S. 155
Hurrell, A. 51, 52, 85, 164, 166–7, 168
Hutu 13

hybridization process 150
Hyndman, J. 74
hyper-globalizers 146, 151

ICARA (International Conference on
    Assistance to Refugees in
    Africa) 142–3, 176
ICC (International Criminal
    Court) 100, 102
ICRC (International Committee of Red
    Cross) 107, 114
identity
  categories 132
  constructivism 41, 132
  nationalism 53
  regional awareness 166–7
  regionalism 169
  shared 46
  and territory 150–1
  trans-national 155
identity formation 41, 103, 132, 157, 158
IGAD (International Governmental
    Authority on Development) 105
IGC: *see* Intergovernmental
    Consultations on Asylum, Refugees
    and Migration Policies
ILO (International Labour
    Organization) 117
imagined community 167
IMF (International Monetary
    Fund) 140
immigration 64, 158
Inayatullah, N. 53
India 10, 34, 71, 128
indigenous peoples 150
Indo-Chinese CPA 82, 90–2, 95, 96–7,
    176
Indochinese refugees 41
Indonesia 91, 155
inequality 66, 155
information, commodified 148
institutions
  choice of 109, 110
  constructivism 86
  global governance 102–3

international 25, 26, 27, 100
multilateral 105
nested/parallel/overlapping 120
power 119–20
refugee protection 123–4
refugee regime 122–3
regional 105
instrumentalism 132
integrated development approach 96
Interahamwe 13, 63
interconnectivity 145–6, 147–8, 160
interdependence 49–50, 58, 59, 164, 169
interest groups 29
Intergovernmental Consultations on
Asylum, Refugees and Migration
Policies (IGC) 122, 123, 177–8
intergovernmentalism 172–3, 180–1
internal flight alternative 122–3, 163
internally displaced persons 1, 6–7
conflict-induced 7–8
containment 57
environmental factors 10
intra-state conflict 132
legal definition 44
safe havens 70–1
securitization 76
soft law 56, 101
sovereignty 56–8, 59
as spoilers 64
states 59
studies on 17
see also development-induced
internally displaced persons
internally displaced persons
protection 81, 159
internally displaced persons
regime 122–4
International Administrative Law 106
International Conference of Refugees in
Central America: *see* CIREFCA
International Conference on Assistance
to Refugees in Africa
(ICARA) 142–3, 176
international cooperation 20, 25–6,
80–1, 93–4, 123, 164

International Criminal Court
(ICC) 100, 102
International Governmental Authority
on Development (IGAD) 105
International Labour Organization
(ILO) 117
international law 46, 47, 100–1
International Monetary Fund
(IMF) 140
International Office for Migration:
see IOM
international organizations (IOs) 8,
33–4, 86–7, 117–19
International Political Economy (IPE)
critical perspective 16, 130–3, 144
global economy 127–9
globalization 145–7
liberal perspective 134–9, 144
North–South relations 127–9, 144
international refugee law 47
International Refugee Organization 38,
88
International Relations (IR) 2–3
debates 19–20
forced migration 3, 14–17
global governance 99, 104
neo-Marxism 34–5
ontology 32
politics 15
regionalism 167
security 60–1
sovereignty 47–53
theories 18–19, 39–40, 42
trade 15
international society 41, 51
International Standards Organization
(ISO) 100, 106
internet 145–6, 150, 151
IOM (International Office for
Migration) 96, 117, 119, 122, 123
IPE: *see* International Political Economy
IR: *see* International Relations
Iran 77
Iraq 57, 66, 123, 132
irredentism 73, 78

Islamic refugees 64
ISO (International Standards
   Organization) 100, 106
Israel 88
issue-linkage 85, 89, 94, 98, 125, 143,
   173
Ivory Coast: *see* Côte d'Ivoire

Jackson, R. J. 47, 53, 72, 73
Japan 116
Jewish resettlement 40
Jews exiled from Spain 55
Jordan 63, 77
Jupille, J. 109, 110
jus inter pares concept 105
Justice and Home Affairs 72, 171, 179,
   181

Kakuma camps 78
Kaplan, R. D. 139–40
Katrina, Hurricane 10
Keck, M. E. 87
Keen, D. 139
Keene, E. 46
Kenya 73, 77, 78
Keohane, R. O. 26, 80, 84–5, 103,
   114, 130, 169
Khmer Rouge 63
Khong, Y. E. 66–8, 69
Kindleberger, C. P. 83
Kiribati island 10
knowledge
   epistemic communities 86
   globalization 155–6
   hegemony 35
   power 35–6, 74
   technological change 148–9, 151
knowledge dissemination 137, 138
Koehler, J. 177–8
Koh, H. H. 111
Korea, South 128
Kosovo 50, 89, 132
Krasner, S. D. 37, 48, 49–50, 57, 81,
   103, 128

labor force 146, 179, 181
labor/capital 34–5
leadership 83, 88, 94–5
League of Nations 24, 28, 37, 40
   High Commissioner for Refugees
      (LNHCR) 100–1, 109–10
Lebanon 63, 77
legitimacy 43, 72–3, 111, 114
lending guidelines 101
Leninism 34, 130
liberal institutionalism 25–7
   Convention (1951) 27
   cooperation 40, 84–5, 89
   institutions 40, 86
   inter-state relations 43–4
   IOs 117–18
   neo-realism 20
   normative debates 113
   regimes 108
   regionalism 169, 170
   sovereignty 47–8
liberalism 27–8, 27–9, 129–30, 134,
   170, 173
liberalization 147
Liberia 165
Lindt, A. 41
Linklater, A. 35
Lisbon Treaty 172
Lischer, S. K. 63
LNHCR (League of Nations High
   Commissioner for
   Refugees) 100–1, 109–10
local population 77–8, 96
   see also host community
Loescher, G. 62, 77, 89, 118–19
Lome Accords 139
London bombings 64, 76

Maastricht Treaty 171, 179, 181
McAdam, J. 101, 176
MacFarlane, S. N. 66–8, 69
McGrew, A. 145, 146, 148, 151, 152
Madrid bombings 64
Malaysia 91

Malkki, L. H. 55–6
Mares, P. 76
marginalized people 70, 153
markets 129–30, 151
Martin, L. 136, 143
Marxism
  base/superstructure 34–5, 130
  capitalism 130
  forced migration 131
  markets 129–30
Mattli, W. 171, 172, 173, 174, 181,
  183
Mearsheimer, J. J. 21, 23, 82–3, 117
media/security 65
Melilla security fence 161
mercantilism 129
MERCOSUR 105, 164
Meunier, S. 121
microeconomic theory 22, 115
migration
  crisis of 131
  and development 159
  globalization 39
  irregular secondary movement
    159, 161–2, 163
  North–South 158
  technological advances 157
  voluntary 4
  see also forced migration
Migration Dialogue for Southern
  Africa 182
Migration Dialogue for West
  Africa 182
Milner, J. 73, 77, 124, 138, 159
Mitrany, D. 172
Momoh, J. 140
monarchy/bureaucracy 45
monetary union 171
monitoring 89, 100
Montevideo Convention on the Rights
  and Duties of States 46
Moravcsik, A. 27–8
Morgenthau, H. 21–2, 48, 61, 99
Moro, L. N. 141–2

multinational corporations 9–10, 11,
  12, 141

NAFTA (North American Free Trade
  Agreement) 105, 122, 164
Nansen Passports 37
Narmada Bachao Andolan
  movement 10, 34
Narmada Solidarity Society 10
national interests 28
national security 61, 62, 65, 70
nationalism 46, 53
nation-states
  bureaucracy 46
  coercion 43
  constructivism 44
  English School 44
  forced migration 158–60
  globalization 146, 163
  non-state actors 36–7
  refugees 56
  regulatory autonomy 151
  self-help 61
  welfare maximization 61
  Westphalian system 36
  world politics 43
NATO (North Atlantic Treaty
  Organization) 165
natural disasters 10, 66
natural resources 139
Nauru 159
neo-functionalism
  cooperation 183
  path-dependency 173
  regional integration 172, 180
  regionalism 169, 170
neo-liberalism 152
neo-Marxism 20, 34–5, 70
neo-neo debate 20, 85–6
neo-realism 20–5
  burden-sharing 88
  cooperation 82–3
  cost-benefit analysis 86
  hegemony 108

neo-realism (*cont'd*)
  inter-state relations 43–4
  liberal institutionalism 20
  refugee regime 40
  regimes 108
  regionalism 168–9
  self-interest 82–3
  sovereignty 47–8
Nepalese 77
net welfare gain 115
network society 148
Neve, R. A. 116
Newman, E. 68, 75
NGOs: *see* non-governmental
  organizations
Nicaragua 12–13, 63, 95, 97
Nigeria 132, 155
Non-Aligned Movement 178
non-entrée regime 138, 161
non-governmental organizations
  (NGOs) 8, 33–4, 87, 170–1
non-intervention principle 47, 51
non-refoulement 6, 27, 33, 75, 87, 124
non-refugee groups 131, 161
non-state actors 32–3, 36–7, 62, 105, 150
norm creation 86, 89–90, 98, 169
normative perspectives
  compliance 111
  DIDR 34
  forced migration 32
  global governance 104, 113–17
  globalization 152–3
  governance 106–7
  international/domestic 170
  legalization 109
North American Free Trade Agreement
  (NAFTA) 105, 122, 164
North Atlantic Treaty Organization
  (NATO) 165
North–South relations
  cooperation 128–9, 134–9
  Doty 137
  forced migration 120, 144
  humanitarian aid 133–4

inequalities 131, 134
International Political
  Economy 127–9, 144
migration controls 158
polarization 142
socioeconomics 128
see also South–North migration
Norway 29
nuclear deterrence 61–2, 66
Numeiry, G. M. 141
Nye, J. S. 130
Nyers, P. 74

OAS (Organization of American
  States) 165
OAU: *see* Organization of African Unity
obligations 53–4, 109
Ogata, Sadako 39, 41, 66, 68
Ohmae, K. 146, 151
oil industry 12, 133, 141, 155
Olson, M. 83, 84
Orderly Departure Procedure 91, 96
Organization of African Unity
  (OAU) 101, 165, 175, 176–7
  Convention 6, 165, 176
Organization of American States
  (OAS) 165
organizational sociology 118
organized hypocrisy model 48, 49–50, 57
otherness, created 53, 56

Pakistan 77
Palestinians 63, 64, 77, 158
Pareto optimality 115
path-dependency 169, 172, 173
patrimonialism 140
patron–client relationships 73
Peace-Building Commission 101
PEC (Programme of Economic
  Cooperation) 92, 94
Peloponnesian Wars 45
persecution 63–4, 156
Phnom Penh 63
Poku, N. K. 68

policy harmonization 177
politics
  domestic level 27–9, 99
  internally displaced persons 1–2
  international 5, 30
  International Relations 15
  micronationalist 150, 155
  securitization 70, 76
  see also global politics; world politics
population movements 68–9, 131
post-colonialism 12, 20, 38–9, 127–8
post-structuralism 20, 35–6, 74–5, 137
poverty factors 66
power
  decentralization 165
  institutions 119–20
  knowledge 35–6, 74
  maximizing 22
  military 21
  plus legitimacy 31–2
  relational 119–20
  see also balance of power
primary product export 133, 155
primordialist perspective 132
principal-agent problem 118–19
Prisoner's Dilemma 84–5, 88, 89,
  134–5, 174, 181
private actors 105–6, 141
private sector 9–10
problem-solving theory 34, 134, 144
PRODERE 94
production processes 148, 149, 155
Programme of Economic Cooperation
  (PEC) 92, 94
protection
  extraterritorial 163
  individual 68
  regime changes 107
  see also internally displaced persons
    protection; refugee protection
Protracted Refugee Situations 77–9
public goods
  global 26, 80–1, 88
  regional 165, 175

Puebla Process 122, 182
Putnam, R. D. 168

quasi-sovereignty 47, 72–3

radicalization 13, 64
rationalist approaches 20, 27, 47,
  48–9, 112
Raustiala, K. 110, 111, 112
RCM (Regional Consultative
  Mechanism) 182
  see also Puebla Process
RCPs: *see* Regional Consultative
  Processes
realism
  classical 21–2, 129
  defensive 23
  security 61–2
  see also neo-realism
receiving states: *see* host community
reciprocity 27, 84–5
referent object 60, 69–70, 79
reflectivist approaches 20
reformism 153
refoulement 72
Refugee Aid and Development
  approach 92–3
refugee camps 5, 13, 75, 77–9
refugee crisis 63–4, 176–7
refugee protection
  asylum/burden-sharing 87–90
  asylum-migration nexus 160–2
  cheque-book role 116
  costs 115–16
  institutions 123–4
  physical role 116
  as public good 81, 88, 165
  regime complexity 121–5
  UNHCR 16, 107, 159
refugee regime 40, 62, 87–90, 110,
  122–3, 175–6
refugee warriors 13, 62–3
refugees 1, 5–7, 62
  citizenship 59

refugees (*cont'd*)
  Communism 25, 158
  conflict 63
  English School 54–5
  EU 175
  foreign policy 29
  human rights 54
  intra-state conflict 132
  and irregular migrants 161–2
  Islam 64
  legal definition 44
  local population 77–8
  nation-states 56
  pluralism/solidarism 51–2
  situational 63–4
  sovereignty 53–6, 59
  state-in-exile 63–4
  terrorism 24, 60, 62, 64
  vulnerability 69
  Westphalian state system 55
regime theory 81, 104, 114–16, 119,
    135, 136
regimes
  complexity 120–5
  cooperation 170
  creation/persistence 108–10
  liberal institutionalism 108
  neo-realism 108
  see also refugee regime
Regional Consultative Mechanism
    (RCM) 182
  see also Puebla Process
Regional Consultative Processes
    (RCPs) 122, 166, 177–8, 181–2,
    183–4
regional integration 167, 171–4, 177,
    180
regionalism 164–6
  collective action 164, 167
  constructivism 169, 170
  East–West relations 165
  EU 100, 122, 164, 172
  forced migration 166, 169–70,
    174–8

  hegemony 168
  identity 169
  interdependence 164, 169
  International Relations 167
  liberal institutionalism 169, 170
  neo-functionalism 169, 170
  neo-realism 168–9
  theories of 166–7
rejectionism 153
religion 45, 69
remittances 13, 131, 157, 158, 161
repatriation 13, 14
resettlement 40, 76, 88, 91–2
resource allocation 78, 116
resource predation 139
responsibility to protect 2, 47, 54, 68
  see also R2P
Revolutionary United Front 139–40
Richards, P. 139, 140
Rome Treaty 171
R2P (Responsibility to Protect) 107
Rwanda 12, 13, 63, 66, 132
Rwandan Patriotic Front 12

SADC (South African Development
    Community) 164, 182
safe havens 70–1
San José 96
Sardar Sarovar Dam 10, 34
Sassen, S. 148
Schengen Agreement 179
Schmidt, A. 107
Scholte, J.-A. 105, 145, 146, 147, 148,
    152, 153, 162
Schuster, L. 161–2
SEATO (South East Asia Treaty
    Organization) 165
securitization 65, 71–2, 75–6, 78,
    133
security
  conflict 60
  depoliticization 65
  displacement 60
  forced migration 24, 62

hard/soft 23
human 61, 66–9
International Relations 60–1
media 65
national/individual 61, 62, 65, 70
non-military threats 64–5
non-state actors 62
realist approach 61–2
referent object 79
societal 71–2
state/individual 67–8
UNHCR 25
see also Traditional Security Studies
(TSS)
sedentarism 159–60
self-interest
Cold War 25
hegemony 88
humanitarian aid 134
mutual 27
neo-realism 82–3
states 22–3, 24–6, 93–4
Sen, Amartya 66
September 11, 2001 64, 75–6
Seville Summit 180, 181, 183
Sierra Leone 12, 132, 139–41, 165
Sierra Ruptile 141
Sikkink, K. 87
Single European Act 179
skeptics 146, 151–2
Skran, C. 94
Slaughter, A.-M. 110, 111, 112, 177–8
smuggling 13, 146, 157, 161, 178
social geography, reconfigured 147
socialization process 111
soft law 56, 101, 122
solidarist perspective 51
Somali asylum seekers 76, 77, 78
Somali refugees 64, 73, 78
Somalia 13, 57, 66, 132
South African Development
Community (SADC) 164
South East Asia Treaty Organization
(SEATO) 165

South–North migration 110, 125, 131,
157, 158–9
sovereignty 43–4, 45–8
citizenship 58
Cold War 47
constructivism 48, 52–3
domestic 49–50, 58
English School 48, 50–2
forced migration 44–5, 58–9
human rights 31, 44, 48, 52
interdependence 49–50, 58, 59
internally displaced persons 56–8, 59
International Relations 47–53
Krasner 49–50, 57
legitimacy 72–3
liberal institutionalism 47–8
neo-realism 47–8
refugees 53–6, 59
Westphalian 49–50, 58, 59
Srebrenica massacre 71
Sri Lanka 158
stateless persons 1
states
absolute/relative gains 25–6
authority 49, 52–3
authority/globalization 49
bargaining 172–3
as black box 22, 23, 26, 32, 48
characteristics 29–30
citizenship 31, 45
conflicts 62, 66
decision-making 50
European Union 171
forced migration 44–5, 58–9
global refugee regime 16
globalization 49
human rights 31, 44
interests 22–3, 24–6, 93–4, 97
internally displaced persons 59
international institutions 27
legitimacy 43
obligations 53–4
population 52–3
relations between 43–4, 117

states (*cont'd*)
  reputation 89
  responsibility 116–17
  territory 52–3
  violence 46
  see also nation-states; sovereignty
states of the exception 74
Stedman, S. J. 62, 64
Stevens, S. 140
Stewart, F. 155
Strang, D. 53
strategic deterrence 66
strategic studies 61–2
structural adjustment 29–30, 73, 127,
  140, 155
Suasion Game 135, 136, 142
Sub-Saharan Africa 155
Sudan 133–4, 139, 141–2, 155
Sudanese People's Liberation
  Movement/Army 141
Sudanese refugees 78, 132
Suhrke, A. 69, 81, 87, 175
Sunshine company 141
supranational organizations 100
supranational regulation 102
supranationalism 173, 181, 183
supra-territoriality 146, 147–8, 149, 160
surplus value 130
surveillance 27, 74, 89, 100
Sweden 123

Talisman 141
Tamil refugees 158
Tampere Summit 180, 181, 183
Tanner, F. 62
Tanzania 73, 77, 107, 138–9
territoriality 52–3
terrorism 24, 39, 60, 62, 64
terrorism recruitment 13, 64
terrorists 75, 76
Thailand 77
Thielemann, E. 89, 177, 180
Third World security predicament
  61, 72–3

Thompson, G. E. 145, 146, 152
threats
  balance of 23
  direct/indirect 77
  referent object 60
  state/individual 70
  transboundary 67
  violent/non-violent 66
Three Gorges Dam 9
Thucydides 45
Timor, East 132
titanium oxide market 140–1
tourists/vagabonds dichotomy 158
trade 15, 128, 145–6, 155
trade regimes 109, 135–6
Traditional Security Studies 61–6
transaction costs 85, 89, 100, 108, 173
trans-boundary movements 152–3
Transformationists 146, 147, 151, 152–3
trans-governmental policy network 182
transit processing centers 159
trans-national advocacy networks 13, 87
trans-national regulation 102
trans-nationalism 102, 157–8
tribalism 132
TRIPS 105–6
tsunami 10
Tunisia 38
Turton, D. 133

Uganda 12, 107
UNCHR (United Nations Commission
  on Human Rights) 9
underdevelopment 127
UNDP: *see* United Nations
  Development Program
UNHCR: *see* United Nations High
  Commissioner for Refugees
UNICEF (United Nations Children's
  Fund) 8
Union of Soviet Socialist Republic 38, 41
United Nations
  establishing 100
  humanitarian aid 7–8

peacekeepers and safe havens 71
refugee regime 110
United Nations Charter
Article 2(4) 46
Article 42 47
Chapter VII 68, 101
United Nations Commission on Human
Rights (UNCHR) 9
United Nations Development
Group 125
United Nations Development Program
(UNDP) 66, 96, 117, 143
United Nations General Assembly 178
United Nations High Commissioner for
Refugees (UNHCR) 6, 7–8, 24
agenda-setting 137
as autonomous actor 118–19, 124
coalitional bargaining 178
Executive Committee Resolutions
90
global refugee regime 121
*Guiding Principles on Internal
Displacement* 7, 8, 56, 57, 68,
122, 176
Humanitarian Evacuation
Programme 42, 89
ICARA 142–3
internally displaced persons 56–8,
124
irregular migrants 161–2
issue-linkage 125
knowledge dissemination 137, 138
national disasters 10
normative function 117, 119
post-colonialism 38–9
post-WWII 38
refugee camps 75
refugee protection 16, 107, 159
regional presence 96–7
security 25, 68
state behavior 33–4
surveillance 27
United Nations Human Development
Report 66

United Nations Relief and
Rehabilitation Agency
(UNRRA) 37–8
United Nations Secretary-General 94,
96, 122
United Nations Security Council 47
United States of America
Afghanistan 12
coercive leadership model 83
and EU 168
hegemony 83, 112, 168
Homeland Security 72
Iraq 12
Mexican border 161
refugee admission quota 75–6
refugee warriors 62–3
refugees from Europe 25
refugees from Indo-China 25, 29
resettlement 88
self-interest 83
Uruguay 128

Van Hear, N. 158, 160–1
Van Selm, 76
Viera de Mello, Sergio 92, 94, 98
Vietnam 41, 63, 88, 91–2, 94
Vietnam War 29, 92
violence 46, 74, 155
vulnerability 69, 162

Waever, O. 71–2
Wales, University of 70
Wallerstein, I. M. 34–5, 130
Walt, S. M. 23
Waltz, K. 20–2, 30
warehousing, refugee camps 77–9
Warsaw Pact 165, 168
Washington Consensus 153
Watson, A. 46
Weber, C. 48, 52, 53
Weiner, M. 62
welfare maximization 61
Welsh School, critical security
studies 70–1

Wendt, A. 32
Westphalia, Peace of 45, 67
Westphalian state system 31, 36,
    49–50, 53, 55, 58–9, 163
WFP (World Food Programme) 8, 117
WHO (World Health
    Organization) 117
Wilson, T. W. 28
World Bank 9, 12, 34, 101
World Commission on Dams 34
World Food Programme (WFP) 8, 117
World Health Organization
    (WHO) 117
world politics
    individual/domestic/system levels 22
    nation-state 43
    power plus legitimacy 31–2

regime theory 119
Wendt 32
see also global politics
world systems theory 34, 130
world trade 128
World Trade Center 64, 75–6
World Trade Organization (WTO) 100,
    102, 109, 117
World War I 37
World War II 37–8, 54, 88, 100
WTO: *see* World Trade Organization

Yugoslavia, former 89

Zaire 63
Zeckhauser, R. 83
Zimbabwe 12